HANDS-ON
GENERAL SCIENCE ACTIVITIES
WITH REAL-LIFE APPLICATIONS

Ready-to-Use Labs, Projects,
& Activities for Grades 5-12

PAM WALKER • ELAINE WOOD

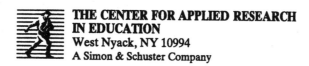

**THE CENTER FOR APPLIED RESEARCH
IN EDUCATION**
West Nyack, NY 10994
A Simon & Schuster Company

Library of Congress Cataloging-in-Publication Data

Walker, Pam.
    Hands-on general science activities with real-life applications :
ready-to-use labs, projects, and activities for grades 5–12 / by Pam
Walker and Elaine Wood.
      p. cm.
   ISBN 0-87628-751-8
   1. Science—Study and teaching (Elementary)—Activity programs.
I. Wood, Elaine . II. Title.
LB1585.W25 1994   94-19238
372.3′5—dc20   CIP

Printed in the United States of America

10 9 8 7 6 5 4

ISBN 0-87628-751-8

**THE CENTER FOR APPLIED RESEARCH
IN EDUCATION**
West Nyack, NY 10994
A Simon & Schuster Company

On the World Wide Web at http://www.phdirect.com

Prentice-Hall International (UK) Limited, *London*
Prentice-Hall of Australia Pty. Limited, *Sydney*
Prentice-Hall Canada Inc., *Toronto*
Prentice-Hall Hispanoamericana, S.A., *Mexico*
Prentice-Hall of India Private Limited, *New Delhi*
Prentice-Hall of Japan, Inc., *Tokyo*
Simon & Schuster Asia Pte. Ltd., *Singapore*
Editora Prentice-Hall do Brasil, Ltda., *Rio de Janeiro*

Dedication

This book is dedicated to Glynda Wood, Assistant Principal of Vocational Instruction at Alexander High School, Douglasville, Georgia, and to Alexander's Science Department faculty. Glynda convinced us that we could write a book that would be useful to other teachers, and she helped us get started. As a mentor and a friend, she supported us with invaluable advice.

Our science department, composed of Peggy Baugh, Jeff Davison, George Hale, Gail Marshall, Dee McDonald, Casey Teal, David Todd, and Ted Wansley, is one of the outstanding lab science departments in the state. These coworkers have shared activities and suggestions with us for years and have been pivotal in the development of our teaching styles. The individuals in this department really care about students and work diligently at developing methods that help students learn. We are indebted to the science department faculty for serving as our teachers, critics, and friends throughout the writing process.

Acknowledgments

We are grateful to everyone who helped us finish this book-writing project. Elaine's mother, Helen Rowe, carefully proofread every word and made invaluable suggestions. Pam's anatomy class critiqued the manuscript from beginning to end, double checking every puzzle and activity. Members of this class include Mindy Beaty, Kristie Boyd, Amy Clavier, Heather Davis, Joann Davis, Kelly Eidson, Chet Kanu, Katherine Lanier, Barbie Matthews, Tameka Mitchell, Jared Moon, Josh Robinson, Laurie Simons, Beth Stepp, and Amanda Willis. Jason Barnes's artwork is featured in the chemistry section.

Ann Bone and Deidre Clines, our librarians, and Mary Brehen, their assistant, helped us locate publishing resources and clarify copyright questions. They have conducted research on many topics for us and have shown incredible patience by answering our questions and offering advice.

Ray Mansfield, our principal, and assistant principals Rodney Davis, Sam Duke, and Glynda Wood have been a supportive and caring group of administrators. The faculty and staff of Alexander High School have helped us in countless ways. The company of these people provided us with a network of contacts and friendships that is conducive to learning.

Connie Kallback and Zsuzsa Neff have given support and guidance and provided notable suggestions. They have not only edited our manuscript but have repaired sections that needed help.

About the Authors

Pam Walker, a science teacher at Alexander High School, Douglasville, Georgia, has been a teacher since 1981. She has taught physical science, biology, applied biology/chemistry, chemistry, human anatomy and physiology, physics, health, and physical education to grades 9 through 12. She earned a B.S. in biology from Georgia College and an M.Ed. and Ed.S. in science from Georgia Southern University. Ms. Walker has conducted numerous seminars and workshops for secondary science teachers and made presentations to educators on the local, state, and national levels dealing with the hands-on approach to teaching applied sciences.

    Elaine Wood earned an A.B. in biology and secondary education in 1971, an M.S. in biology in 1988, and an Ed.S. in science education in 1993, all from West Georgia College. She interned at Georgia State University, conducting research in genetic engineering. Her ten years of teaching experience in secondary science include physical science, biology, chemistry, and applied biology/chemistry. Ms. Wood currently teaches at Alexander High School, Douglasville, Georgia, conducts teacher workshops for teachers, and often makes presentations on the state and national levels.

    Ms. Walker and Ms. Wood are coauthors of *Handbooks for Applied/Biology Chemistry,* which accompany the Center for Occupational Research and Development (CORD) modules in applied biology/chemistry. They have also formed Atlanta West Science Education Consultants. Their consultant group provides seminars and workshops for educators across the United States using hands-on, student-centered activities to link science and society in the high school classroom.

    Both educators strive to provide other teachers with ideas, techniques, and methods to help students understand the importance of science. They believe educators can and should provide instruction that links science and everyday life.

About This Resource

"Why do I have to know this information, and how will I ever use it in the future?" Science teachers hear this question from students on an almost daily basis. This resource was created to help you answer that question to students' satisfaction.

The truth is that science issues are a part of the everyday world. Consequently, basic science education can help everyone make more intelligent decisions. To be tomorrow's successful adults, today's students will need an understanding of science topics as diverse as genetic engineering and natural resource conservation just to be able to vote, shop, and work in a responsible manner.

But what commonly happens with the teaching of science in today's schools may stem from the fact that the body of knowledge in science has grown to an unmanageable size: Students are sometimes smothered in science content, much of which is highly theoretical and abstract. Instructors often spend time teaching useless details, causing some students to feel discouraged. As a result, students often give up on science at the secondary level.

Hands-on General Science Activities with Real-Life Applications, a practical, easy-to-use resource for grades 5 through 12, is designed to meet the needs that students will have in the adult world and also to spark the interest of students who may have been turned off by science in the past. It has several attractive features:

- Hands-on activities, modeled after real-life situations, focus on concrete, applicable science that is interesting and relevant. The content relates to daily life experiences and answers the question, "Why do I need to know this?"

- Labs and activities that are inexpensive and require little specialized equipment and no scientific expertise. Even out-of-field teachers will be comfortable with these labs. Most materials needed for labs can be bought in places like grocery and general merchandise stores. All lab and activity materials are nonhazardous.

- The lessons require very little advance preparation by the teacher. Lab and activity worksheets are reproducible for class use, and the labs lend themselves well to either individual or cooperative group work.

This teaching tool also emphasizes critical thinking, values clarification, and problem-solving skills. For example, one unit explores current issues in water shed management, while another looks at up-to-date information on plotting earthquake epicenters.

Five units feature earth science, physics, astronomy, chemistry, and biology—a total of twenty-two lessons in all. Each lesson is introduced by a concise section of content, with science vocabulary developed through games and puzzles that are both fun and interesting. Vocabulary words are synthesized with debates and role-playing situations. Activities and labs reinforce the content and help students explore the topic in more detail.

We have found the materials in this resource to be a valuable supplement in our science classes in a comprehensive high school and recommend them to any science teacher in grades 5 through 12.

Pam Walker
Elaine Wood

Table of Contents

SECTION 1: EARTH SCIENCE—*1*

SECTION 4: CHEMISTRY—*163*

SECTION 5: BIOLOGY—*209*

SECTION 1

Earth Science

LESSON 1: PLATE TECTONICS

1–1 AS THE EARTH MOVES
Content on Plate Tectonics

Moving Plates

Sit very still for a few seconds and try to detect any motion or movement around you. You probably don't feel a thing unless an airplane is passing overhead or your stereo is thumping out some extra loud vibrations. Nevertheless, scientists know that the surface of the earth is divided into pieces called plates. These plates are in constant motion. So why can't you feel the motion? The average movement of a plate is estimated to be about the rate at which the human fingernail grows. Since you can't feel your fingernails in motion, it makes sense that you can't feel the plates of the earth in motion either.

The study of the formation and the movement of these plates is called plate tectonics. The latest scientific data indicates that about one dozen plates exist. Some plates are moving apart (diverging), some are moving together (converging), and some are colliding and sliding under and past each other. Why are these plates moving? What is providing the power to push them along? To understand this concept, you must know a little about the composition of the earth.

Probing Deep into the Earth's Interior

The earth is divided into the crust, the mantle, and the core (see Figure A). The crust is the solid portion on which we stand. The mantle is a plastic but solid material under the crust that can flow and move about. And finally, the core is the innermost part of the earth made of solid and molten iron. Today scientists speak of the lithosphere (the crust and the upper portion of the mantle) as being broken into plates that are capable of motion. The lithosphere and its plates rest on top of the asthenosphere (layer within the mantle). This portion of the earth is plastic and able to flow by means of convection currents. Convection currents are created when heating causes material to expand and rise, and cooling causes material to contract and sink (see Figure B).

Scientists believe that the convection currents bring new material to the surface of the earth and push older material aside. This motion pushes the plates of the lithosphere apart, as is occurring between the South American plate and the African plate. Plates come together and collide when the cooler currents are sinking. For example, the Nazca plate and the South American plate are colliding, and one plate is sliding beneath the other plate.

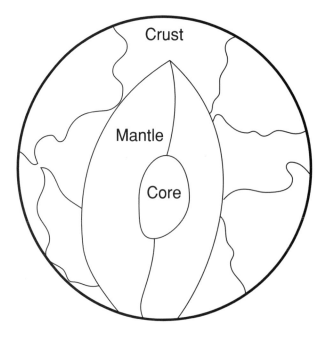

FIGURE A

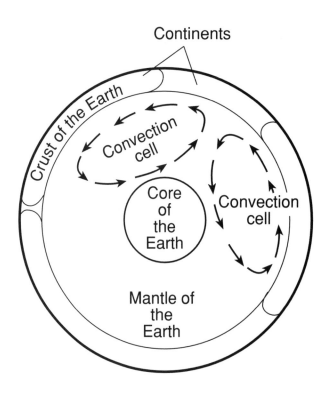

FIGURE B

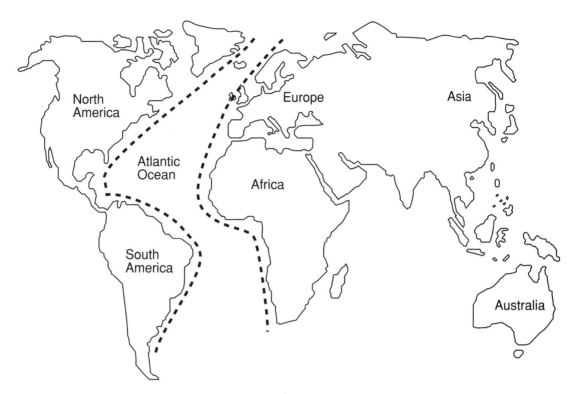

The East and West Coast lines of the Atlantic Ocean seem to fit together.

FIGURE C

Supporting Evidence for Plate Tectonics

Does all this seem a little far fetched? Many scientists laughed at this theory for years, but today it has gained widespread acceptance. What caused the reversal of opinion in the scientific community? Several factors contributed to the acceptance of this theory. One piece of supporting evidence comes from viewing the shape of South America's eastern coast and the western coast of Africa. The two borders seem to fit together like a jigsaw puzzle (see Figure C). This gave rise to the belief that at one time they were joined together and formed one large body. But as years have passed, they have broken apart and formed two continents. This idea became known as the theory of continental drift. Later, this theory was reinforced when scientists discovered the remains of a reptilian fossil called *Mesosaurus* both in Brazil and in South Africa, but nowhere else in the world. If these two continents were joined together at one time, it would explain why this reptilian fossil would only be found in both South America and Africa but nowhere else in the world. Since that discovery, the theory of continental drift has been expanded and has become known as the theory of plate tectonics.

The theory of plate tectonics explains the occurrence of volcanoes, earthquakes, and reversal of magnetism in the earth. Earthquakes and volcanoes do not just occur randomly throughout the earth. Their occurrence is limited to specific areas (or belts) that mark the exact location of plate boundaries. As these

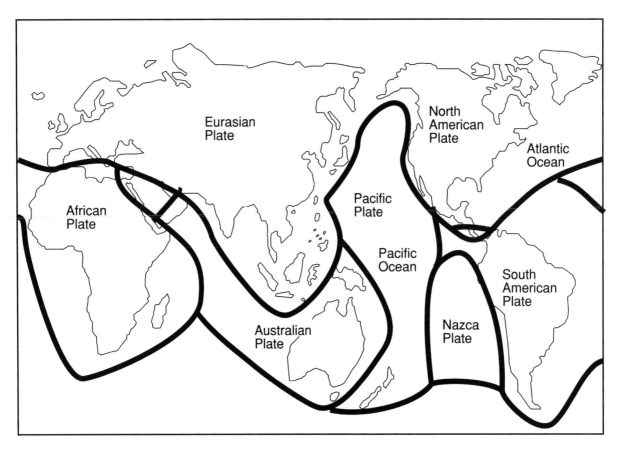

FIGURE D

boundaries move relative to one another, stresses build up and fractures occur. Earthquakes result from this event, and the high heat flow in these areas can give rise to upward movement of molten rock known as volcanoes. The largest belt is located in the Pacific Ocean, and about 90% of all earthquakes occur in this zone (see Figure D).

Scientists have also discovered that the earth's magnetic poles have been reversed at least four times over the past 4 million years. They believe that in areas where the plates are moving apart, lava wells up from within the earth and forms new rocks. Older rocks move away from the boundary. This is called sea-floor spreading. This spreading carries the continents with them and creates areas called midocean ridges (spreading centers). These spreading centers have higher elevations than surrounding areas. That is why certain areas of the sea-floor are elevated.

Cracking, Rumbling, and Erupting

When lithospheric plates slide past each other, a break or crack in the earth can occur. These breaks or cracks are called faults. Movements called earthquakes occur along these fault lines. One famous fault line in southwest California is called the San Andreas fault. Its average rate of movement is about 5 cm per year.

Mountains can be built from plates that converge or collide. The collision may cause the lithosphere at the boundary to be pushed upward into a mountain range. The Himalayan mountains are an example of this process, which occurred as India pushed into China.

Volcanoes usually occur when one plate is plunging beneath another by a process known as subduction. When two ocean plates come together, a deep sea trench (called a subduction zone) is formed. The deep sea trench that forms in the subducting plate is accompanied by the formation of volcanic islands on the overriding plate. Most of the world's active volcanoes occur at subduction boundary eruptions.

It is important to note at this time that all scientists do not advocate complete acceptance of the theory of plate tectonics. But for now, it is the most widely accepted explanation for the occurrence of phenomena such as earthquakes and volcanoes, reversal of the magnetic poles of the earth, similarity of the borders of continents, and fossil remains on seemingly unrelated areas of the earth.

ACROSTICS—VOCABULARY ACTIVITY ON
As the Earth Moves

Directions

After reading the content on plate tectonics, answer the following questions. Enter your answers vertically in the blanks. The numbers are written across the top of the puzzles. When you finish, you will form a two-word message horizontally in the boxes in the puzzle.

Clues

1. Breaks or cracks in the lithospheric plates that may result in earthquakes as the plates slide by each other.

2. Specific locations at the boundaries of the plates that mark the location of the volcanic and earthquake activity.

3. A _____ can be caused by subduction of plates. Hot molten rock then moves upward toward the surface of the earth.

4. Scientists believe that the earth has spreading centers where _____ wells up from within the earth to form new rocks and push older material aside.

5. The partially melted layer of the mantle that is able to flow due to convection currents and carry the plates along with it is the _____.

6. The crust and the upper portion of the mantle that is rigid in consistency is the _____.

7. When plates converge or collide, the lithosphere may be pushed upward at the boundary into the formation of _____.

8. Over the past 4 million years, the _____ poles of the earth have been reversed.

9. The appearance of one of these in both Africa and South America, but nowhere else in the world, supports the plate tectonic theory.

10. This is the semisolid layer beneath the crust but above the core.

11. Convection currents within the earth bring new materials to the surface of the earth and _____ older material aside.

12. This ocean has the majority of volcanic activity.

13. Plate _____ is the study of formation and movement of the plates of the earth.

14. Preceding plate tectonics was the theory of continental _____.

15. During convection currents of the mantle, the cooler currents are _____ and the plates are being pulled together in some plates.

Vocabulary Acrostics

1 2 3 4 5 6 7 8   9 10 11 12 13 14 15

1–2 ROCKIN' AND ROLLIN' IN THE U.S.A.
Lab on Earthquake Epicenters

Objectives

Students will calculate the epicenter of a hypothetical earthquake by using data and information on the primary and secondary waves collected at three seismographic locations.

Teacher Notes

A lesson on wave motion preceding this activity might facilitate a more thorough student understanding of this material.

ROCKIN' AND ROLLIN' IN THE U.S.A.
Lab on Earthquake Epicenters

Background Information

Whenever objects are subjected to extreme amounts of pressure or stress, they build up potential energy. This potential energy can be released in a variety of ways. The crust of the earth, for instance, can release its stress in the form of vibrations, which we call earthquakes. Earthquakes can result from sudden movements along a fault or from volcanic activity.

The potential energy contained within the earth can be released in the form of wave energy. These shock waves spread out in all directions during an earthquake. Some of the waves cause the rocks of the earth to vibrate from side to side, while other waves cause a backward-and-forward vibration. The various shock waves travel through rock material at different speeds. The P waves (primary waves) travel at 6.1 km/sec, and the S waves (secondary waves) travel at 4.1 km/sec. The P waves, causing backward-and-forward vibrations, can travel a distance of 100 km (about 62.5 miles) in 16.4 seconds; while the S waves, creating side-to-side vibrations in the earth, require 24.4 seconds to travel 100 km.

Instruments called seismographs are used to measure the arrival time of both the P and S waves at various locations around the world. This arrival time can then help geologists predict the exact location of an earthquake. The point of origin of an earthquake (the place where the stress energy changed to wave energy) is called the focus. The point or area of the earth's surface directly above the focus is called the epicenter. Seismologists (scientists who study earthquakes) can pinpoint the exact location of the epicenter of an earthquake by calculating the difference in the arrival time of the two types of shock waves.

Seismographic stations are located in various places around the world to collect the shock-wave data on their seismographs. Seismologists then compute the arrival time of the shock waves at three or more stations around the world to calculate the exact epicenter of the earthquake. The greater the difference in the arrival time in the P and S waves to a station, the farther that station is from the epicenter of the earthquake.

Seismologists also determine the energy given off by an earthquake by a special rating scale called the Richter scale. This scale ranges from 1 to 10. Each step indicates a tenfold increase in energy, which means that an earthquake of 5 on the scale is 100 times more powerful than an earthquake of 3.

Prelab Questions

1. Explain how a seismologist determines the exact location of an earthquake.

2. What is the difference between a seismologist and a geologist?

3. How long would it take a P wave and an S wave to travel 500 km?

4. What does the difference in arrival time of the P and S waves at a seismographic station indicate about the distance of the epicenter from that station?

5. How are the epicenter and focus of an earthquake different?

6. What is meant by potential energy?

7. Besides arrival time of the shock waves, what else does the seismologist measure at a station about the earthquake?

Materials

Figure A of hypothetical shock waves

Figure B of map of eastern United States

Compass and ruler

Calculator (optional)

Procedure

1. You and your partner are training to be seismologists for the U.S. government. You will analyze data from various seismographic stations in the United States on shock-wave arrival time and use your math skills to determine the epicenter of a hypothetical earthquake.

2. To begin, find Figure A on the records of earthquakes. This illustration shows the arrival time of the P and S waves at three different seismographic stations in the United States. The peak of the P and S waves corresponds to the number of seconds on the line beneath the reading. You will notice that the S wave always arrives later than the P wave. The difference in seconds in arrival time will help you determine how far the earthquake is from each of the stations recording the data. Calculate the difference in time for the P and S waves at each of the three stations and record this number of seconds in the data table.

3. Take this information and use it to compute the distance of the earthquake from each of the three recording stations. To accomplish this task, you will use this formula:

$$\frac{\text{Difference in time between P and S waves} \times 100 \text{ km}}{8 \text{ seconds}} = \text{unknown distance.}$$

This formula is applicable because the difference in the amount of time required for a P wave to travel 100 km and an S wave to travel 100 km is 8 seconds. Look at the example in Figure A. If a P wave arrived in Pittsburgh at 4:10 P.M. and 0 seconds on the clock and the S wave arrived at 4:10 P.M. and 35 seconds on the clock, you can calculate the distance of the earthquake from Pittsburgh by using the above formula. Your answer would be

$$\text{Unknown distance} = \frac{35 \text{ seconds} \times 100 \text{ km}}{8 \text{ seconds}} = 437.5 \text{ km.}$$

The earthquake would be located 437.5 km from the Pittsburgh station. However, to be exact on the location, you will need the readings of two other cities to pinpoint the precise location of the epicenter. Use your P- and S-wave time difference in the data table and the formula provided above to calculate the distance of each

© 1994 by The Center for Applied Research in Education

of the three stations from the earthquake epicenter. Record your findings in the data table under the heading "Distance."

HYPOTHETICAL RECORDS OF EARTHQUAKES FROM THREE STATIONS IN THE UNITED STATES

New York Station (Station A)

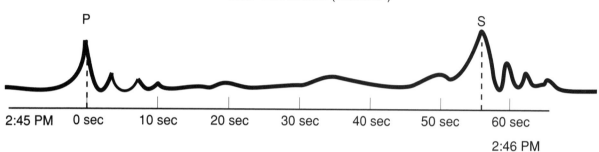

Louisville Station (Station B)

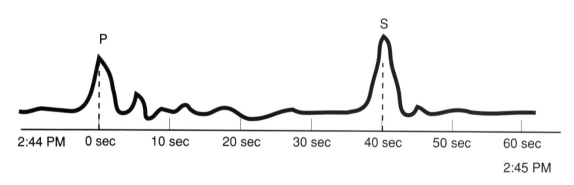

Pittsburgh Station (Station C)

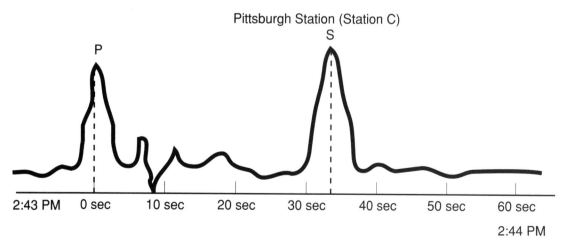

FIGURE A

4. Locate the map of the eastern United States (see Figure B), a compass, and a ruler. Use the information in the data table to locate the epicenter of your earthquake. Notice the kilometer line chart at the bottom of the map. The markings on the chart give a scaled-down representation of distance. Each 100 km is represented by about 1 cm in distance. Consult the data table for the distance to the epicenter. Place the compass point on zero of the "km" scale at the bottom of the map. Maintaining this position on the scale, place the compass pencil on the distance (km) of the earthquake from New York. Remove your adjusted compass, and place the point of the compass on the dot representing New York City on the map. Draw a circle around New York using the compass. Repeat this step for Pittsburgh and for Louisville.

FIGURE B

5. If you have done your computations and drawings correctly, you will notice that the three circles intersect at one point. This one point marks the exact epicenter of the earthquake.

6. Answer the postlab questions that follow.

DATA TABLE

City	Difference in P- and S-wave arrival time	Distance (km)
New York City		
Louisville		
Pittsburgh		

Postlab Questions

1. Which of the three cities above was the closest to the earthquake? Which of the three cities was the farthest away?

2. What state was the focus of the earthquake?

3. If a seismographic station in Savannah, Georgia detected the earthquake you measured, would it receive its reading before or after 2:45 P.M.? Explain your answer.

4. Using the map on which you determined the epicenter, determine the distance in kilometers that the earthquake was from New Orleans. Now put this information into your formula for lag time and calculate the difference in arrival time between the P and S waves in New Orleans. Draw a sample wave reading for New Orleans, like the ones in Figure A, from the information you just calculated. Use the other side of this page if you need more space.

LESSON 2: ROCKS AND SOIL

2–1 THE SCOOP ON SOIL
Content on Rocks and Soil

※)(※

Why Rocks Crack

It would be nice to age without changes occurring in our appearance. Unfortunately, human flesh deteriorates over time, and we witness this deterioration as alterations in our appearance. Changes in appearance can be seen in non-living things as well as living things. The earth has changed in its appearance over the passage of time. Like the flesh of the human body, the rocks that compose the earth are worn down and deteriorate with age. Many factors contribute to the breakdown of the rocks of the earth. The process of breaking down the rocks that compose the earth is called weathering. Weathering can be chemical or physical.

Physical and Chemical Weathering

Physical weathering changes the size of a rock but does not alter the composition of the rock. Temperature changes can cause physical weathering to occur. Rocks expand in the summer and contract in the winter. If you are unclear on the terms *expansion* and *contraction,* think about how tight your rings feel in the summer and how loose they feel in the winter. In other words, the fingers swell (expand) in hot weather and shrink (contract) in cold weather. This alteration of expanding and contracting in rocks weakens the rock and can cause it to crack and break into pieces. Roots from shrubs and trees can also grow between the openings in rocks, causing them to break apart. This also represents physical weathering.

    Chemical weathering may change not only the size but the composition of a rock. In this type of weathering a new material is formed. Oxidation and carbonization are two forms of chemical weathering. Oxidation is the process of combining oxygen with other materials to form new substances. Some rocks can appear to have a black, brown, or orange coloration because of oxidation. Iron oxide (rust) has developed on these rocks when the iron mineral in the rock is exposed to the atmosphere to form iron oxide. In effect, the rock has rusted. Carbonization is another agent of chemical weathering. Carbonization forms limestone caves when the carbonic acid (formed from the union of rainwater and carbon dioxide in the atmosphere) reacts with limestone rock to dissolve it slowly. Over thousands of years a cave is formed. As time goes by, the cave will increase in size.

16

From Where Do We Get Soil?

What determines the speed and intensity of the weathering process? These factors include (1) the type of rock, (2) the type and hardness of the materials in the rock, and (3) the climate. Rocks that dissolve easily in water or acid weather much more quickly than insoluble rocks. Sedimentary rocks generally weather more quickly than igneous or metamorphic rocks. Sandstone weathers more quickly than granite. This is because the sandstone is sand grains cemented together with natural materials and is more porous than granite. The more precipitation in an area, the more quickly the rock weathers. (The amount of precipitation can affect weathering.) A lot of weathering, occurs in areas with hot, humid climates.

Weathering can create and shape structures. Mountains can be shaped through the weathering process. Weathering can also break down rocks into useful materials such as soil. Over time, weathering causes the bedrock of the earth to decompose. With the passage of years, soil is formed. The formation of soil occurs in soil horizons or layers. The uppermost layer (Horizon A) is composed of the nutrient-rich topsoil. It is here that plants are nurtured with essential minerals. Decayed plants and animals form humus, which enriches the topsoil. The layer beneath the topsoil is the subsoil (Horizon B). This layer has some nutrients, but certainly not to the extent found in the topsoil. Horizon B has an orange coloration due to the high content of clay particles. Water and most plant roots have great difficulty penetrating through the subsoil. Horizon C is the layer below the subsoil and just above the bedrock. It is composed of broken pieces of rock. When the process of soil formation is completed, all three soil layers exist. When rock has not been sufficiently transformed by weathering into all three layers, it is called immature soil. As time passes, weathering will change immature soil into mature soil (soil with all three layers present).

As weathering occurs, pieces of rock break off and fall to the ground. Some of these pieces remain in that location, and other pieces are carried away by natural agents such as wind or water. The transportation of these broken pieces of rock to other locations is called erosion. The four most common agents of erosion include running water, glaciers, gravity, and wind.

Erosion by Water

In most areas, running water is a dominant agent of erosion. Rivers and streams transport eroded material. All material transported by rivers and streams is called the stream load. The composition of the stream load is dependent on the speed and volume of water in the stream. Heavier particles of material bounce along the bottom of the stream, grinding and wearing down surfaces they strike. This action is called abrasion. Lighter particles become suspended in the water and are eventually dropped when the stream slows in velocity. The weight and composition of these particles influence the order in which the deposition of particles takes place. Running water can even be so powerful that it creates new landscapes. Rainwater carries particles down mountain slopes and forms river valleys between two mountains.

Erosion by Glaciers

Glaciers (mounds of sliding snow on top of ice) can cause erosion. The icy bottom of the glacier causes it to flow smoothly. It may move only an inch a day, but this is enough to carry along particles underneath it. Glaciers can transport small particles and large boulders, but they cover much less area than running water.

Erosion by Wind

Wind can pick up and move sediments easily because of the great velocity it can generate. These traveling sediments suspended in air rub against rocks and other surfaces. This can be very dangerous. If you have ever been in a wind gust on a sandy ball field or playground, you know that the whirling sand particles sting as they strike your body. Think what damage huge dust storms might do to plants, animals, and buildings. In the 1930s a huge dust storm occurred in the Great Plains. Long dry spells in that area had killed the vegetation and left the topsoil exposed to the air. Violent winds came along and picked up the topsoil and bombarded nearby crops and buildings. The abrasive action of these storms caused massive devastation.

The clay and silt particles in soil can damage some structures, but the most devastating culprit is sand particles. Sand grains are much larger and much more abrasive. They can damage structures and grind giant boulders and small rocks into shapes called ventifacts. Sand particles can wear away materials to form smooth surfaces called facets.

As wind carries particles of sand along, it will eventually lose energy. When the wind loses energy and slows, it drops the sand in mounds called sand dunes. These dunes can migrate over time, covering and destroying objects in their path.

Erosion by Gravity

Gravity is the last and most influential agent of erosion. This is so because gravity is the underlying force behind all erosion. Gravity causes water to run downhill, it causes glaciers to flow, and it produces winds by pulling heavy colder air beneath lighter warm air. Gravity is the factor responsible for phenomena such as landslides, rock slides, and snow slides.

Preventing Soil Erosion

What effect does erosion have on the surface of the earth? Valuable topsoil is carried away by erosion. This loss of topsoil reduces soil fertility and lowers crop production. This can cause severe environmental and economic problems in a region. This depletion of topsoil can be controlled by a variety of methods. Use of these methods is called soil conservation.

Farmers practice soil conservation techniques daily. They use vegetation to cover topsoil and prevent erosion. The roots of the vegetation extend down into the soil and hold the soil in place. When farmers do not have crops planted in their fields, they allow wild vegetation to grow there as a protective measure.

Lumber companies can practice wise soil conservation by replanting trees after cutting down trees for lumber. Selective cutting of mature trees, as opposed to clear cutting of all trees in an area, is a form of soil conservation.

Soil conservation is important to our future and our food supply. Some methods employed by farmers to conserve the topsoil include the following:

1. *Planting windbreaks:* Belts of trees are planted along the edge of a field to slow wind erosion.

2. *Contour plowing:* Crops are planted in rows parallel to the contour of the land to prevent rapid flow of water downhill.

3. *Terracing:* The slope of a hill is flattened by building small terraces or ridges that resist erosion.

4. *Strip cropping:* Alternating crops are planted next to one another, rather than having bare ground in between rows (an example is corn and alfalfa planted side to side with no uncovered soil in between).

5. *No till:* An area is plowed, planted, and fertilized all at once, so the ground is not disturbed again until harvest.

Even though the earth changes with age, humans can help to control some undesirable alterations. Uncontrolled erosion is a change in the earth that humans can help to slow. Soil conservation is important to our generation and future generations. Our food supply depends on it.

THE SCOOP ON SOIL—VOCABULARY ACTIVITY ON
THE SCOOP ON SOIL

Directions

After reading the introductory material, complete the following sentences. Locate each of your answers in the word trace puzzle. Trace over the word in an unbroken line.

Questions

1. The material that is found beneath soil Horizon C and that is broken down into soil is called the _____.

2. The decayed plant and animal material found in the topsoil is called _____.

3. Horizon A is also called _____. It is rich in nutrients and minerals, which plants need to grow.

4. A(n) _____ is an agent of erosion composed of packed snow on a layer of moving ice.

5. _____ is the grinding down of a surface due to the friction caused by contact.

6. _____ is the underlying force behind all erosion. It causes water to run downhill.

7. Shapes created by sand abrasion are called _____.

8. When sand dunes are moved from one location to another by the wind, this is called dune _____.

9. A belt of trees planted outside a field to block the wind is called a _____.

10. Most wind abrasion is caused by larger particles of soil called _____.

11. Structures, called _____, are composed of sand that has been dropped in one location as the wind lost its energy.

12. A _____ _____ is material transported by a stream from one location to another.

13. _____ is planted on top of soil to prevent erosion.

14. _____ of soil includes practices employed by persons who wish to prevent erosion of the soil.

15. _____ plowing is the planting of crops in rows parallel to the contour of the land to prevent the flow of water down hillsides.

16. _____ is the flattening of a slope on a hill to prevent erosion.

17. When all three horizons are found in the soil, the soil is said to be _____.

© 1994 by The Center for Applied Research in Education

18. _____ is the process of breaking down rocks that compose the earth.

19. _____ of a plant can cause physical weathering as they enter the cracks of the rock.

20. _____ is a rock that weathers very slowly because it is not a porous rock material.

21. _____ is the process of combining oxygen with another material to produce chemical weathering.

22. _____ is a form of chemical weathering that results when carbonic acid reacts with limestone to make caves.

23. _____ is another name for iron oxide.

24. _____ _____ is the orange-tinted coloration formed on rocks as chemical weathering occurs.

Word Trace Puzzle

Example

```
b i o m t z
k m l z b t
u t o r e b
k m g y b v
j w p c v t
```

The study of life is called biology.

```
K J D F B W B I R O N O X I D D U D
S A O V M E E D R O A B R T E L N C
C N X E T A M N B C G L A E B T E R
O D I G K T A T U K L R S R K V S T
N P D E Z H E R R H A E I R M J D V
T R A T A T T I E U C I O A B N L W
O U T I O I O N R M U S N C I N G Y
U S T D N O P G R O O T S V E N T Z
R S C I O N S O I L W I N D B R I B
N T O T N G M I G R A T N G V E F T
D R N A Q R A V I T Y I O R F A A X
V E S V D P C O R N Z O I A K K C M
K A E R L J A K M U M N T N B R T L
J M L O A D R B O N I Z A I T E S D
```

2–2 BREAKING UP IS EASY TO DO
Lab on Weathering of Rocks

Objectives

Students will observe the mechanism behind the physical and chemical weathering of rocks into soil.

Teacher Notes

The rocks listed in the materials are common rocks suggested for your use, but you may substitute other rocks if this is more convenient for your location. This lab is written to be conducted for 48 hours, but the results will be adequate if you want to do only a 24-hour reading. You also can wait several days and still get good results if you cannot observe the results the day immediately following the start of the activity.

BREAKING UP IS EASY TO DO
Lab on Weathering of Rocks

Introduction

As time passes, objects change. The rocky materials composing our earth are subjected to a variety of environmental factors. These factors contribute to the wearing away and break down of these rocks into soil. This process is called weathering, and it can be of either the physical or chemical variety.

Physical weathering results only in the alteration of the size of the rock, not the composition of the rocky material. As the roots of plants push into the cracks of rocks, the rocks fracture and break apart over time. The abrasive forces of wind and water also are physical factors that wear away rocky materials. Water can be a source of physical weathering when it seeps into the cracks of rocks and freezes. The freezing of water inside the rock results in the expansion of the water into ice. The force exerted on the walls of the rock can result in cracking and fractures in the rock. This process is called ice wedging. Certain rocks are more susceptible to this process than others. Sedimentary rocks like sandstone are very porous and absorb water more easily than other rocks. This tendency for rocks to absorb water and then become exposed to freezing temperatures results in the process of ice wedging.

Chemical weathering alters the composition of a rock. In chemical weathering, a new substance is formed in the process. An example of chemical weathering is the process of carbonization. In carbonization, carbon dioxide from the atmosphere is dissolved in water to form carbonic acid. The strength of carbonic acid is equivalent to the strength of acid in carbonated beverages. Over time this acid reacts slowly to dissolve minerals in certain rocks. Limestone is an example of a sedimentary rock composed of calcium carbonate from the remains of dead animals. This calcium carbonate in the limestone is acted on and dissolved by the carbonic acid. The process of carbonization is the method by which caves are formed in limestone deposits over hundreds or even thousands of years.

The speed at which rocks weather depends on the type of rock, the type and hardness of materials in the rock, and the climatic conditions. As rocks weather, soil is formed.

Prelab Questions

1. Explain the differences between physical and chemical weathering.

2. Explain ice wedging.

3. Explain carbonization.

4. Why is sandstone more prone to ice wedging than granite?

5. Why is limestone more prone to carbonization than granite?

6. What three factors determine the rate of weathering a rock undergoes?

BREAKING UP IS EASY TO DO *(continued)*

Materials

Limestone (two rocks)	Vinegar
Marble (two rocks)	Eight small containers
Granite (two rocks)	Platform balance
Sandstone (two rocks)	Water
Grease pencil	Towel

Procedure

1. Label the eight containers A, B, C, D, E, F, G, and H with a grease pencil.

2. Find the mass of the following rocks, record this mass in the data table, and place the rock in the designated container:

   Limestone rock _____ Container A

   Marble rock _____ Container B

   Granite rock _____ Container C

   Sandstone rock _____ Container D

   Limestone rock _____ Container E

   Marble rock _____ Container F

   Granite _____ Container G

   Sandstone _____ Container H

3. Add water to Containers A, B, C, and D. Place enough water in these containers to cover the rock completely.

4. Add vinegar to Containers E, F, G, and H. Place enough vinegar in these containers to cover the rock completely.

5. Set these eight containers aside for 24 hours.

6. Remove each rock from its container one at a time and towel dry the rock. Weigh the rock on the platform balance and record the mass in the data table under the heading "Mass After 24 hours." Do this for rocks A through H. Return each rock to its proper container when you finish measurements.

7. Set the containers aside for 24 more hours and repeat the process used in step 6. Record the mass in the data table under "Mass After 48 hours."

8. Clean up the containers and answer the postlab questions.

© 1994 by The Center for Applied Research in Education

BREAKING UP IS EASY TO DO *(continued)*

DATA TABLE

ROCKS PLACED IN WATER			
Container	Initial Mass	Mass After 24 Hours	Mass After 48 Hours
A Limestone			
B Marble			
C Granite			
D Sandstone			
ROCKS IN VINEGAR			
E Limestone			
F Marble			
G Granite			
H Sandstone			

© 1994 by The Center for Applied Research in Education

Postlab Questions

1. Which rock would be the best candidate to undergo ice wedging? Explain your answer.

2. Which rock would be most likely to undergo carbonization? Explain your answer.

3. Which rock seemed unchanged by either water or vinegar?

4. Explain why vinegar rather than carbonic acid (carbonated drink) was used in this lab.

5. List the sedimentary rocks and the metamorphic rocks used in this lab.

6. Do you think smog and humidity can affect details in rocklike statues? Explain your answer.

7. Explain what the water and vinegar in this lab represent in a real-life situation.

Lesson 3: Weather

3–1 WEATHERING THE STORM
Content on Weather

Weather Indicators

Have you ever seen a bee buzzing around in a rain shower? You probably can't remember a single time you've witnessed this because bees are sensitive to humidity in the air. As soon as the humidity rises and rain is near, bees seem to know that it's time to head back to the hive.

Humidity is just one of the indicators of weather conditions. Weather is the state of the atmosphere at a given time and place. Mark Twain once said, "If you don't like the weather, wait a few minutes." The conditions that control weather patterns can fluctuate quickly, changing the weather outlook just as quickly. If you take into account the incorrect weather projections made by meteorologists (scientists who study the weather), you can agree with Mark Twain's statement.

Meteorology is the study of the entire atmosphere, including its weather. To understand the weather, meteorologists must understand how the atmosphere heats and cools, how the clouds form and produce rain, and what makes the wind blow. To predict weather patterns, they use a variety of instruments.

Tools of the Trade

One instrument used by meteorologists is the barometer, which is used to measure air pressure. Rising air pressure is usually a sign that the weather is going to improve. When the air pressure falls, it is a sign of approaching bad weather. Animals such as bats and swallows don't need barometers to detect low air pressure. These animals know when the air pressure is low and do not attempt flying during these conditions. Bats rely on the higher air pressure to help get them off the ground during flight. But humans need barometers to help detect air pressure changes.

© 1994 by The Center for Applied Research in Education

Thermometers are used by meteorologists to determine the temperature of the atmosphere. Fluctuations in the temperature of the air directly influence many other weather conditions. As the temperature of the air changes, the capacity of the air to hold water changes. The warmer the air becomes, the more water vapor the air can hold. Specific humidity is the name given to the amount of water vapor actually present in the air. A more useful term dealing with this concept is *relative humidity*. During a weather forecast, the relative humidity is given as a percentage that compares the actual amount of water vapor in the air to the maximum amount of water vapor the air can hold at that temperature. Relative humidity is calculated by dividing the specific humidity by the maximum water-holding capacity of the air at that temperature. Instruments such as hygrometers and psychometers are used to detect relative humidity. The point at which the atmosphere can accept no more water vapor is known as 100% humidity. This is a saturated condition. It is easy to detect 100% humidity by feel, because when coupled with warm temperatures, this condition prevents sweat from evaporating from your skin. You recognize high humidity as a sticky, uncomfortable feeling.

The direction and the speed of the wind are two more factors that influence weather patterns. Wind information is gathered from weather ships, weather stations, and satellites in space. That data is then used to predict the weather. Differences in the air pressure influence the wind patterns. Air pressure is normally the same in all directions, but if pressure becomes greater in one direction than in another, some kind of movement will result. Air movement is wind. Wind vanes are simple mechanisms used to determine the direction from which the wind blows. The direction of the wind can be a key in weather predictions. In the northeast part of the United States, a winter wind from the northeast can mean a blizzard. In the summer, an east wind may bring rain.

The speed of the wind is another good weather predictor. An instrument called an anemometer is used to find the speed of the wind. In 1806 an English admiral called Sir Francis Beaufort worked out a scale from zero to 12 to indicate the strength of the wind. A zero on the scale was calm wind with speeds under 2.5 miles per hour. At the other extreme of his scale are hurricanes. These storms carry a rank of 12 with winds above 95 miles per hour.

Interrupting for a Weather Center Bulletin

Anyone who has watched TV for any length of time has probably had his or her favorite show interrupted by a thunderstorm watch or warning. Thunderstorm watches indicate to the viewers that conditions where they live are favorable for a thunderstorm to develop. A warning indicates that a storm has been sighted in the area. A thunderstorm is a small-area storm formed by strong upward movements of warm, moist air. Two major types of thunderstorms exist: air mass thunderstorms and frontal thunderstorms. An air mass thunderstorm is formed from warm, moist air masses. These begin when a surface is strongly heated, and they last less than an hour. They usually occur in the summer and spring and are widely scattered over land. The frontal thunderstorms form in warm, moist air on or ahead of cold fronts. These thunderstorms often occur in lines along the frontal surface. Slow-moving fronts on squall lines can produce heavy rain and flooding. Frontal storms are stronger and of longer duration than air mass thunderstorms.

Both types of thunderstorms are accompanied by lightning and thunder and usually produce rain. Strong versions of thunderstorms produce high winds, hail, and even tornadoes. The lightning from thunderstorms comes from a discharge of electricity between a thunder cloud and the ground or from one cloud to another. The high temperatures in the lightning bolt heat up the air, causing a sudden, explosive expansion of the air called thunder. Since sound travels much more slowly than light, one sees lightning before hearing thunder. Since light travels at 186,000 miles per second, lightning can be seen immediately. Sound (thunder) takes about 5 seconds to travel 1 mile. To determine how far away (in miles) lightning strikes are, count the seconds between a flash and a boom and divide by 5.

Violent Storm—Take Cover

Tornadoes may accompany violent thunderstorms. They are more frequent in the United States than any other place in the world. Most tornadoes occur in the Mississippi River valley and the Great Plains. Warm air from the Gulf of Mexico moves northward into the Mississippi River valley and into the Great Plains, fueling these storms. The funnel in a tornado is a mixture of clouds and dust. The air pressure is low near the center of a tornado. The low pressure of the tornado causes the condensation level to dip downward, forming a funnel. This funnel-shaped column of spiral winds extends downward from the cloud base toward the ground. The strength of a tornado varies greatly. The strongest winds in a tornado can be between 360 and 500 km/hour. A tornado normally follows an irregular path of less than 25 km long and usually survives no longer than an hour before running out of energy. These storms are often accompanied by heavy rain, lightning, and hail.

Hurricanes are violent storms that occur most often on the Gulf and Atlantic coasts. These storms have intense tropical low pressure with sustaining winds of 120 km/hour or greater. The winds in a hurricane spiral toward the center. A hurricane grows larger and more powerful from the vast amounts of energy released in it by condensing water vapor. Hurricanes have a central area of sinking air called the eye (about 15 to 50 km in diameter). You may have heard someone say that the eye of a hurricane is calm. This is true.

As the air in the eye sinks, it produces no rain and little wind. In comparison, winds just outside the eye are the most violent and can reach up to 240 km/hour. In fact, winds and rain increase toward the center of a hurricane. The average diameter of a hurricane is about 300 to 600 km.

You may wonder where the custom of naming hurricanes originated. World War II pilots began the tradition by naming hurricanes after their girlfriends and wives. They even went as far as naming one hurricane after President Truman's wife, Bess. Later in 1950, the Weather Bureau began issuing an alphabetical list of women's names for the hurricanes they expected each year. Finally, in the late 1970s, after some objections from the female population, the Weather Bureau began naming hurricanes after both men and women.

WEATHER OR NOT—VOCABULARY CROSSWORD PUZZLE ON *WEATHERING THE STORM*

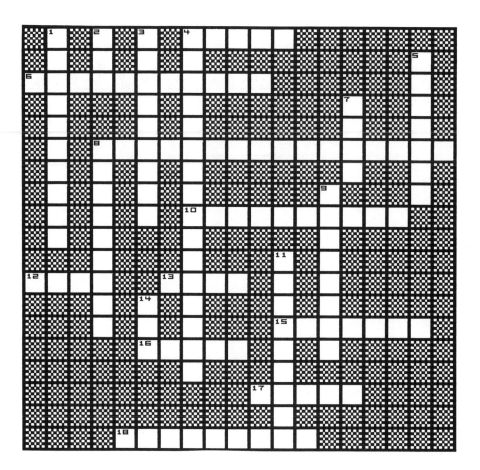

Across

4. When the air pressure _____, it is usually a sign that better weather is approaching.

6. The study of the weather and the atmosphere is _____.

8. The name given to the amount of water vapor actually present in the air is _____.

10. This is the name of the instrument used to detect humidity.

12. The funnel of a tornado is a mixture of clouds and _____.

15. The type of thunderstorm that lasts less than an hour and starts when a surface is strongly heated is _____.

16. A thunderstorm or tornado _____ means that conditions are right for these storms to develop.

17. This travels at 186,000 miles per second and allows us to see lightning before hearing thunder.

18. Winds in these storms spiral toward the center and are named for both men and women.

Down

1. This instrument is used to detect wind speed.

2. This is the central area of sinking air in a hurricane.

3. This instrument is used to measure air pressure.

4. A percentage that compares the actual amount of water vapor in the air to the amount the air can hold is _____.

5. This is the type of thunderstorm that lasts several hours and forms ahead of cold fronts.

7. The eye of a hurricane has little wind and no _____.

8. This condition results when the relative humidity is 100%.

9. This is the scale that ranges from 0 to 12 to indicate the strength of winds.

11. In storms, when the air is heated by lightning, _____ occurs.

14. When the air pressure is _____, it may be a sign the weather is going to turn bad.

Word List

AIRMASS	FRONTAL	RELATIVE HUMIDITY
ANEMOMETER	HURRICANE	RISES
BAROMETER	HYGROMETER	SATURATED
BEAUFORT	LIGHT	SPECIFIC HUMIDITY
DUST	LOW	WATCH
EXPANSION	METEOROLOGY	WIND
EYE	RAIN	

3–2 HYGROMETER ENGINEERING
Lab on Measuring Relative Humidity

Objectives

Students will construct and use a hygrometer to measure relative humidity.

Teacher Notes

None

HYGROMETER LAB
Lab on Measuring Relative Humidity

Objective

In this lab you will construct and use a hygrometer.

Background Information

Visualize this situation:

Terri gets up on Saturday morning about 8:00 to get ready for her 9:30 step aerobics class. She flips on the television to find out if she needs to wear long pants over her leotard this morning. The weather station indicates that the temperature is 60 degrees Fahrenheit and the relative humidity is 97%. Terri decides it is cool enough to wear sweat pants because it is just 60 degrees outside, but she does not take into consideration the humidity reading.

Once Terri gets to the health club, she goes to the aerobics room. She arrives just in time for class and decides not to take off her sweat pants until she warms up. After only about five minutes of aerobics, Terri notices she is dripping with sweat and does not seem to be cooling off as easily as usual. She dislikes this hot, sticky feeling and wonders why she is so soaked with sweat this morning.

In the preceding description, Terri's body is not cooling off as quickly as usual because of the high humidity. When the humidity is high, sweat does not evaporate from your body as quickly as usual. This occurs because the atmosphere is already full of water vapor. When the relative humidity is 100%, the atmosphere is saturated (completely full of water vapor at that temperature). In the preceding example, the 97% reading means that very little water vapor can enter into the atmosphere, and therefore sweat stays on the skin and does not evaporate. This, in turn, prevents cooling because heat is not drawn away from the skin. The result is a hot, dry, sticky feeling.

The relative humidity compares the actual amount of water vapor in the air with the maximum amount of water vapor the air can hold at that temperature. This can be calculated by dividing the specific humidity by capacity. For instance, 1 kg of air at 15.5 degrees Celsius can hold 11 grams of water vapor. If you have 5.5 grams of water vapor in the air, the relative humidity is 5.5/11, or 50%.

People usually feel good when the humidity is low, even if the temperature is high. But when the humidity is high, it can be very uncomfortable. The humidity allows you to predict how comfortable or uncomfortable you will be during the day.

Hygrometers are instruments used to find the relative humidity. A simple type of hygrometer is a hair hygrometer. It works on the principle that human hair stretches when it is humid. Human hair is attached to a fixed point on one end and a pointer on the other end. When the hair stretches, the pointer moves up. When the hair gets dry, the pointer moves down. Another type of hygrometer is a psychrometer. It works on the principle that evaporation causes cooling. A simple version of this can be constructed by using wet- and dry-bulb thermometers and comparing the difference in temperature of these two thermometers. In the following activity, you will construct a psychrometer to detect relative humidity.

Prelab Questions

1. What is relative humidity?

2. What does it mean when the relative humidity of the air is 75%?

3. Would it be more comfortable to jog in weather that is 60 degrees at 98% relative humidity or 70 degrees at 20% relative humidity? Explain your answer.

4. What is meant by saturated conditions of the atmosphere?

5. Explain why you get hotter and stickier in humid weather than in dry weather.

Materials

Two standard thermometers (Fahrenheit)
Cotton or cotton fabric about 3 to 4 inches long (it will be dampened before use)
Narrow-mouth bottle (like a soda bottle)
Water
Table of relative humidity
Tall container
Rubber bands
Modeling clay

Procedure

1. Wrap the bulb end of a thermometer with cotton fabric that has been soaked in water. Use a rubber band to secure the cotton fabric to the thermometer.

2. Lower the cotton-wrapped end of the thermometer into a soda bottle that is about one fourth full of water. Submerge only the part of the thermometer covered with fabric into the water. The water will travel up through the cotton fabric to keep the bulb wet.

3. Take the modeling clay and secure the thermometer in that position in the bottle to keep the thermometer from slipping down deeper into the water.

4. Take the bottle with the thermometer (called a wet-bulb thermometer) and position it in a convenient location in the room.

5. Do the same for another thermometer, but do not wrap the bulb or place it in water. Just lower the thermometer into the soda bottle and attach it with clay. This is a dry-bulb thermometer.

6. Place the wet- and dry-bulb thermometers beside each other (see Figure A) and observe their temperature readings over the next several days. Record your data in Table 1. Record in the blanks at the bottom of the table the way you feel during those

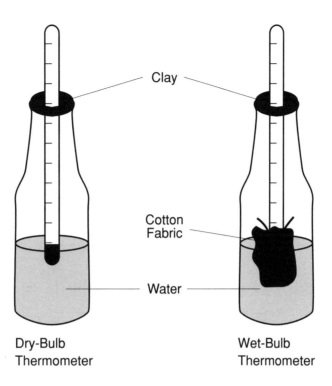

Clay

Cotton
Fabric

Water

Dry-Bulb
Thermometer

Wet-Bulb
Thermometer

FIGURE A

days. Could you tell if the humidity was high or low? Did you sweat a great deal or were you feeling sticky? and so on.

7. Use the difference in the two temperature readings to calculate the relative humidity. Read this answer from the relative humidity chart provided in Figure B.

8. Answer the postlab questions.

Hygrometer Lab *(continued)*

TABLE 1

Day of week	Dry-bulb temp.	Wet-bulb temp.	Difference in wet- and dry-bulb reading	Relative humidity

Notes on how you felt each day:

_____

_____

_____

_____

_____

_____

HYGROMETER LAB *(continued)*

Relative Humidity Chart

Use the left column in this chart to find the dry-bulb reading in degrees Fahrenheit. Subtract the difference in the dry-bulb and wet-bulb reading on that day, and locate that number along the top horizontal column. At the intersection of these two readings, you will find the relative humidity.

Example: If the dry-bulb temperature was 72 degrees Fahrenheit (F), you would locate 72 under the dry-bulb column. If the wet bulb had been 68 degrees F, subtract 72 from 68, and you get 4. Locate the 4 along the top of the chart for difference in wet and dry. Then intersect the two readings. You will find 82% as your answer. If you do not get any difference in readings, the humidity is 100%.

RELATIVE HUMIDITY CHART

Dry Bulb Reading	Difference Between Dry and Wet Bulb											
°F	1	2	3	4	5	6	7	8	9	10	11	12
66	95	90	85	80	75	71	66	61	57	53	48	44
68	95	90	85	80	76	71	67	62	58	54	50	46
70	95	90	86	81	77	72	68	64	59	55	51	48
72	95	91	86	82	77	73	69	65	61	57	53	49
74	95	91	86	82	78	74	69	65	61	58	54	50
76	96	91	87	82	78	74	70	66	62	59	55	51
78	96	91	87	83	79	75	71	67	63	60	56	53
80	96	91	87	83	79	75	72	68	64	61	57	54
82	96	92	88	84	80	76	72	69	65	61	58	55
84	96	92	88	84	80	76	73	69	66	62	59	56
86	96	92	88	84	81	77	73	70	66	63	60	57
88	96	92	88	85	81	77	74	70	67	64	61	57
90	96	92	89	85	81	78	74	71	68	65	61	58

FIGURE B

HYGROMETER LAB *(continued)*

Postlab Questions

1. Will the temperature on the dry bulb or wet bulb usually be higher? Explain why.

2. Will the humidity be higher when there is a slight or great difference in the temperature readings of these two thermometers? Explain your reasons.

3. Why will the humidity be 100% when the readings show no difference in temperature?

4. As the temperature of the dry bulb increases and the difference in temperature decreases, will the humidity tend to increase or decrease? Choose an answer and explain.

5. Add together the humidity readings for all five days or more, and divide by the number of days to get your average humidity for that week.

6. Describe any days on which you could tell the humidity was high or low, and tell why.

LESSON 4: WATER

4–1 THE WATER PLANET
Content on Water

Water Everywhere

Fresh water, salt water, water table, water works, water hazards, potable water, bath water, boiling water—our lives are built around this essential compound, water. Earth is often called the water planet because three quarters of its surface is covered with water. Throughout their existence on earth, humans have taken the plentiful water supply for granted. Only recently have humans come to regard this renewable resource with the respect it deserves.

We do not have an endless water supply. Even though planet earth is very wet, 97% of all the water on earth is salt water and cannot be used by terrestrial plants and animals. Of the remaining 3% of fresh water, 2% is tied up in glaciers around the polar caps. That leaves 1% of the earth's total water that is available for human use. Water occurs in all three states of matter—solid, liquid, and gas—and is distributed throughout the earth in terrestrial, oceanic, and atmospheric reserves.

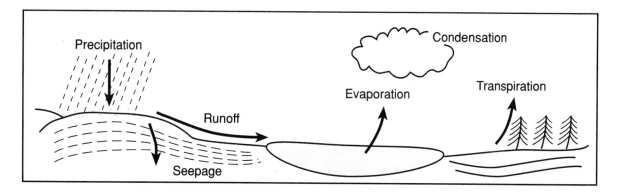

FIGURE A. The Water Cycle

Water Cycle

The water, or hydrologic, cycle has moved water from one part of the earth to another since the existence of the earth. New water is never created, and the total volume of water has remained constant for millions of years. We are using the same water in which bacteria evolved and that the dinosaurs drank. Water molecules spend thousands of years circulating from the bodies of living things to surface water, to water vapor and back to the ocean or glaciers.

Figure A illustrates the water cycle. This cycle is sustained by energy from the sun. The sun's heat causes water to evaporate (or change from a liquid to a gas) from the land and seas. Water also enters the atmosphere by transpiration, an evaporative process in which plants lose water. Water frozen in glaciers can evaporate to a gaseous form by the process of sublimation.

Water vapor in the atmosphere condenses into a liquid again and forms clouds. From these clouds, water falls in various forms of precipitation and replenishes supplies in the ground, in rivers, and in oceans. Rain, snow, sleet, and hail are forms of precipitation.

Once precipitation reaches the earth's surface, it follows one of several possible routes. In one route, water percolates through the soil to become ground water. Most of the unfrozen ground water in the United States is in underground reservoirs. Ground water within 1000 feet of the earth's surface can be recovered economically. The volume of this ground water is about nine times the volume of water in the Great Lakes. Fifty percent of the U.S. population gets it water from ground water, and the primary use of ground water is for irrigation.

Ground Water

Ground-water supplies can be depleted if the rate of withdrawal exceeds the natural rate of recharge or replenishment. Under the Great Plains of the United States, a huge aquifer, or underground reservoir, exists called the Ogallala aquifer. Humans have removed water from the Ogallala since the 1930s to irrigate the dry land of the Great Plains regions, converting this area to the lush "breadbasket of America." Water has been pumped from the Ogallala for the last 60 years and has been used primarily to irrigate fields. The removal of water from this aquifer is 50 times faster than can be replenished by rain. The water table is dropping drastically as the reservoir is emptied. Consequently, farmers are changing their farming methods to raise crops that require little or no water.

Water that does not infiltrate the ground becomes runoff, which travels as streams and rivers to the sea. The land area that delivers the water and its load of sediment and dissolved minerals is called the watershed or drainage basin. Water flows from high elevations to lower ones due to the force of gravity. Rapid flow over steep terrain often erodes and reshapes the land. Materials washed into a river from the land, together with the sediment that eroded from the channel, make up a river's load. The kinds and amounts of substances dissolved in water depend on the climate, the rock and soil composition, and human activities in the basin. Pollutants in the drainage basin can include gas and oil from road surfaces, fertilizers from fields, animal manure from feedlots, and pesticides from farms.

Water that falls as precipitation can also rejoin existing water bodies such as rivers, lakes, and oceans. Water molecules that fall into fresh water systems are available to plants and animals, which must have water to survive. These molecules will one day be excreted from the animals and evaporated from the plants to reenter the atmospheric water supply.

WATER WORDS—VOCABULARY ACTIVITY ON
THE WATER PLANET

Using the following clues, complete the words in the raindrop.

1. The _____ provides energy that drives the water cycle.
2. A river's _____ is composed of sediment plus materials from the watershed area.
3. Running water can cause soil to _____.
4. In the atmosphere, water vapor condenses to form _____.
5. A large, underground resevoir is a(n) _____.
6. Rain helps refill or _____ an aquifer.
7. The land area that delivers water and its load to a stream is the _____.
8. Runoff may include oil, gas, fertilizer, and other _____.
9. _____ occurs when ice changes to a vapor.
10. The water cycle is also called the _____ cycle.
11. Water can _____ into the atmosphere from lakes and rivers.
12. _____ means to change from a gas to a liquid.
13. A _____ is a large body of ice.
14. Water can exist as a solid, _____, or gas.
15. Because of the water _____, water changes from a gas to a liquid and back to a gas.

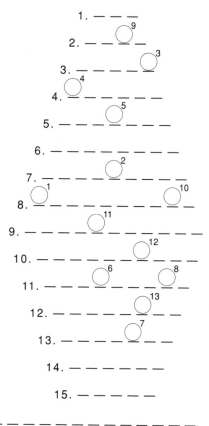

4–2 BEARLY RAINING
Lab on Drainage Basins

Objectives

Students will read a topographic map, determine the volume of rain that falls on an area, and explore ways a drainage basin affects water quality.

Teacher Notes

A hypothetical school campus is used in this example. However, you can determine the volume of water that falls on your campus by measuring the area with a trundle wheel or tape measure. An estimate of school ground size is also acceptable for an activity such as this. The amount of annual rainfall in your area can be obtained from almanacs, newspapers, and TV weather stations. Or you can determine the volume of rain that falls during one rainfall event with a rain gauge.

BEARLY RAINING
Lab on Drainage Basins

Introduction

    Figure A is a topographic map that shows the Little Dipper High School (LDHS) campus and surrounding area. You can determine elevations on the topographic (topo) map by reading the numbers written on one of the topo lines. Each line represents a 50-foot change in elevation. Creeks and rivers are on the lowest elevations, and roadbeds are generally built on ridges.

    The school campus is marked with four X's. The campus width is 320 yards, and its length is 599 yards. The annual rainfall for this locale is 59 inches per year.

    The Bear Creek drainage basin includes all that land area from which runoff flows to Bear Creek. Water always flows downhill, and since LDHS is on the top of a hill, the rain that falls on campus flows toward both creeks. The quality of this runoff from the school campus is affected by the activities of people in the drainage basin.

Materials

    Topographic map
    Colored pencils

Procedure

1. The average volume of rain that falls on this campus per month can be determined by multiplying the length of the campus by the width of the campus by the depth of rain each month. Divide annual rainfall by 12 to determine average monthly rainfall. Be sure to change all numbers to the same units. Record your answer in Table 1.

   Area = Length × width × height

2. How much does this monthly rain weigh? One cubic foot of water weighs 62.5 pounds. Convert this weight to kilograms. There are 0.454 kilograms in one pound. Record your answer in Table 1.

3. Determine the elevation of the school by reading one of the marked topo lines and counting the number of 50-foot lines between the one marked and the school.

4. Where does the water that falls on the school campus eventually go?

5. Shade the Bear Creek drainage basin in yellow and the Little Bear Creek drainage basin in pale blue.

6. On your map, add some features that will affect the quality of the water in the Bear Creek basin and the Little Bear Creek basin. These could include, but are not limited to, homes, roads, pastures, barns, businesses, and parks. (See the key for appropriate symbols.)

7. Indicate with dots areas that might support wildlife.

© 1994 by The Center for Applied Research in Education

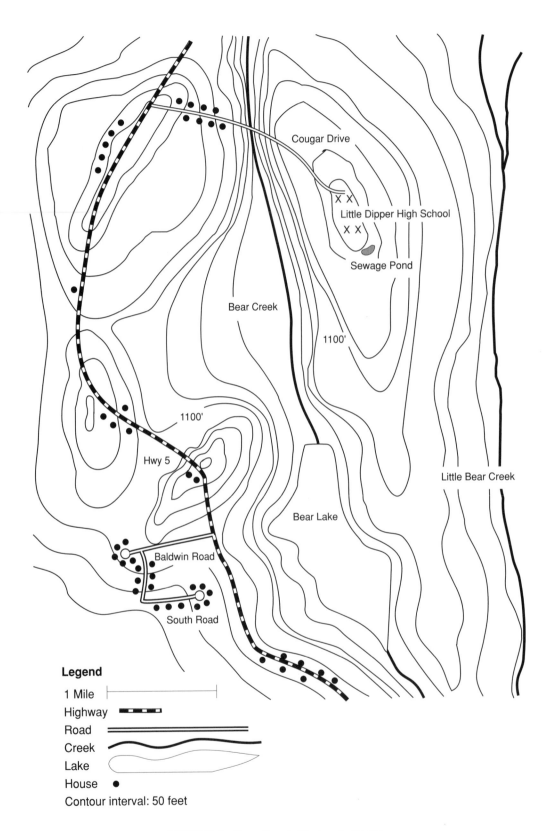

FIGURE A. Bear Creek Drainage Basin

BEARLY RAINING *(continued)*

Conclusions

1. Complete Table 1 with data from your calculations.

TABLE 1
Rain on Little Dipper High School Campus

Annual rain volume	Monthly rain volume	Weight of annual rain in pounds	Weight of annual rain in kilograms	Weight of monthly rain in pounds	Weight of monthly rain in kilograms

2. What is the elevation of Little Dipper High School?

3. What did you add to the drainage basin of Bear Creek? How will your additions affect the quality of water in the creek?

4. What did you add to the drainage basin of Little Bear Creek? How will your additions affect the quality of water in the creek?

5. How will wildlife in the area be affected by changes in the runoff of these two creeks?

6. If all of the vegetation between LDHS and Bear Creek was removed, how would the runoff and the creek be affected? Explain your answer.

SECTION 2

Physics

LESSON 5: WAVE ENERGY

5–1 WAVE ON
Content on Wave Energy

What Wave?

Have you ever done the wave at a baseball game? That undulating motion produced by spectators standing, one after another, in sequence reminds us of the motion of waves in nature. Waves are difficult to see because most of them are invisible. But like the wave at a baseball game, the energy in waves moves from one place to another.

If you drop a marble into a pool of water, you create a wave. The marble has kinetic energy because it is moving, and it transfers some of this energy to the water particles, causing them to move. The particles of water transfer this energy to adjacent particles, and the wave moves outward from the center.

A Disturbance

A wave is a disturbance that moves energy through matter or space. The matter or space through which a wave moves is described as the medium. Air is a medium for sound waves. Light waves do not need a medium because they can travel through a vacuum. As a wave travels through a medium, the medium does not move along with the wave. Only the energy is transmitted. To see this, tie a string to a doorknob, and move it up and down to form a wave (see Figure A). The string is not moving toward the doorknob, but energy is moving along the string. The wave moves from your hand to the doorknob. But the medium, a string in this case, moves up and down.

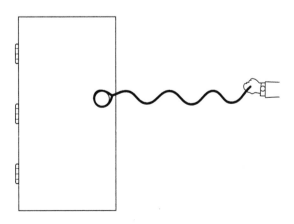

FIGURE A

Transverse and Longitudinal Waves

There are two types of waves: transverse and longitudinal. An ocean wave is a transverse wave because the medium (the ocean) moves at right angles to the wave. Just like the string you tied to a doorknob, the ocean moves up and down, but the wave moves toward the shore. The crest of a transverse wave is the high point, and the trough is the lowest downward point (see Figure B).

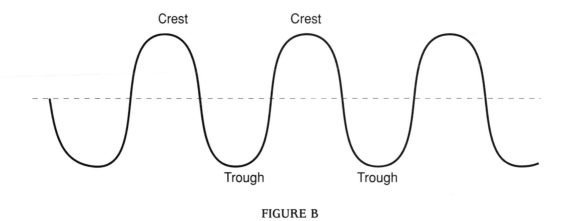

FIGURE B

In longitudinal waves, the medium moves back and forth in the same direction as the wave travels. Ask a friend to hold one end of a Slinky®. When you push your end of the Slinky® in and out, you are creating a longitudinal wave. Particles of the medium are compressed or pushed together in areas called compressions. As a compression moves forward, it leaves behind a space containing fewer particles, called a rarefaction. Sound waves travel in this manner.

Wave Characteristics

There are many types of waves: sound waves, light waves, radio and television waves. All waves have some common characteristics.

Amplitude. This characteristic refers to the maximum distance molecules of the medium are displaced from their original position. If you push the Slinky® very gently, the waves you create will have a small amplitude. However, if you shove the Slinky® forward with a lot of force, you can create waves with large amplitudes.

Wavelength. All waves are measured by wavelengths. A wavelength is the distance between two consecutive crests or between two successive identical wave parts. Wavelength is usually measured in meters or centimeters. However, wavelengths of light are measured in millionths of a meter (micrometers).

Frequency. The number of waves that pass a point per unit of time is called frequency. For example, if 1000 complete waves passed a point in one second, the waves would have a frequency of 1000 cycles per second. Wave frequency is measured in units called hertz (Hz). A frequency of 1 Hz is equal to one wave per second. Higher frequencies are measured in kilohertz (kHz), and extremely high frequencies are measured in megahertz (MHz). AM radio waves are broadcast in kilohertz, but FM waves are broadcast in megahertz. If a station is 104 MHz on the FM radio, it is broadcasting waves with a frequency of 140,000,000 hertz. These waves are produced by electrons vibrating at the same frequency in the radio station's transmitting antenna.

Sound

Sounds are produced by vibrating objects that cause the surrounding medium, air, to vibrate. The speed of sound in air is about 340 meters per second. You can determine how far you are from a bolt of lightning by counting the number of seconds between the time you see the lightning and the time you hear the thunder. Multiply the number of seconds between the lightning and the sound of thunder by 340 meters, and you know how far you are from the storm. Thunder is a compression of air molecules caused by the heat of the lightning bolt. Light travels about a million times faster than sound, so the light from the lightning bolt reaches your eyes almost instantly.

Sound has two important components.

Intensity. The amount of energy in a sound wave is referred to as that wave's intensity. Intensity determines the loudness of a sound, and is measured in units called decibels. The decibel scale begins at zero, the point at which we can just hear. The sound of a rocket engine is deafening and is 200 on the decibel scale. All sounds with intensities near 120 decibels can cause pain to humans. Sounds above 85 decibels can damage hearing. Loud music, especially played through earphones, damages many people's hearing.

Pitch. Sound waves also have pitch, which is determined by how fast the molecules of the medium are vibrating. The frequency of a sound wave determines the pitch of a sound. High-frequency sound waves have high pitches. A high note by a female singer may be about 1000 Hz, and a male bass may sing at 70 Hz. Humans can hear sounds between 20 Hz and 20,000 Hz. Ultrasonic sounds are those waves whose frequencies are above 20,000 Hz. Dogs can hear pitches up to 25,000 Hz, and porpoises can hear them up to 150,000 Hz. Some bats produce their own ultrasonic frequencies, which they use for navigation.

The Doppler Effect

Have you ever listened to the sound of a siren approaching you? The pitch of the siren gets higher as it approaches you due to the Doppler effect. When there is motion between the observer and the source of sound, the frequency of sound waves changes. As the sound approaches the observer, the waves are compressed closer together, and waves reach the observer sooner than they would have if the source of sound had not been moving. Therefore, sound waves that reach the observer seem to have a higher pitch because their frequency has increased. As the source of sound moves away from the observer, the sound waves are farther apart, and the pitch drops.

WAVES—VOCABULARY ACTIVITY FOR
WAVE ON

Select a word from the wave below that fits in the following sentences. Some words can be used twice.

wave   amplitude   bats
medium   rarefraction   hertz   intensity
transverse   compression   frequency   sound
longitudinal   trough   Doppler   decibels
crest   ultrasonic

1. The _____ of a sound wave determines a sound's pitch.

2. Ocean waves are _____ waves because the water and the waves move at right angles to each other.

3. In a longitudinal wave, the space where there are few particles of medium is called a _____.

4. Some _____ can produce ultrasonic sounds, which they use for navigational purposes.

5. A _____ is a disturbance that moves energy through space or matter.

6. Sound is a _____ wave because the medium moves back and forth in the same direction as the wave travels.

7. The _____ of a transverse wave is the highest point, or point of maximum displacement, of the wave.

8. The sound of an approaching train whistle increases in pitch because of the _____ effect.

9. Sounds that people cannot hear are called _____ sounds.

10. Air is one _____ through which sound can travel.

11. The frequency of sound waves is measured in units called _____.

VOCABULARY ACTIVITY *(continued)*

12. In a sound wave, the space where air particles are pushed together is called a

    _____.

13. A _____ wave is produced by a vibrating object that causes the air molecules to vibrate.

14. The intensity or loudness of a sound is measured in units called _____.

15. Wave _____ refers to the maximum distances medium molecules are displaced.

16. The lowest displacement of a wave is called the wave's _____.

17. A rocket engine produces a wave of high _____, which registers 200 on the decibel scale.

18. Dogs can hear _____ sounds in the 25,000-Hz range.

19. FM radio stations broadcast at frequencies in the mega-_____ range.

20. Sounds above 85 _____ can damage our ears.

5–2 GOOD VIBRATIONS
Lab on Wave Energy

Objectives

Students will create a musical instrument composed of strings that vibrate at different frequencies. In addition, students will relate the pitch of a vibrating string to the number of times the string vibrates.

Teacher Notes

Students do not receive explicit directions for construction of their musical instruments—they can be creative in their design. If you have other materials available beside those suggested in the Materials section, please let your students choose from a variety of supplies when they are in the planning stage. Foot-long pieces of lumber ($2'' \times 4''$) are suggested as the base of the musical instrument. However, different sizes of wood are just as useful. Anything that can support four strings can be used in this lab.

© 1994 by The Center for Applied Research in Education

GOOD VIBRATIONS
Lab on Wave Energy

Introduction

A sound is considered music if it has a pleasing quality, an identifiable pitch, and a repeated timing or rhythm. People have made musical instruments for centuries. Woodwind instruments such as flutes and clarinets produce their sound by vibrating a column of air within the instrument. Drums and other percussion instruments vibrate when they are struck. Stringed instruments vibrate when they are either rubbed or plucked. Guitars, violins, and pianos produce sounds when their strings are vibrated. The pitch of a stringed instrument can be changed by changing the length, tightness, or thickness of the string.

A short string vibrates at a higher frequency than a long one and thus produces a higher pitch. Musicians change the pitch of a string by placing their fingers along it, thus altering its length. A finger placed near the far end of a string shortens it slightly, raising the pitch one or two steps. A finger placed near the center of an instrument shortens the string much more, producing a very high pitch.

The tighter a string, the higher the frequency of its vibration. Pianos, guitars, and violins are tuned by tightening or loosening the strings. When a string is tightened, it produces a higher pitch.

Thick strings vibrate slower, and thus at a lower frequency, than thin strings. The strings on a bass guitar are much thicker than those on the lead guitar. Likewise, the strings on the bass (low) keys of a piano are thicker than those on the treble (high) keys.

In this lab, you will create a four-stringed musical instrument.

Materials

Four pieces of monofilament fishing string or thin wire

Piece of wood (1-foot piece, 2″ by 4″)

Eight tacks

Tape

Procedure

1. Use the materials available from your teacher to create a stringed musical instrument.

2. Your instrument must produce sounds of four pitches. The first string should have the lowest pitch. The second string should have a higher pitch; the third string, a still higher pitch; and the fourth string, the highest pitch.

Conclusion

1. (a) What are some problems you encountered in construction of your instrument?

   (b) How did you solve these problems?

2. Ukuleles are small, guitarlike instruments that have four strings. The first string has the lowest pitch and the last string the highest pitch.

   (a) Which string is probably the tightest?

   (b) Which string is probably the thickest?

3. What other materials might make good strings for musical instruments?

   Why?

LESSON 6: HEAT

6–1 DOING THE ATOMIC SHAKE
Content on Heat Energy

The Heat Is On

Matter is classified as anything that has mass and occupies space. All forms of matter are made up of atoms and molecules. What do you visualize when you think of an atom or a molecule? Some people might say that they see little round dots stacked side by side in nice ordered rows. This isn't the case. The molecules in all forms of matter are constantly moving and jiggling about. All this shaking and moving is due to the kinetic energy these molecules possess. The amount of kinetic energy in these molecules can be detected by the amount of heat given off by a particular form of matter. As the temperature of something increases, the kinetic energy increases.

It is easy to increase the kinetic energy in matter. Hit a baseball hard with an aluminum bat and then feel the point of impact on the bat. The bat has gotten warmer.

This impact has caused the molecules in the metal bat to move and shake faster. Take your hands and rub your palms together quickly. Notice that they begin to get warm. This warmth was the result of speeding up the molecules in your hands. As they speed up, they give off heat.

The Temperature Is Rising

Temperature is the measurement quantity that tells how warm or cold a body is with respect to some standard. A thermometer is an instrument that measures temperature. A thermometer contains either mercury or colored alcohol. These substances expand (rise up the thermometer) when temperature is raised and contract (sink lower on the thermometer) when the temperature is lowered. Thermometers can be marked in the Fahrenheit scale, Celsius scale, or Kelvin scale.

On the Celsius scale (the metric scale most often used to measure temperature), 0 degrees represents the point at which water freezes and 100 degrees represents the point at which water boils. On the Fahrenheit scale, 32 degrees represents the freezing point and 212 degrees represents the boiling point. Kelvin is also a metric scale used to measure temperature. On this scale, temperature is measured in units called kelvins (K). This is a particularly useful scale because 0 K is the lowest possible temperature that anything can reach; furthermore, 0 K is known as absolute zero and is the temperature at which all molecular motion stops.

Temperature measures the motion of molecules or atoms in a substance. Heat is the energy that is transferred from one object to another because of temperature difference between objects. An increase in temperature indicates the addition of heat. A decrease in temperature represents the removal of heat. The calorie is one of the units used to measure heat. One calorie is defined as the amount of heat required to raise the temperature of 1 gram of liquid water 1 degree Celsius. The amount of heat needed for a given temperature change depends on the mass of the water being heated and the specific heat of a substance. Specific heat is the ability of a substance to absorb heat energy. In fact, the specific heat of a substance is the number of calories needed to raise the temperature of 1 gram of that substance 1 Celsius degree. Water has a specific heat rating of 1.0 calorie per gram of Celsius degree. Mercury has a specific heat of 0.03, and wood has a specific heat of 0.42.

Bulging Cans and Sagging Lines

As the temperature of a substance is increased, its molecules move faster and farther apart. The result of this movement is expansion. Have you ever left an aluminum can of soda unopened in your car on a sunny day? Chances are that the can

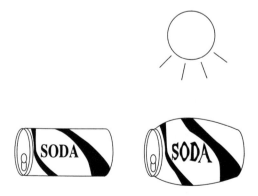

expanded and possibly exploded by the end of the day. This is why warnings are put on aerosol spray containers not to expose them to extreme heat.

The opposite of expansion is contraction. Cold weather slows the molecular motion of substances, and the molecules move closer together. These concepts of expansion and contraction must be considered when buildings are being designed and constructed. The amount of expansion of a substance depends on the amount of heat it absorbs. Why are telephone lines allowed to sag when they are strung between the poles in the summer? The answer lies in expansion. In the summer, when it is warm, the lines are longer; in the cold of winter, they are shorter. If the lines are strung too tightly, they might snap in the winter because they contract when it is cold.

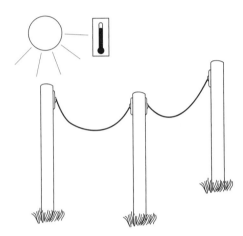

How do liquids fit into the concept of expansion? Almost all liquids expand when they are heated. I bet you have already thought of an exception to that statement. Place some water in your ice trays and pop them in the freezer. What happens? The water freezes and expands. When heat is added, the water will contract. Normally this does not occur with other liquids. The odd crystalline structure of ice explains the expansion of water upon freezing.

Up, Up, and Away

What effect does temperature change have on gases? Gases expand much more than solids and liquids for comparable increases in temperature. But when gases are expanded they do not get warm; they get cooler. When gases are compressed, they do not get cool; they get warmer.

Have you ever thought about why warm air rises? When air is warmed, it expands and becomes less dense than the surrounding air and is buoyed up like a balloon. The buoyancy is upward because the air pressure below a region of warmed air is greater than the pressure above. Thus the warmed air rises because the buoyant force is greater than its weight. If this is true, why is the temperature not warm at high altitudes? Why are the mountain tops usually cool and covered with snow? The warm air moves from a region of greater atmospheric pressure on the ground to a region of less pressure above it. Because it is moving to a region of less pressure, the gas expands and the temperature drops.

ATOMIC SHAKE—VOCABULARY CROSSWORD PUZZLE ON
DOING THE ATOMIC SHAKE

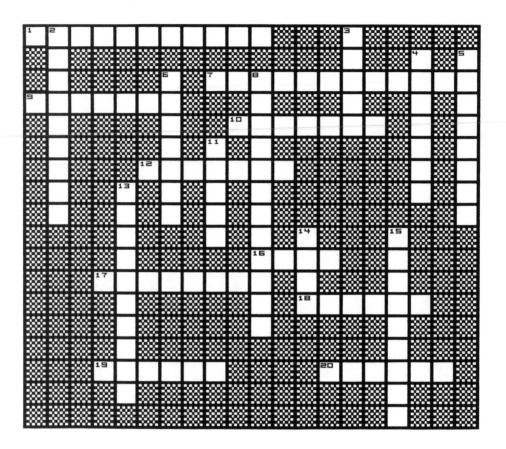

Across

1. The quantity that tells how warm or cold a body is with respect to some standard.

7. This is the lowest possible temperature anything can reach—it is 0 degrees Kelvin.

9. The amount of heat required to raise the temperature of 1 gram of liquid 1 degree Celsius.

10. A metal used in thermometers—responds to temperature change by contracting and expanding.

12. This energy can be detected by the amount of heat given off by the form of matter.

16. This is the energy transferred from one object to another because of temperature change.

17. This is lower below a region of warmed air than above it, causing warm air to rise.

18. During this season, power lines will often sag due to expansion.

19. Metric scale used to measure temperature—absolute zero is found on this scale.

20. When gases are expanded, their temperature will become _____ than when it is contracted.

Down

2. When the temperature of substances increase, _____ of the substance may occur.

3. The specific heat of this substance is 1.0.

4. The units used in the Kelvin scale.

5. This occurs when substances are cooled and decrease in size.

6. Metric temperature scale most often used to measure temperature (100 is boiling).

8. The ability of a substance to absorb heat energy.

11. Warm air is less _____ than cold air, so it rises above it.

13. When gases are _____, they do not get cool, they get warmer.

14. The amount of heat needed for a given temperature change depends on the _____ of water heated.

15. These move and shake due to kinetic energy in forms of matter.

Word List

ABSOLUTE ZERO	EXPANSION	MOLECULES
CALORIE	HEAT	PRESSURE
CELSIUS	KELVIN	SPECIFIC HEAT
COOLER	KELVINS	SUMMER
CONTRACT	KINETIC	TEMPERATURE
COMPRESSED	MASS	WATER
DENSE	MERCURY	

6–2 UP, UP, AND AWAY
Lab on Heat Energy

Objectives

Students will discover how hot air causes objects to rise by building a hot air balloon.

Teacher Notes

None

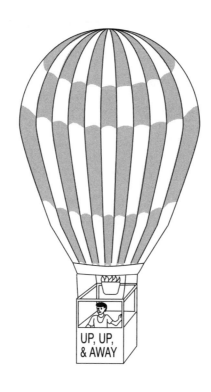

UP, UP,
& AWAY

Up, Up, and Away
Lab on Heat Energy

Introduction

If you were to hold a piece of tissue paper above a radiator that was emitting warm air, you would see the tissue begin to float upward. This is caused by warm air currents pushing up on the tissue paper. Warm air is lighter than cold air and will rise. The cold air will then move under the warm air to take its place. This is one reason that the top floor of two-story homes is hotter than the bottom floor in the summer.

As the colder air moves in underneath the rising warm air, currents of air result. Birds take advantage of these currents and float for long distances with little effort. Gliders also use this mechanism to stay airborne. They use the rising currents of warm air once they are high enough in the sky to manage this technique.

When air is warmed, it will expand. If you don't believe this, blow up a balloon and hold it over the top of a radiator. Before too long, the balloon will burst due to expansion.

In this activity, you will make a hot air balloon. In real life, hot air balloons are filled with hot air. The hot air is lighter and less dense than the air around the balloon. The hot air balloon is buoyed upward because the air pressure below a region of warmed air is greater than the pressure above it. The modern-day version of the hot air balloon has a gas burner to heat the air inside the balloon. The wind then carries the balloon along.

Prelab Questions

1. Explain why hot air rises.

2. Describe how hot and cold air can cause currents in a home or outdoors.

3. How is pressure related to the rising of hot air?

4. Explain why a bottle of hair spray might explode if left in a hot car all day.

5. If you were to put a balloon over a bottle placed in hot water and one over a bottle placed in ice water, which balloon might get larger? Explain.

Materials

One sheet of tissue wrapping paper for each group of two or three

Glue

Hair dryer

Scissors

UP, UP, AND AWAY *(continued)*

Procedure

1. Each group needs one large sheet of the tissue wrapping paper, some glue, and scissors.

2. Groups will compete to design the best hot air balloon.

3. Dimensions and shape do not matter.

4. The balloon will be filled with hot air from the hair dryer. It then should be able to float up to the ceiling.

5. Competitions will be held to see which group can construct the balloon that can float to the ceiling in the least amount of time. The winning team will get extra points on the next test.

6. Each group will be allowed to test out its creation. The teacher will designate a day for the competition in which each group will have its balloon timed.

7. After all balloons have been launched, a class discussion can be conducted.

Postlab questions

1. Describe the balloon that floated to the ceiling the fastest.

2. Explain why you think the balloon you described in question 1 was the best constructed balloon.

3. Explain what problems you encountered with your balloon.

4. How would you build your balloon next time if this experiment was repeated?

5. Summarize in one sentence what you learned from this lab.

© 1994 by The Center for Applied Research in Education

LESSON 7: MOTION

7-1 LET'S GET MOVIN'
Content on the Energy of Motion

It Depends on How You Look at It

Look over at someone's desk in the classroom. Is it moving? Do you witness any motion from the desk? If you answered yes or no to those questions, you are right. This is because the motion of an object depends on the frame of reference you use to evaluate that object. The desk is at rest if you judge it relative to the floor or to yourself; but it is in motion relative to the sun. Since it is located on the earth, the desk is revolving around the sun continuously. Actually, no object on the earth is ever at rest relative to the sun.

For the purpose of our discussions on motion, we will use the earth rather than the sun as our frame of reference. When objects on the earth are placed in motion, they travel certain distances in a given time. The distance an object travels in a given time frame is called speed. Speed is determined by the following formula: speed = distance divided by time $(S = d/t)$.

Is It Speed or Is It Velocity?

There are two types of speed we need to consider in our discussion—instantaneous and average. Instantaneous speed is an easy concept to grasp if you think of a speedometer on a car. The speedometer is registering the speed at that particular instant you are looking at the dial. Unless the car has a cruise control monitor, there will be some fluctuations in the speed over time. Red lights and stop signs and slower motorists dictate that the instantaneous speed will vary. Average speed is the concept that we discuss more often when traveling. Average speed is the total distance an object travels over the total time span it took to achieve this distance. If you went on a trip across the country and wanted to figure your average speed, you could do this by watching your odometer (distance dial on the speedometer) and your watch. Let's say you went 80 miles in 90 minutes. What would your average speed be? Eighty miles divided by 90 minutes would give you speed in miles per minute. Your average speed was 0.89 miles/minute, or you could figure your answer in miles per hour by dividing 80 miles by 1.5 hours. Your average speed would be 53.33 miles/hour.

Most people think of speed and velocity as the same concept. And to everyone but the physicist, this may be true. In physics, velocity is the speed in a given direction. Velocity is determined by dividing the displacement by the time. Displacement is the length and direction of an object's path from its starting point straight to its ending point.

This means that the speed and velocity of an object may be different depending on the route you took to get to your destination. It might be easier to understand this if you pictured a walk with your beagle dog from your house to your grandmother's house. You would probably stay on the sidewalk and walk directly from your house to your destination by using the shortest route. Your beagle would probably veer off the sidewalk and sniff a few trees and run after a couple of rabbits on the trip. This would increase the distance the dog traveled but not his displacement. Therefore, the speed of the dog would be different from your speed, whereas the velocity for both of you would be the same if you both arrived at the house at the same time.

When computing velocity, you not only state the magnitude of the velocity but also the direction traveled. Magnitude and direction traveled are called vector quantities in physics, whereas magnitude without direction is called a scalar quantity. Speed is a scalar quantity and velocity is a vector quantity.

Let's return to our walk with the beagle to reinforce these concepts. It is 4 miles to your grandmother's house by the shortest route you can travel. She lives due west of your home. You and your dog, Doc, accomplished this mileage in 60 minutes. You took the straight path of 4 miles, but Doc logged in 6 miles as he veered off the path for some rabbit-hunting adventures. Your speed was 4 miles/hour. Your velocity was 4 miles/hour west. Doc's velocity was 4 miles/hour west, but his speed was 6 miles/hour (distance traveled divided by time).

There's No Cruise Control on Roller Coasters

Another vector quantity we need to mention is acceleration. Acceleration is the rate of change in velocity. Since acceleration is a vector quantity, it can involve a change in speed, a change of direction, or both. Have you ever experienced or felt acceleration? If you have braved the amusement park's roller coaster rides you have experienced acceleration. Changes in speed can be detected easily as you feel your body jarred about as the roller coaster slows down and speeds up. The formula for finding the magnitude of acceleration is as follows: acceleration equals change in velocity divided by time, or a = final velocity – initial velocity/time for change in velocity. Acceleration can be represented by either negative or positive numbers. When objects speed up, you have positive acceleration. When objects slow down, you have negative acceleration (known as deceleration). Think about the next three situations.

Situation 1—You have a new set of "wheels." You want to try them out to see what the new car can do. You begin at a stop sign and press the accelerator as you move south on Main

Street. You find that your speedometer reaches 60 miles/hour after 4 seconds. What was the acceleration of your new car?

Situation 2—You are out for your nightly jog. You are jogging along at a constant 3 meter/sec pace. A car turns sharply in front of you, and you have to stop suddenly to avoid being struck. Your sneakers skid to a dead stop in 0.9 seconds. What was your deceleration?

Situation 3—You go to the oval-shaped dirt race track to do a little practice driving. You keep your car at 90 miles per hour for 10 seconds without changing your speed. Was the car accelerating? If so, explain why.

You have jostled your brain cells to solve these problems. Let's see if your solutions were correct. In situation 1, you should have answered that the acceleration of the car would be 0.00417 miles per second square. In situation 2, your acceleration was negative. You should have come up with a negative 3.3 meters per second^2. Finally, in situation 3, the car was accelerating due to a change in direction on the oval track.

Solutions

Situation 1—To solve this problem, you must change miles/hour to miles/second or either change seconds to hours. Let's change miles/hour to miles per second. 60 miles/hour divided by 3600 sec = 0.01667 miles/sec. Now use the miles per second in the acceleration formula:

$$a = 0.01667 \text{ miles/sec} - 0/4 \text{ sec} = 0.00417 \text{ miles/sec}^2.$$

Situation 2—$a = 0 - 3$ miles/sec/0.9 sec = $-3/0.9 = -3.3$ miles/sec^2.

Situation 3—The car was accelerating even though the speed was not being changed, because acceleration is a vector quantity. Vector quantities are also affected by changes in direction, which occurred on the oval track.

Free Fall

The last concept we want to examine is free fall. Objects that fall downward toward the earth due to the pull of gravity fall with the same acceleration regardless of their mass. This is acceleration due to gravity, *g*. Ten meters per second squared is the acceleration due to gravity for objects falling toward the earth. If you were to climb to the highest building in your town and drop a tennis ball and a bowling ball off the building at the same time, they would both hit the ground at the same time. This is because they both maintain equal accelerations due to the pull of gravity and the effects of inertia. Later in this lesson we will work out some problems dealing with this concept.

Inertia and Newton

No discussion of motion is complete without the mention of Newton's three laws of motion. Newton's first law of motion is called the law of inertia. It states that an object at rest will remain at rest and an object in motion will remain in motion unless some outside force acts on it. The term *inertia* means "a resistance to change" and often is the measure of the mass of a substance. To understand the first law of motion, imagine a boulder on the edge of a cliff. It remains perched on the edge unless something or someone nudges it forward. This force could be a person pushing it or a vibration of the earth. Or imagine that your car hits the car in front of you and you lunge forward until the force of your seat belt stops your forward motion.

It's a Matter of Mass

The second law of motion says that the acceleration produced by the net force on a body is directly proportional to the magnitude of the net force, in the same direction as the net force, and inversely proportional to the mass of the body. Or, to shorten this explanation, think of this formula: acceleration = net force/net mass $(a = f/m)$. You can turn this formula around and say that $F = m \times a$ or $m = F/a$. To understand this concept, think of a golf ball on a tee. The more force you use to strike the golf ball, the greater the acceleration of the ball. Now think of a lead ball on the tee. You might increase the force you use to hit the ball but not reach the acceleration you did before because of the great increase in mass of the object being moved. In other words, acceleration is directly proportional to force (if you increase one, you increase the other). Mass is inversely proportional to acceleration (if you increase the mass, you will decrease the acceleration if the force is not altered upward). The second law of motion might help to explain why race cars are built of light-weight materials like fiberglass to hasten acceleration. It is important to remember that forces applied to an object may be resisted by friction. Friction is a force that always acts in a direction to oppose motion. Greater masses may experience more friction when being moved than lighter masses. The surface on which the object is resting will dictate the amount of friction involved. Air resistance is also a type of friction. For objects that fall downward through the atmosphere, air resistance does not present a problem unless the mass of the object is so light that air currents can slow its progress (like feathers and pieces of paper).

Actions and Reactions

The third law of motion is the law that is mentioned most often. It states that whenever one body exerts a force on a second body, the second body exerts an equal and opposite force on the first. In laypeople's terms, for every action there is an equal and opposite reaction. Forces always occur in pairs. As you walk across the floor, you push down on the floor and the floor pushes back up on you. As a rocket fires out gases that push on the air molecules, the air molecules push back, propelling the rocket upward. The force that initiated the reaction is called the action force. The force that responded to the initial action is called the reaction force. You might have experienced this law of motion in a frightening way the first time you jumped from a row boat toward the bank of a pond. As you jumped forward off the front of the boat, the boat floated backward in response to your forward push. Hopefully, you took this into account as you leaped forward, or you might have gotten a little wet on your journey.

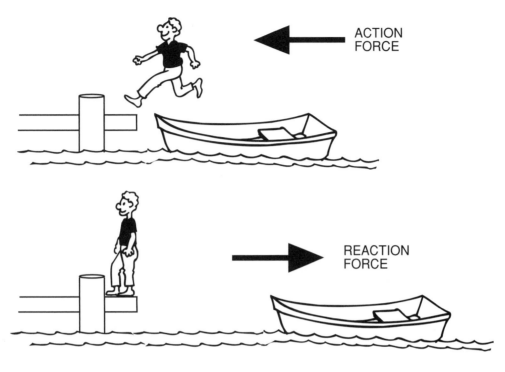

THIRD LAW OF MOTION

WORD FIND—VOCABULARY ACTIVITY ON
LET'S GET MOVIN'

Directions

Read the following statements and determine the best word to complete each statement. Circle the word on the Word Find Puzzle that completes each statement. If you cannot find a word horizontally, vertically, or diagonally in the word find, you probably have an incorrect answer for the statement.

1. Distance divided by time is known as _____.

2. What device on a car registers the magnitude of the distance you have traveled on a trip? _____

3. What type of speed is determined by dividing the total distance traveled by the total time it took to travel that distance? _____

4. Another term for resistance to change or a measure of mass is _____.

5. The second law of motion is stated as _____ equals mass times acceleration.

6. According to the second law of motion, the mass of an object is _____. proportional to the acceleration of that object.

7. When deciding if an object is in motion, it is important to determine your _____ by which to judge the relativity of that motion.

8. Velocity is defined as the _____ divided by the time.

9. When a quantity requires both the magnitude and the direction, it is classified as a(n) _____ quantity.

10. The change in velocity divided by the time required to achieve that is known as the _____ of that object.

11. The speed of an object at that moment in time only is called the _____ speed.

12. 10 m/sec^2 is known as the acceleration of an object due to _____.

13. In the third law of motion, the force that is a response to the initial force is called the _____ force.

14. Negative acceleration is called _____.

15. The force that opposes motion when moving objects over a surface is called _____.

16. The quantity that expresses magnitude but does not express direction is called a _____ quantity.

17. The first law of motion explains that forces are required to initiate motion for objects at _____.

© 1994 by The Center for Applied Research in Education

18. Which law of motion explains why football players who are running backs weigh less than linebackers due to the need for acceleration? _____

19. What object is used for the frame of reference if you were to say that a dead mosquito is in motion even though it is lying still on the ground? _____

20. Inertia is really a measure of the _____ of an object. Objects with greater inertia are often harder to move.

```
E  I  A  D  S  S  A  M  O  G  R  A  V  I  T  Y
C  N  V  T  M  K  V  J  D  S  R  D  B  D  R  U
N  V  E  P  O  K  M  P  O  A  E  E  K  E  Z  S
E  E  R  L  B  C  S  Q  M  I  A  E  M  C  M  U
R  R  A  F  I  R  S  T  E  T  C  P  Z  E  K  O
E  S  G  R  S  T  L  J  T  R  T  S  R  L  C  E
F  E  E  M  E  B  B  V  E  E  I  R  V  E  B  N
E  L  J  D  L  S  R  S  R  N  O  O  U  R  O  A
R  Y  B  N  J  V  T  K  B  I  N  T  S  A  L  T
F  T  V  L  B  N  K  S  M  P  U  C  T  T  P  N
O  S  M  C  R  O  F  U  D  R  V  E  L  I  D  A
E  P  E  C  R  O  F  N  K  S  K  V  B  O  F  T
M  D  I  S  P  L  A  C  E  M  E  N  T  N  J  S
A  S  E  C  O  N  D  R  D  K  J  M  L  T  S  N
R  N  O  I  T  A  R  E  L  E  C  C  A  B  R  I
F  F  R  I  C  T  I  O  N  J  R  A  L  A  C  S
```

7–2 SOLVING YOUR PROBLEMS IN MOTION
Activity on the Energy of Motion

Objectives

Students will solve physics problems on speed, velocity, and acceleration using the appropriate formulas.

Teacher Notes

Students must read "Let's Get Movin' " to complete this activity. Students may find a calculator helpful. You might want to solve some sample problems on the board before making this assignment.

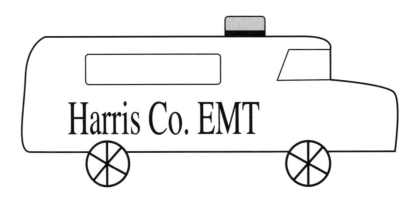

Solving Your Problems in Motion
Activity on the Energy of Motion

Directions

Use the information and formulas discussed in the content of *Let's Get Movin'* to solve the following motion problems. Please show your work for each problem in addition to the final answer. If you need additional room for your computations, you may use the back of the worksheet.

   I. Read the information below and consult the map to answer the following questions about this paragraph:

Joe works for the Emergency Medical Technician (EMT) team in Atlanta. He is often called on to use his superior driving skills when rushing to the scene of an accident and then delivering the patient back to Hardy Hospital in Atlanta. On May 14, Joe received a call that a car collision had occurred on Radburn Road in Douglasville. Joe knew he must cover the 25-mile distance in as little time as possible. He jumped into his car at 10:00 P.M. and arrived at the scene of the accident at 10:15 P.M. He spent from 10:15 to 11:00 P.M. getting the patient ready to transport. At 11:00 P.M., Joe jumped into his EMT vehicle and started back toward Atlanta with his patient. As he started the engine to leave the scene of the accident, he went from 0 to 60 miles per hour in 2.5 seconds. He had almost made it back to the hospital when a green Volkswagen darted in front of him. Joe slammed on the brakes and went from his 120-mile-per-hour speed to stop in 4 seconds, barely avoiding an accident. Finally at 11:20, Joe arrived safely at Hardy Hospital with his patient.

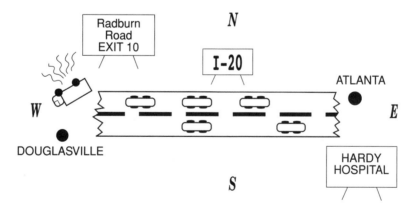

Questions

   1. Give the speed of the trip from Atlanta to Douglasville in (A) miles/min, and (B) miles/hour.

   2. Give the speed of the trip from Douglasville back to Atlanta in (A) miles/min, and (B) miles/hour.

3. Give the velocity of the trip from Hardy Hospital in Atlanta to Douglasville in miles per hour (be sure to include both magnitude and direction).

4. Give the velocity of the trip from Douglasville back to Hardy Hospital in miles/hour (be sure to include magnitude and direction).

5. Give Joe's acceleration in that 2.5-second period when he started from the scene of the accident in Douglasville. Give your answer in (A) miles/hour^2, and (B) miles/sec^2.

6. Give Joe's deceleration as he slowed to avert the accident with the Volkswagen as he returned to the hospital. Give the answer in miles/hour^2.

II. Look at the drawing below and answer the following questions:

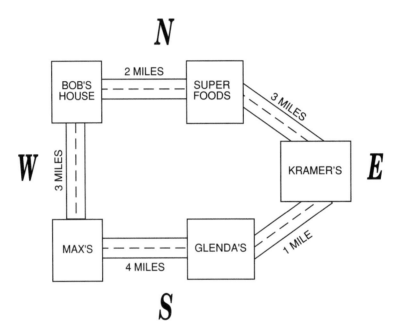

Information: Bob leaves home at 9:00 A.M. to run some errands on his bike. He goes directly from his house to Super Foods to pick up some jelly beans. He leaves Super Foods and travels to Kramer's to return some plastic bags for recycling which he received on his last shopping trip. He goes directly from Kramer's to Glenda's clothing store to pick up some black socks. And finally he leaves Glenda's and goes directly to Max's. He arrives at Max's at 11:00 A.M. Now answer the following questions as you look at the map above.

7. Give the distance Bob traveled.

8. Give the displacement of Bob's journey.

9. Give the average speed of Bob's trip in miles/hour.

10. Give the velocity of Bob's trip in miles/hour (be sure to include both magnitude and direction).

III. For the problem below, use this formula to find final velocity: final velocity = initial velocity + (acceleration)(time). Also remember that acceleration of an object that is falling toward the ground due to gravity is 10 m/sec^2.

11. An amateur cliff diver plans to jump off a cliff into the river below. She realizes that injury can result from too high a dive. She needs to know the velocity with which she will strike the water below to judge the danger of the dive. She makes this judgment by dropping a heavy rock off the cliff to the water below. It takes the rock 2.5 seconds to reach the water. Now give her final velocity just before she struck the water.

IV. For the following questions, use the speed = distance/time formula to figure the distance traveled.

12. An airplane travels at 250 miles/hour for 90 minutes. Give the distance the plane traveled in miles.

13. A car travels at 60 miles per hour for 20 miles. Give the time it took for the trip in minutes.

7–3 THE BALL DROP
Lab on the Energy of Motion

Objectives

Students will apply the physics formula relating acceleration, time, and distance in determining the height of a structure by dropping a tennis ball.

Teacher Notes

The structure you select to have the ball dropped from should allow this to be performed without any obstructions to the ball prior to it reaching the ground. Suggestions include the top of the football stadium steps (off the side), top of the basketball bleachers (off the side), from the press box, etc. You will need to do some looking around to find the best location. It is also wise to choose a location that has some data on its actual height when it was constructed. Your administrators might be able to help with this. In this lab the students use tennis balls, but any object heavy enough to overcome air resistance can be used. It's a good idea to work out some problems in class using the distance formula before conducting this lab.

Extension

Give students the actual value of the structure they measured in the lab and have them figure out their percent of error. They should use this formula: observed value – accepted value ÷ accepted value × 100%. For example, if the student found the stadium to be 225 meters tall and you were told by the administration that it was really 260 meters tall, this formula could be used: 225m – 260m/260m × 100% = –35/260 × 100% = –0.142 × 100% = –14.2% error. A discussion could then follow about what caused the error and how to make the measurement more exact.

© 1994 by The Center for Applied Research in Education

THE BALL DROP
Lab on the Energy of Motion

Introduction

Formula use is an integral part of physics. It is very important not only to be able to learn formulas and use them in solving word problems, but to be able to apply them to real-life situations. Sometimes distances cannot be measured easily using basic measurement tools (such as the tape measures, rulers, etc.) because measurements can be very inconvenient to make. Let's say you were asked to measure the height of the tallest building in Atlanta, Georgia. You would look pretty funny using a tape measure to achieve that task. But if you knew a little physics, you could achieve a fairly accurate measurement in a matter of seconds. You may be saying, "That's impossible." Let's look at how it might be done. You would need to take the elevator (or stairs) to the roof of the building. You also would need an object such as a golf ball or tennis ball, a stop watch, and a calculator. To conduct your measurement, you would drop the ball off the top of the building and start the stop watch at exactly the same time. As soon as you see the ball strike the ground below, you hit stop on the stop watch. You have just measured the time it took the ball to fall from the building to the ground under the influence of gravity.

This time can then be used in a physics formula that gives you distance. The following formula is used: displacement = 1/2 (acceleration due to gravity) (time) (time), or $\Delta X = 1/2 (gt^2)$. In this formula, displacement represents the distance from the top of the building to the ground (that is what you are trying to find!). In addition, g represents acceleration due to gravity. As we mentioned earlier, all objects fall toward the earth at the same acceleration due to the pull of gravity if they can overcome air resistance. This g value is always about 10 meters/sec/sec. Time is the number of seconds it took to complete the fall. When using this formula your answer will come out in meters.

Here is some sample data to help you learn this formula. When you went to the top of the building, let's say it took 15 seconds for the ball to drop to the ground. You would use the formula like this: $\Delta X = 1/2 (10 \text{ m/sec/sec}) (15 \text{ sec}) (15 \text{ sec}) = 5 \text{ m/sec}^2 (225 \text{ sec})^2 = 1125$ meters. You have thus determined the height of the building using this simple method. You need to remember when performing such an experiment that you cannot use objects like a feather or piece of paper because air resists this acceleration. Obviously, that is an important fact for a person who parachutes out of airplanes. But if you could eliminate air resistance in a container such as a vacuum, you would see that all objects fall at an acceleration of 10 m/sec^2 toward the earth in response to gravity and the inertia of the object. This is certainly a different value on different planets because of the factor of gravity.

Now that you know a little more about height, let's practice using this formula.

Prelab Questions

1. A diver is planning a dive from a cliff into the river below. He knows that dives are safe only from certain heights. He does not know the height of this cliff, but he knows his physics. He drops a large rock from the top of the cliff into the water below. It takes 8 seconds for the rock to hit the water. Give the height of the cliff in meters.

2. Explain why a feather cannot be used in question 1.

3. Explain what acceleration is.

4. Why is the *g* value different on Earth than on Jupiter?

5. Explain why using this formula is only moderately accurate. What are some problems you might encounter when using this formula that would cause some error?

6. List three professions that might use this physics formula, and explain how they would do so.

Materials needed

Stop watch
Tennis ball or golf ball
Calculator
A tall structure

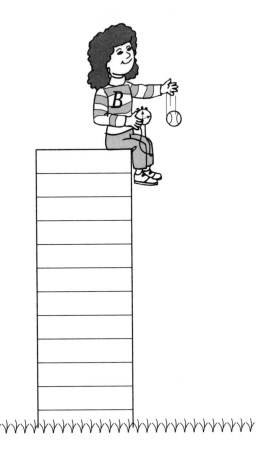

Procedure

1. Go to the top of your tall structure (such as the top of the stadium steps) with a tennis ball and stop watch.

2. Standing on the top step, drop the ball off the side of the steps so it can fall toward the ground without being obstructed during its fall.

3. As you release the ball, start your stop watch. Stop it as the ball hits the ground below. Enter this value in the chart that follows.

4. Repeat this process three more times and enter each time in the chart.

5. Find the average number of seconds from your four trials and enter it in the chart.

6. You will use the average number of seconds to determine the height of the steps above the ground.

7. Answer the postlab questions.

THE BALL DROP (*continued*)

CHART FOR DATA

Trial number	Number of seconds required for fall
1	
2	
3	
4	
Average	

Postlab Questions

1. Take the average number of seconds and use your formula to determine the height of your structure.

2. Cite any problems you encountered in this lab and explain how they might have skewed your results.

3. Do you think the use of this formula is more accurate on fairly short structures or on taller structures? Explain why.

4. You are standing at the base of a tree with a ball. You want to know how tall the tree is. You have a stop watch and a calculator. You toss the ball straight up in the air to almost exactly the height of the tree and time the number of seconds it takes to go up and return to the ground below. You note that it took 8 seconds from the time the ball left your hand until the time it returned to the ground. You remember that time going up will be equal to time coming down. With this in mind, figure out the height of the tree.

7–4 TAKE 1
Project on the Energy of Motion

Objectives

Students will apply their knowledge of the three laws of motion to create commercials that describe how their original products are based on Newton's laws of motion.

Teacher Notes

Students must be familiar with the three laws of motion before they attempt this project. You may want to reserve one or more video cameras for student use. A video camera must be available on the day of presentations.

Some suggestions for evaluation have been given, but you may prefer to devise your own evaluation sheet.

TAKE 1
Project on the Energy of Motions

Introduction

Divide into groups of three or four students each. You will devise a 1-minute commercial that describes a product you invent. Your group will attach a two-page written description of your original product to this activity sheet and present information about your product to the rest of the class. You should be prepared to discuss why your product is better than other products presently on the market based on the principles of Newton's three laws of motion.

Procedure

1. Your team is employed by a large corporation that specializes in manufacturing high-tech products.

2. Because of your science background on the three laws of motion, you know that the product must satisfy all the laws of motion to be marketable.

3. Your product should be able to outsell all other like products on the market.

4. Unfortunately, the president of the company does not have a very diverse background in science. In fact, he does not recognize much value in scientific principles. His sole concern is to sell, sell, sell and make more and more money. But recently, the company has been losing money. Lack of planning and research has caused the company to market some malfunctioning products. Some of the clients are getting agitated over this matter. Your boss has agreed to a meeting with your team of researchers in order for you to present the importance of the laws of motion. In this time frame, you must convince the boss that your product is superior, functional, and marketable.

5. For your presentation, your boss asks your team to make a commercial that you would air on television to promote your product. Your commercial should last about 1 minute. Your team should conduct the commercial in a professional manner. Special emphasis should be given to how your product works according to one or all of the three laws of motion.

6. Appropriate dress and background scenery are essential.

7. Be creative and imaginative. Explain how one or more of the laws of motion would be applicable to your new product.

8. You should have a representation of your product on the commercial. You might want to build a model of your product, do a computer printout drawing, do a poster, etc. Be neat and very creative in this area.

9. You can choose to be videoed the day of your presentation or you can video your presentation prior to the due date. Then just bring your ready-made video with you.

10. Examples of high-tech equipment presented in the past include golf clubs that fold up into your glove compartment and shoes with built-in springs for basketball players. This is your own creation, so you will want to choose something that is of interest to you. Be sure you can connect your creation to one of the three laws of motion. Be inventive and convincing. Your job may depend on this presentation.

11. Be prepared to answer questions from the class after your presentation. Everyone on your team must participate in the video.

Evaluation

Grading will be based on imagination and creativity, dress, props, relevance to the three laws of motion, ability to discuss the material, and ability to answer questions at the conclusion of the project.

LESSON 8: ENERGY, WORK, POWER, AND MACHINES

8–1 FULL OF ENERGY
Content on Energy, Work, Power, and Machines

Going the Distance to Do Work

Have you ever heard someone describe another person as "full of energy"? Or perhaps you've even described yourself as having no energy on a particular day. Actually, all persons, places, and things have energy. The sun can give energy as well as the food we eat. Energy is only evident to the observer as work is being done. In fact, most people define energy as the ability to do work.

Work itself is the transfer of energy. Think about step aerobics. Do you think doing step aerobics is a form of work? Let's take a look and find out. In order for work to be done, a force must be present and an object must be moved a certain distance by that force. The food you eat provides the energy for the aerobics. The participant in the aerobics class moves his or her body weight up and down on a step (about 8 inches is standard). Moving your body weight requires a force (newtons is the unit), and the up-and-down motion is your distance (usually figured in meters) upon which the force is applied. Yes, you have done work in the case of step aerobics.

Let's go to the free weight room and see if work is being done. First, we see a woman doing bicep curls with the free weights. She is lifting 35 pounds in each hand. As she curls the bar up and down, she is doing work (supplying force to move the weight a certain distance). Nearby we see a man holding a 200-pound weight bar over his head. You see him grimacing from the load. Is he doing work? Although it sure looks like work, he is not doing any. This is because he is not moving the object through a distance. (Better not tell him that at this particular time!)

More Power to You

The formula for work is work = force × distance. Force is calculated in units of newtons, and distance is calculated in meters. Thus work is a newton-meter, also called a joule. You'll notice that the formula for work says nothing about how long it takes you to perform that task. If I told you that you did the same amount of work running up the stadium steps as you did walking slowly up the steps, you'd probably ask me if I had run those steps lately.

The concept we are talking about here is power. Power is the rate at which work is done. Power equals the amount of work done divided by the amount of time during which the work is done. In formula format, it looks like this: $P = f \times d/t$ or $P = W/t$. The units for power are joules per second (also called a watt). The unit called *watt* is a metric unit named after James Watt (the eighteenth-century developer of the steam engine). When James Watt was trying to sell his steam engine, he had to tell his customers how many horses his engine could replace. To do this, he had to find out how much work a good horse could do. He found that on an average, a horse could lift 550 pounds 1 foot in 1 second, and this became known as horsepower. One horsepower is the same as 0.75 kilowatts (a kilowatt is 1000 watts). So an engine that is rated as a 134-horsepower engine is really a 100-kW engine. According to the definition for power, engines that are high in horsepower can do work rapidly. This does not mean that these engines do more work or necessarily go faster; they do the work in less time. This means they accelerate faster.

Energy Stores and Conversions

With all this talk about energy, do you wonder if it can be stored? We store it every day. As we eat, our cells stockpile energy in our muscles and in our fat cells. *Potential energy* is the term used to describe energy that is stored and held in readiness. It has the potential for doing work. Would you be willing to walk under a piano suspended 20 meters above the ground by a single rope? I doubt that I would take the chance because the piano is loaded with potential energy. With a slight failure of the rope, that energy could be changed into work and move downward. The piano is an example of an object with gravitational potential energy. The amount of gravitational potential energy it possesses is equal to the work done against gravity in lifting it to that position. The formula for gravitational potential energy is gravitational potential energy = (mass) (acceleration due to gravity) (height) or $PE = m \times g \times h$. Mass is calculated in Kilograms, acceleration due to gravity is always 110 m/sec^2, and the height is calculated in meters. Look back at the piano example. If the piano had a mass of 2300 kg and was suspended 20 meters above the ground, what would be its potential energy? PE = 2300 kg $\times$ 10 m/sec2 $\times$ 20 m = 460,000 joules. Once again, the product is a newton-meter, which is a joule.

Once the potential energy is set into motion, it is called kinetic energy. Kinetic energy is defined as the energy of motion. The kinetic energy of an object depends on the mass of the object as well as its speed. It is equal to half the mass multiplied by the square of the speed. The formula is written kinetic energy = 1/2 mass $\times$ velocity^2 or $KE = 1/2\ mv^2$. If and when the rope on the suspended piano breaks, the potential energy becomes kinetic energy as work is done. To use the KE formula, you must know the velocity with which an object is traveling at that time. You can find the velocity of an object by using the formula $V_f = V_i + (a)\ (t)$, or final velocity equals the initial velocity plus the acceleration multiplied by the time. The final answer for kinetic energy is also given in joules.

Lightening the Load with Machines

Some of the objects that perform work are machines. Machines are devices for multiplying forces or changing the direction of forces. There are six simple machines that do this. Each of the six types makes work easier for the person doing the work. If you don't believe it, think of unscrewing a bolt without a screwdriver or lifting up a car without a jack. The six families of simple machines are levers, pulleys, wheels and axles, inclined planes, screws, and wedges.

A lever helps you move objects by increasing the force you exert. A lever is a long, rigid bar with a support that allows the bar to pivot. The point of rotation is called the fulcrum. Think of a seesaw. This is a lever, and the balance point is the fulcrum. Crowbars and screwdrivers used to pry the top off objects are also levers. Pulleys are machines that consist of a rope passing over a grooved wheel. Think about an example of a fixed pulley. This would be like an old water well. The rope is connected to the bucket and passes over the pulley. You pull down on your end of the rope and the bucket of water comes up toward you. A fixed pulley does not decrease the force needed to do the job, but it changes the direction and makes work easier. When several pulleys are used together to make work even easier, this system is called a block and tackle. This combines both fixed and movable pulleys. The wheel and axle is a simple machine consisting of a wheel and a shaft. As you spin the wheel, the axle turns. Doorknobs and eggbeaters are examples of this.

An inclined plane is a slanting surface that allows you to apply less force in lifting an object to the desired height. Just think of a moving van with pull-down ramps at the back of the truck. These ramps are inclined planes that allow the movers to deliver furniture into the van. They increase the distance the movers travel but decrease the amount of force they must supply to lift each object. The wedge is a type of inclined plane with either one or two sloping sides. The point of a needle or the blade of a knife are examples. A screw is an inclined plane in a spiral form. It makes work easier by pressing against the material around it as it moves into the wood. The ridge that spirals around the screw is called its thread, and the pitch is the number of threads in a given length. When you turn a screw, the direction of force is changed and multiplied. The force you need to apply decreases as the threads get closer. You have to make a lot of turns with your hands, but the work is much easier than if you did not have the screw.

When evaluating a piece of machinery, the concept of mechanical advantage (MA) is often used. MA is the value that tells the number of times a machine increases the applied force. For example, if the MA was 4 when you used a screwdriver to pry the lid off a paint can, that meant that the screwdriver multiplied your force by 4. Each type of simple machine has a formula for figuring the MA of that machine. This will be dealt with in Lesson 8–4, *Machines Made Simple*.

Fact or Friction

Simple machines combined to form more complex pieces of equipment are called compound machines. The value of a compound machine is often based on its efficiency. The efficiency of a machine is the amount of useful work obtained from the machine as compared to the work put into the machine. It is important to note that no machine has 100% efficiency. Why? Friction is the culprit. Remember, friction is the force that opposes motion. The formula for determining the efficiency of a machine is as follows: efficiency = useful work/work put in × 100%. For example, if you put 200 joules of work into a machine and the machine did 30 joules of useful work, its efficiency is 30/200 × 100% = 15%. This would mean that 85% of the work you put into the machine was wasted, probably in overcoming friction. And many complex machines have very low efficiency ratings. Cars have a low efficiency rating (below 35%), not because of bad design but because some of the energy converted to heat goes into the cooling system and is wasted through the radiator to the air. Some energy will go out the exhaust, and much is wasted in friction of the moving parts. Substances (such as grease and oil) that reduce friction on moving parts are important to the efficiency rating of the car. When these are utilized, friction is reduced and efficiency is increased.

Energy Unscramble—Vocabulary Activity on *Full of Energy*

Directions

After reading *Full of Energy,* unscramble the words below to complete the statements.

1. _____ (oewrp) This is described as work divided by the time it takes to perform that work.

2. _____ (nnweot) This is also known as kgm/sec^2. It is the unit used to measure force.

3. _____ (inciket) This is the energy of motion.

4. _____ (ipcht) When this is closer together on a screw, the screw is easier to turn.

5. _____ (rontifci) This is one of the major reasons that machines never can reach a 100% efficiency rating.

6. _____ (uojel) This is the unit used to designate work done.

7. _____ (eitraloenacc) This is the advantage of a high-horsepower automobile over a lower-horsepower automobile.

8. _____ (yrgnee) This is the ability to do work.

9. _____ (ressoh) James Watt compared his steam engine to these when he was trying to market the new engine.

10. _____ (iehhgt) To determine the potential energy of an object, you must know the acceleration due to gravity, mass, and the _____.

11. _____ (yveticol) To compute a kinetic energy, you need mass and _____.

12. _____ (ihmnceas) These are devices for multiplying force or changing the direction of a force when moving an object.

13. _____ (elerv) These simple machines have a fulcrum on which a long, rigid bar rests and pivots freely.

14. _____ (fnike) This is an example of a wedge.

15. _____ (oerhrwsope) This unit was selected by Watt to describe his steam engine, and it is still used in car descriptions.

16. _____ (ientdrcio) A fixed pulley does not increase the force needed to do the job, but it does alter the _____ in which the job is being done.

17. _____ (eeswas) This is an example of a type of lever.

18. _____ (orkw) This is determined by multiplying the force times the distance in which an object is moved.

19. _____ (islmoagkr) Mass is calculated in units of _____ when determining potential energy.

20. _____ (iflan elvcotiy) This is equal to the initial velocity plus acceleration multiplied by time.

8-2 GOLF BALLS AND THEIR POTENTIAL
Lab on Potential Energy

Objectives

Students will observe how potential and kinetic energy can perform work. They will evaluate the effect of changing heights on potential and kinetic energy.

Teacher Notes

Golf balls are only one of a variety of balls that can be used in this activity. Paper cups are just one of a variety of containers that can be used.

GOLF BALLS AND THEIR POTENTIAL
Lab on Potential Energy

Introduction

The potential energy of an object is found by multiplying the mass × height × acceleration. If the object moves downward due to the pull of gravity, then 10 m/sec^2 is used as the acceleration. In this lab you will be judging the movement of a golf ball down a ramp. In this case, you should use 10 m/sec^2 due to downward tug of gravity. The unit to denote potential energy (stored energy) is a newton-meter (joule).

Kinetic energy is the energy of motion. When an object begins to move, the potential energy of that object changes into kinetic energy. The formula for kinetic energy is 1/2 mv^2. The unit to denote this is also the joule. Remember that kg is the unit for mass.

Work is also denoted in units of joules (found by force × distance). Potential energy is calculated in joules (mass × acceleration × height).

Prelab Questions

1. A ball (2 kg) is resting on top of a fence 20 meters above the ground. Answer these questions about the ball:

   a. What is its potential energy?

   b. When is the potential energy greater: when the ball is on top of the fence or when the ball has fallen 10 meters from the fence?

   c. When is kinetic energy greater: near the top or the bottom of the fence? Explain why.

2. Make a word problem and a drawing for a problem on (A) work, (B) power, (C) efficiency, (D) kinetic energy, and (E) potential energy. Use the back of this page to do this if you do not have enough room below. Be sure to make an answer key to go with this.

Materials

Golf balls

Paper or plastic cups

Two meter sticks per student or two same-size pieces of wood

Tape

Clay

GOLF BALLS AND THEIR POTENTIAL *(continued)*

Procedure

1. Tape the underside of two meter sticks together lengthwise so they have a slit left between them to form a groove. The golf ball can roll down this groove like it is on a track.

2. Use the clay to construct a support on one end that is 8 cm above the ground (see Figure A). On the other end of the meter sticks, place a paper cup with the open side facing toward the slit on the meter sticks.

3. Hold the ball at the top of your ramp. Release the ball and let it roll down the ramp and into the cup.

4. Measure the distance the cup moved along the floor. Record the measurement in Data Table 1.

5. Repeat the above steps, but vary the height of the ramp each time as shown in Data Table 1. Complete the data table as you go.

6. Use the platform balance and determine the mass of the ball you used and the mass of the cup you used. Record these masses in Data Table 2.

7. Calculate the potential energy of the ball for each of the heights in Data Table 1. Show your work (be sure to use kg, m/sec^2, meters).

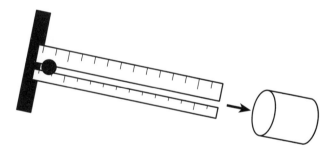

FIGURE A

DATA TABLE 1

Height of ramp	Distance cup traveled	Potential energy of the ball
8 cm		
18 cm		
28 cm		
40 cm		

DATA TABLE 2

Mass of ball	Mass of cup

Postlab Questions

1. As the potential energy of the ball increased, what happened to the amount of work done on the cup? What makes you think that?

2. Explain how the potential energy will become kinetic energy as it rolls down the ramp.

3. Explain what type of simple machine was represented in the lab.

4. If we had greased the ramp, what do you think might have happened to our results?

8–3 PROBLEMS WITH ENERGY
Activity on Energy, Work, Power, and Machines

Objectives

Students will apply their knowledge of formulas for solving problems relating to energy, work, power, and machines.

Teacher Notes

Students should read Lesson 8, *Full of Energy*, before they attempt to solve these problems. The following formulas are needed to solve these problems:

$W = f \times d$

$P = W / t$

$KE = 1/2 \ mv^2$

$PE = mgh$

$E = \text{output/input}$

Problems with Energy
Activity on Energy, Work, Power, and Machines

Directions

Read over the following problems and solve them using the formulas discussed in *Full of Energy.* You may use the formulas $PE = mgh$; $KE = 1/2\ mv^2$; $W = f \times d$; $P = W/t$; efficiency = work output/work input. Be sure to give the proper units with your answer, as discussed in *Full of Energy.*

1. That famous barefoot football kicker, Rocky Nails, can kick a football with a force of 20 N. He can kick it 80 meters. Give the work that Rocky does on the ball.

2. Give the power Rocky uses in question 1 if he can accomplish this feat in 6 seconds.

3. Killer has reached up to speeds of 2 meters/sec on a good day. Killer has a mass of about 10 kg. Give his maximum kinetic energy on his good days.

4. Sue Ellen is carrying a present for her boss, who is about to retire. She thought of filling the box with rocks, but she decided on a popcorn popper instead. She is not very anxious to get to her boss's retirement party, so she slides across the floor at 1.2 m/sec speed. Sue Ellen weighs 70 kg, and the present she is carrying weighs about 2 kg. Give the total kinetic energy Sue Ellen reaches on her trip across the floor.

5. Rover was thrown from his owner's airplane after the owner discovered that Rover was not "plane broken" (house broken on the plane). Luckily, Rover thought to wear his parachute on the plane. He opened it immediately as he was hurled out the door. After several seconds, Rover has drifted to a position of 200 meters above the ground. Compute (if possible) his potential energy at this location above the ground. Rover has a mass of 4 kg. Explain your answer.

6. Bill dashes up the stadium steps during football practice. Bill has a mass of 80 kg. He must travel from the base of the steps to the top (a distance of 70 meters). It takes him an average of 3.5 seconds to achieve this.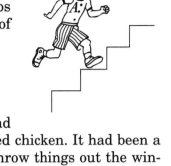

A. Give the work he does to do this.

B. Give the power he uses to do this.

7. Jill lives at the top of a high-rise condo. One day Jill got mad at her husband because he forgot to bring home a pail of fried chicken. It had been a bad day for Jill, so she went a little berserk. She began to throw things out the window at her husband, Jack. Jack stood on the ground outside the window looking up at an irate Jill. Jill began to hurl some of Jack's prize belongings out toward him. Find the potential energy of the three objects at the point they are shown suspended in the diagram. Their height and mass are shown.

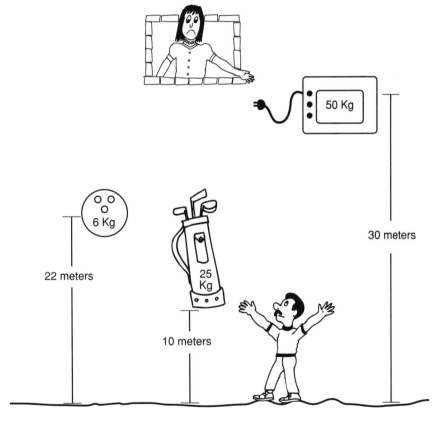

8. Your lawnmower requires that you put 500 joules of work into it to make it function. From this you get 100 joules of work. Give the lawnmower's efficiency and explain why it seems so low.

8–4 MACHINES MADE SIMPLE
Project on Machines

Objective

Students will evaluate the differences in simple machines.

Teacher Notes

1. Write the names of the six simple machines on slips of paper (one machine per slip). Include enough slips of paper for each student or pair of students in your class. Place these slips of paper into a paper bag.

2. As students enter the room, have them draw out a slip of paper from the bag. The slip they draw will be the simple machine they research. After each student receives the name of the machine he or she is to research, distribute a handout explaining this project. (A copy of the student handout is included at the end of this activity.)

3. Provide the students opportunities to go to the library to research their simple machine. They must develop one visual aid and bring in one example of their machine on the day of their presentation.

4. The visual aid must include the following things:

   A definition or description of the simple machine

   Some examples (drawings, photos)

   The use of the machine in society (include both everyday use and technical use)

   How one calculates the mechanical advantage of that machine and an example of such a calculation

   Interesting facts or trivia about the machine

5. During the oral presentation, the visual aid should be shared with the class. At the end of the presentation, the example of the simple machine should be displayed and explained.

6. The student should also provide the teacher with five multiple-choice questions that are appropriate for the rest of the class to answer after hearing the presentation.

© 1994 by The Center for Applied Research in Education

Evaluation Criteria

Is the visual aid neat and colorful? (10 points)

Did the visual aid contain all the material requested? (10 points)

Was the information presented accurately? (30 points)

Was the presentation technique acceptable? (the student displayed a serious manner and did not read all material but explained parts of it in his or her own words) (15 points)

Was an example brought in and explained? (15 points)

Were five multiple-choice questions provided? (20 points)

_____

Total for one test grade (100 points)

MACHINES MADE SIMPLE
Project on Machines

Name of simple machine _____

Due date for presentation _____

Library research dates _____

Directions for Presentation

You will research a simple machine in the library. After the research is completed, you should create a visual aid explaining the simple machine. The visual aide should include the following components:

A definition or description of the simple machine

Some examples (drawings, photos)

The use of the machine in society (include both everyday use and technical use)

How you calculate the mechanical advantage of that machine and an example of such a calculation

Interesting facts or trivia about the machine

On the presentation date, you will share the visual aid with the class. You should bring in an object that is an example of the simple machine and provide the teacher with five multiple-choice questions that are appropriate for the rest of the class to answer after hearing the presentation.

Evaluation Criteria

Is the visual aid neat and colorful? (10 points)

Did the visual aid contain all the materials requested? (10 points)

Was the information presented accurately? (30 points)

Was the presentation technique acceptable? (you displayed a serious attitude and were able to talk about the machine without reading each word) (15 points)

Was an example brought in and explained? (15 points)

Were five multiple-choice questions provided? (20 points)

_____

Total for one test grade (100 points)

8–5 MORE POWER TO YOU
Lab on Energy, Work, and Power

Objectives

Students will calculate their work performed and power attained in climbing activities.

Teacher Notes

This lab can be done outdoors or indoors, depending on your location and the weather conditions. The lab directions are geared toward indoor work, but if you wish to take your students outside, there are many options available. You could choose to have the students climb to the top of the stadium steps and measure their power in this manner. They would need to measure the distance they travel in climbing up each step to the top. This could be done by measuring the first step and multiplying by the total number of steps in the stadium. Ask whether any students may have medical problems that would prohibit their participation.

MORE POWER TO YOU
Lab on Energy, Work, and Power

Introduction

Work is defined as the product of a force exerted over a distance. Power is the rate of work being done or the product of the force exerted over a distance divided by the time.

Work is measured in units called joules, and power is measured in units called watts. In order to do work or display power, an object must possess energy. The food you eat each day provides you with that energy. This is evident when people are sick and cannot eat for a few days. When they try to get up and move about, they discover that their energy stores are low. Extreme dieting can cause this same feeling.

When you take in adequate food, your body changes that food into energy. You store that energy in various places in your body for future use. In fact, that is one major role of your fat stores. The fat in your body is holding energy in reserve for you. This energy will then be available if your body has to go without fuel for a time. If this occurs, you must call upon the fat stores to provide energy. This is the principle behind taking in less calories and thus losing weight and reducing the fat percentage in the body.

Your body takes the energy provided by the digestion of food and turns it into kinetic energy. Remember, kinetic energy is the energy of motion. Respiration, digestion, circulation, etc., all require some energy even if you never get up off the couch. The more movements you perform, the more energy your body needs. In this lab, you will look at an activity that requires a substantial amount of energy.

You may be familiar with the term *step aerobics* or *bench*. This is a cardiovascular activity that requires large quantities of energy to perform work for extended periods of time. As you perform this activity, you use your energy to perform work. If you time how much work you did, you could find your power. In step aerobics, the participant steps up and down on a platform called a bench or step. Most benches are anywhere from 4 to 12 inches in height depending on the aerobic conditioning of the participant. Lifting your body weight up and down on a bench requires a force. So if you multiply the force required to overcome gravity to lift the body times the distance or height of the step, you can calculate the work performed. If you figure the amount of time required to step up completely one time onto the bench, you can calculate the power you used to do this.

Prelab Questions

1. Explain why the units for work, potential energy, and kinetic energy are the same (joule).

2. Would power or work be a better indicator of the intensity of an exercise? Explain your answer.

3. Solve this problem: A man has a mass of 100 kg. He pulls himself up on a chin-up bar a distance of 2 meters. How much work did he do? [*Hint:* When converting mass to force, you multiply the mass $\times$ 10m/sec^2 (acceleration due to gravity).]

© 1994 by The Center for Applied Research in Education

4. Calculate the power the man used in question 3 if it took him 2 seconds to accomplish this. (Remember, units for power are watts. A watt is a joule/sec.)

5. Calculate the potential energy the man possesses when he is suspended at the top of the chin-up bar 2 meters from the ground. (*Hint:* potential energy = mass × acceleration due to gravity × distance.)

Materials

Bench or step (anywhere from 4 to 12 inches). A higher step is better for this activity. If a step is not available, you can use a stool or a chair. *Be very careful if a step height over 12 inches is used in this activity*

Meter stick

Kilogram bathroom scale or a standard pound scale and conversion table

Watch or clock with a second hand

Procedure

1. The teacher divides the class into pairs. Each pair should obtain a step, meter stick, and watch.

2. Find your mass on the kilogram scale, or take the number of pounds you weigh and multiply this number by 0.454 to convert your weight to kilograms. Record your kilogram weight on the chart on page 102.

3. Measure and record the height of your step or stool in meters. If you know the number of inches of the platform, you can divide the number of inches by 39.37 to get the number of meters.

4. As your partner holds the stool or step steady, you will step up and down on it: right foot up, left foot up, right foot down, left foot down. Practice a couple of times to get the hang of it. *(Caution: Do not perform this activity if you have any type of medical condition that might be aggravated by this exercise.)*

5. You will step up and down as many times as you can in 1 minute. Your partner will count the total number of times you step up onto the step. This should be recorded on the chart.

6. Reverse roles and let your partner do the same activity. You will count and record for him or her this time.

CHART FOR PARTNERS A AND B

	Mass in kg	*Distance of step from floor*	*Number of up steps in 1 minute*
Partner A			
Partner B			

Postlab Questions

1. Calculate the work done by Partner A and Partner B. (Remember, to find force you must multiply the mass × 10 m/sec^2.)

2. Calculate the power both partners exerted while stepping up onto the stool. The work you did (your answer to question 1) divided by time will give you this answer. To calculate the time to use in the formula, take the number of steps you completed in the 1-minute (60-second) time span and divide that number into 60. This will give the amount of time it took you to complete one complete step cycle or up, up, down, down. Now take this number and divide it by 2. This will give you the amount of time it took you to go up onto the step. This is the number of seconds you will use in the formula $P = W/t$.

3. Compare the amount of work both partners did. Do heavier people have to work harder than smaller people. Predict if heavier people burn more calories when working than smaller people.

4. Compare the amount of power both partners used in this activity. Explain why a person with a higher power rating might expend more energy than a person with a lower power rating, even if the amount of work they both did was almost equal.

© 1994 by The Center for Applied Research in Education

LESSON 9: ELECTRICITY

9–1 DANCING ELECTRONS
Content on Electricity

© 1994 by The Center for Applied Research in Education

We Take It for Granted

Look around the room. How many objects, devices, or appliances require electric energy to operate? What happens to our daily lives when we suffer a power outage? Americans are very dependent on electricity. We often take this invisible force for granted. Where does it come from? Who makes it?

Electrical energy is produced by converting some other form of energy into electricity. For example, some power plants convert the force of steam into mechanical energy, which causes a turbine to rotate. The turbine is connected to an electrical generator that produces current. Electrical current travels along wires to our homes and businesses.

Current

An electrical current is the flow of electrons through a wire. Electrons can travel within a wire because they are free to move throughout the atomic network. Current, abbreviated I, is measured in amperes (A, or amp). One ampere of current equals 1 coulomb (6.25 billion billion electrons) flowing past a point in 1 second. Current travels differently in different materials. Some materials are good conductors; that is, the current travels easily through them. Copper, silver, and aluminum are examples of good conductors. Insulators are materials through which a current cannot travel.

Resistance

The ability of a current to travel through a material depends on that material's resistance, or opposition, to the flow of electrons. Resistance is abbreviated as R and is measured in units called ohms. The resistance of an electrical wire depends on the material from which the wire is made, its length, thickness, and temperature. Electrons can travel more easily along a thick wire than a thin one. Long wire offers more resistance than short wire. The filament in a light bulb is a thin wire that offers a lot of resistance to the flow of electricity. As the electrons attempt to travel through this filament wire, they heat up, producing light and

103

heat. The lamp cord, on the other hand, has very low resistance and remains cool while electricity travels along it.

People can be electrocuted or shocked because they accidentally lower the resistance of their body to the flow of electric current. Normally, when our skin is very dry, our bodies have a resistance of about 50,000 ohms. However, if we are wet, our resistance drops sharply to about 100 ohms. Normal household current can be very dangerous to a person standing in a puddle of water because wet skin conducts current well, and it can travel easily through our bodies to the ground.

Voltage

Not all electrical current has the same amount of push or strength. The amount of electricity available to push electrons along a wire is the voltage (V) or potential difference. When each electron traveling along a wire carries a lot of energy, the voltage is high. However, if each electron is only carrying a little energy, the voltage is low.

The current in a wire can be determined by dividing the voltage of electricity in that wire by the resistance of the wire. This rule, called Ohm's Law, is stated as

$$I = V/R$$

To determine the amount of current flowing through a wire that has a resistance of 25 ohms when voltage is 50, divide 50 volts by 25 ohms:

$$I = V/R$$
$$I = 50 \text{ volts}/25 \text{ ohms}$$
$$I = 2 \text{ amps}$$

Notice that current is expressed in amps, or amperes.

Direct Current

Electrical currents are produced in various ways. DC, or direct, current is produced by dry-cell batteries, wet-cell batteries, and thermocouples. Flashlight batteries are dry-cell types that change chemical energy to electrical energy. Zinc casing around the battery surrounds a paste made of various chemicals. This zinc casing serves as a negative pole for the battery. A carbon post in the center serves as a positive pole. Chemical reactions between the paste and the zinc cause electrons to build up around the zinc pole. If the two poles are connected by a wire, electrons will flow from the negative to the positive pole. If the wire contains a small light, electrons will flow through that light bulb filament and cause it to give off heat and light.

Wet-cell batteries operate in a similar fashion. Your car battery is a wet-cell battery composed of two metal poles (electrodes) and an acid (electrolyte). The chemical reaction between the acid and the metal at the negative pole causes an accumulation of electrons. A wire between the two poles allows electrons to flow, producing an electric current.

Thermocouples

Heat energy can be changed to electrical energy. When two different kinds of wire, such as iron and copper, are connected to form a loop, a current can be produced by heating the wires at one junction and cooling them at another. Such devices are called thermocouples, and they are used as thermostats on car engines. By placing one junction inside the engine and the other junction on the outside, a temperature difference is created when the engine becomes hot, and a small electrical current is generated. The hotter the engine becomes, the more current is generated. This current operates the temperature gauge on the car's dash.

Alternating Current

AC, or alternating current, changes direction 60 times per second. This type of electricity is produced by power plants and runs into our homes on long transmission wires. Most homes, businesses, and industries rely on alternating current.

Circuits

A circuit is the path along which electrons flow. The parts of a circuit include the source of electrons (e.g., battery, power plant), the load (e.g., light, radio), the wires, and a switch. The switch opens and closes the circuit.

In order for electricity to flow, the electrons need a closed path to follow. In other words, electrons can only travel along a circuit that begins at a negative pole and ends at a positive pole. In Figure A, both wires are connected to the battery, and electrons can flow along the path of the wire and operate the stereo headset, which represents the load. However, when one wire is not connected to the battery, as in Figure B, the circuit is incomplete and electrons will not move. Removing one wire from the battery has the same effect as opening a switch.

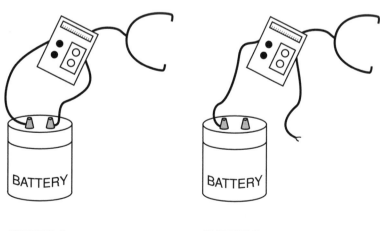

FIGURE A   FIGURE B

There are two types of circuits, depending on how the parts are connected. In a series circuit (see Figure C), there is only one path for electrons to follow. If there is a break anywhere in the circuit, current cannot pass along the circuit. Christmas tree lights are commonly wired in series, and if one light bulb is defective, none of the lights in the string will work. Household light circuits, however, are wired in parallel (see Figure D). If the bulb in one lamp burns out, other lights on that same circuit continue to burn.

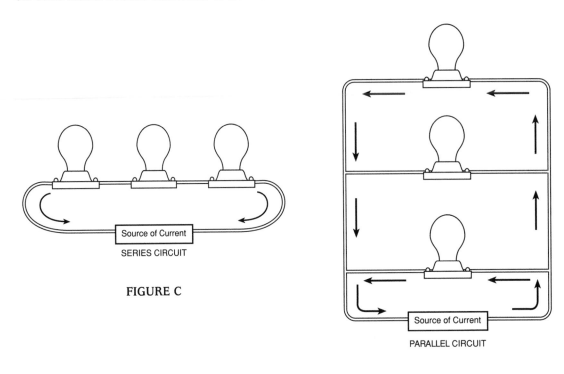

FIGURE C

FIGURE D

Electrical Power

Every month, most people receive an electric power bill. We must pay for the electricity we use in our homes and businesses to perform work. Electric power is a measure of the rate at which electricity does work or provides energy. Electric power can be calculated by multiplying voltage used by the amount of current:

$$\text{Power} = \text{voltage} \times \text{current}$$
$$P = v \times I$$

Power is expressed in watts (W) and kilowatts (kW). A kilowatt is 1000 watts and is used to measure large amounts of power.

To determine how many watts of power are used by a light bulb on a 120-volt circuit with 0.5 amps of current, multiply voltage by amps.

$$P = v \times I$$
$$P = 120 \text{ volts} \times 0.5 \text{ amps}$$
$$P = 60 \text{ watts}$$

Different appliances have different power ratings. The higher the rating, the greater the amount of electricity needed to run the appliance. Some common appliances and the power (watts) they use are as follows:

Clock	3 watts
Radio	100 watts
Hair dryer	1000 watts
Dishwasher	2300 watts
Clothes dryer	4000 watts

Our electric power bills are based on the total amount of energy a household uses. This amount depends on the total amount used by all appliances multiplied by the time they were used.

$$\text{Energy} = \text{power} \times \text{time}$$
$$E = P \times t$$

Electric energy is expressed in kilowatt-hours (kWh). One kWh equals 1000 watts used for 1 hour. To get an idea of how much energy 1 kWh represents, image ten 100-watt light bulbs burning for 1 hour. Or think about the power used to operate a 500-watt TV for 2 hours.

The Cost of Electricity

When we pay our electric bill, we multiply the amount of energy used in kilowatt-hours by the cost of energy per kilowatt-hour. An average household might use 1000 kWh in a month. If the local utility company charges $ 0.7/kWh, multiply 1000 kWh by $ 0.7/kWh to determine the family's power bill.

$$1000 \text{ kWh} \times \$ \, 0.07/\text{kWh} = \$70.00$$

AC-DC—Vocabulary Activity on
Dancing Electrons

Following is a list of terms. Put terms that relate to alternating current (AC) in the circle. Put terms that relate to direct current (DC) in the box. Put terms that relate to either AC or DC in the area where the circle and box overlap.

circuit	thermocouple	turbine
appliance	flashlight	wet-cell battery
generator	car thermostat	power plant
ohms	transmission lines	current
light bulb	voltage	watts
power	electricity	conductor

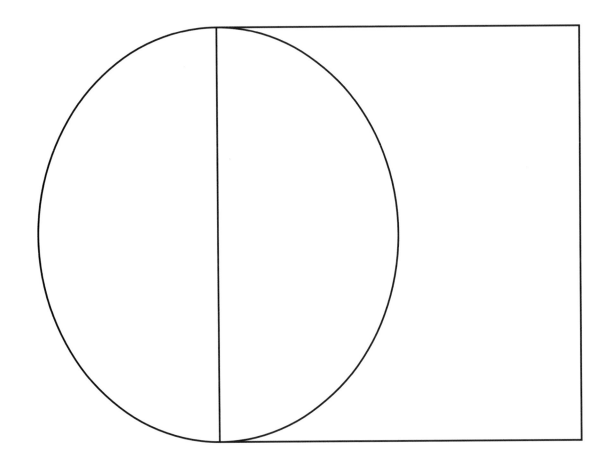

9–2 PAYING THE BILLS
Activity on Calculating the Cost of Electric Power

Objectives

Students will calculate the cost of electricity and analyze the way utilities charge customers for use of electricity.

Teacher Notes

Rates from Georgia Power have been used in this activity as representative rates. Not all utilities charge the same rates, so the information included here may not apply to every locale.

PAYING THE BILLS

Activity on Calculating the Cost of Electric Power

Introduction

Georgia Power, the major electric utility in Georgia, sends a monthly bill to its customers based on how much electric power they have used. Utilities charge different rates for winter (October through April) and summer (June through September) seasons. In the summer, customers are charged an escalating rate, whereas in the winter they are charged a declining rate. Examine the chart below.

Utility Rate

kWh	Summer	Winter
First 650 kWh	$.04782	$.04782
Next 350 kWh	$.07948	$.04104
Over 1000 kWh	$.08184	$.04040

The base rate each month is $7.50 whether customers used any electricity or not. In addition, customers pay 5% sales tax and a fuel recovery cost of $.015 per kilowatt-hour.

Questions

1. In December, the Kendrix family stayed at home for two weeks to celebrate the Christmas season with family and friends. The regular group of two adults and three teenage children was augmented with visiting grandparents and plenty of spend-the-night friends. Meals were cooked at home, and laundry was done daily. At the end of the month, Mr. Kendrix was suprised to see his electric bill, which stated that 3233 kWh of electricity had been used.

Calculate the Kendrix family's power bill using the sample bill on the next page.

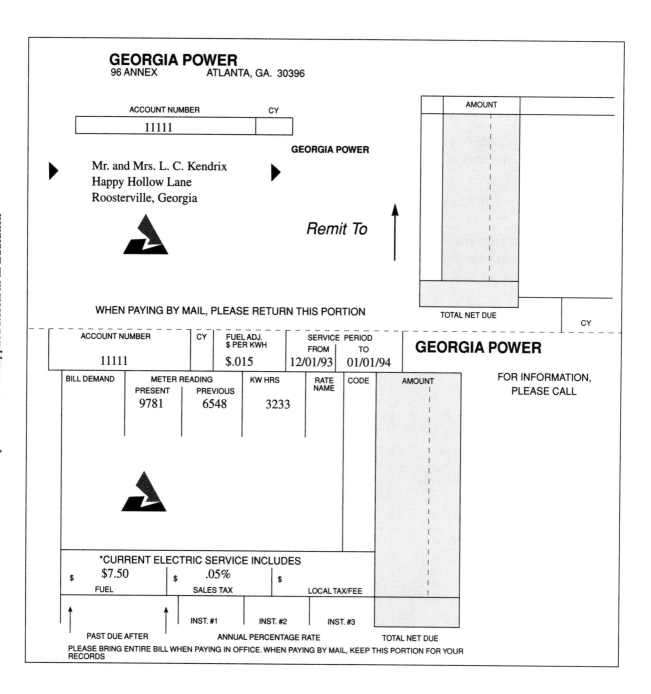

GEORGIA POWER
96 ANNEX   ATLANTA, GA. 30396

ACCOUNT NUMBER	CY
11111	

GEORGIA POWER

Mr. and Mrs. L. C. Kendrix
Happy Hollow Lane
Roosterville, Georgia

Remit To

AMOUNT
TOTAL NET DUE

CY

WHEN PAYING BY MAIL, PLEASE RETURN THIS PORTION

ACCOUNT NUMBER	CY	FUEL ADJ. $ PER KWH	SERVICE PERIOD FROM	TO
11111		$.015	12/01/93	01/01/94

GEORGIA POWER

FOR INFORMATION, PLEASE CALL

BILL DEMAND	METER READING PRESENT	PREVIOUS	KW HRS	RATE NAME	CODE	AMOUNT
	9781	6548	3233			

*CURRENT ELECTRIC SERVICE INCLUDES

$ $7.50	$ .05%	$
FUEL	SALES TAX	LOCAL TAX/FEE

	INST. #1	INST. #2	INST. #3
PAST DUE AFTER	ANNUAL PERCENTAGE RATE		TOTAL NET DUE

PLEASE BRING ENTIRE BILL WHEN PAYING IN OFFICE. WHEN PAYING BY MAIL, KEEP THIS PORTION FOR YOUR RECORDS

2. In April, the entire Kendrix family took a trip to Washington State, and the house was empty for three weeks. The monthly power bill stated that they had used only 630 kWh. Calculate their power bill.

3. In July, the heat wave and summer drought brought daily temperatures into the nineties. Mrs. Kendrix set the air conditioner on 76 degrees Fahrenheit. The power bill stated that 2995 kWh of electricity were used. Calculate the Kendrix power bill for July.

4. During which season is electricity expensive to use? Does the amount of electricity one uses affect the cost of this energy to the customer?

5. How could a family conserve electricity in the summer?

6. Do utilities encourage or discourage customers to use a lot of electricity in the summer? Explain your answer.

SHOCKING SOLUTIONS
Math Problems Involving Electricity

1. Brad has a new flashlight that runs on one 8-volt battery. How much current flows through this circuit if the bulb has 2 ohms of resistance?

2. If your fingers are damp and offer a resistance of only 1200 ohms, how much current will pass through them if you touch the terminals of a 6-volt battery?

3. If your hair dryer draws 10 amps of current on a 120-volt circuit, how much power does it use?

4. Shane's 100-watt radio draws 7 amps of current on a 120-volt circuit. What is the resistance in the radio?

5. It is Lisa's night to clean up the kitchen, but she's anxious to get started on her physics homework. While loading the dishwasher, she calculates how many amps of current it uses on a 120-volt circuit. What did she find?

6. Audrey fell off her horse during riding lessons and got all of her clothes dirty. How much energy is used by an 1800-watt washing machine that runs 30 minutes and a 4000-watt clothes dryer that runs for 1 hour? If electricity costs $0.06 per kilowatt-hour, how much did it cost Audrey to wash and dry her clothes?

SECTION 3

Astronomy

LESSON 10: PLANETS

10–1 A SPACED-OUT FAMILY
Content on the Planets of Our Solar System

Siblings of the Solar System

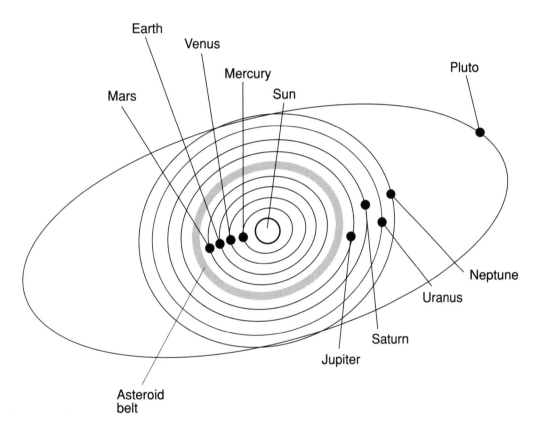

A family is a group that can share a common location. The solar system is the location for our planet, earth. Also within our solar system are planets and their satellites, asteroids, comets, and meteoroids. These objects move in a gravitational field around the central body called the sun. There are nine major planets that exist in our solar system, and thousands of minor planets we call asteroids. Most asteroids are less than a few miles in diameter, and many scientists believe they are chips broken from the major planets. Comets are bright objects with glowing tails that travel in long and narrow orbits. Comets consist of frozen

117

gases and rocks. As the comets come near the sun, the frozen gases are heated. These changes produce the glow we see. Meteoroids are tiny particles of matter (often less than 1 gram) that travel at high speeds.

Inner and Outer Space

The nine planets of our solar system are often divided into two categories. The first category is the inner or terrestrial planets (earthlike planets). This category includes the four planets closest in proximity to the sun. The second category is the outer planets. These five planets move in orbits of vastly greater diameter than the inner planets.

The planets (with the exception of Uranus) all rotate in a uniform direction; they all revolve about the sun in the same direction; and all have orbits within a few degrees of each other. Gravitational attraction pulls the planets toward the sun and keeps them moving through space.

A Close-Knit Family

The planet closest to the sun is Mercury (about 36 million miles from the sun). The side of Mercury exposed to the sun can reach temperatures of up to 770 degrees Farhenheit, while the shaded side of Mercury can drop to absolute zero. No other planet has this extreme temperature range. Scientists believe that pools of molten metal might exist on the hot side of Mercury. Mercury takes about 88 days for one revolution around the sun, and it has no satellites. Mercury has craters and a terrain very much like our moon. No discernable atmosphere exists on Mercury. The average density of Mercury is about that of earth, which suggests that it may have a core of iron.

Venus is the second planet from the sun (about 67 million miles away from the sun). This planet is often called the morning star or evening star because it is the brightest object in our sky, besides the sun and our moon. Venus requires about 225 days to revolve around the sun. Venus is much like the earth in mass, size, and density; but it is much hotter than the earth (temperatures can soar to 570 degrees Farhenheit). The atmosphere of Venus is extremely dense because it is composed primarily of carbon dioxide (with very little oxygen). The air pressure on the surface of Venus is about 90 times that of the earth. Its atmosphere is filled with pale yellow clouds composed of extremely corrosive sulfuric acid.

Earth is the third planet from the sun and the fifth largest planet in size. More than 75% of the surface of the earth is covered with water. One revolution around the sun requires 365 days. The tilt of the earth on its axis causes seasons to occur around the planet. The atmosphere of the earth is 79% nitrogen, 20% oxygen, and 1% trace elements. The temperatures of the earth are variable but moderate. At this time, the earth is the only planet known to be capable of supporting life.

Mars is the fourth or last of the inner planets. The length of the Martian day is about the same length as that of earth, while a year on Mars is about twice as long as a year on earth. The air pressure on Mars is extremely thin (about 166 times less than that on earth). In fact, Mars is close to having no air at all. The air that does exist is primarily carbon dioxide. Mars has cold and warm seasons like those on earth, but to a much greater extreme than the temperature range on earth. At night temperatures on Mars can dip to -170 degrees Farhenheit. A variety of terrain that appears red upon observation is evident on Mars. This red coloration is due to the iron oxide (rust) found on the surface of Mars. Sand dunes, craters, mountains, and volcanoes can all be found on Mars.

Distant Relatives

Jupiter is the largest planet in our solar system, with 125 times the surface area of earth but one quarter the density of earth. Jupiter is orbited by 16 moons. A day on Jupiter lasts only about 10 hours, but a year on Jupiter lasts about 12 times as long as a year on earth. The planet is almost all gases, mostly hydrogen and helium. The atmosphere of Jupiter consists of ammonia and methane but no oxygen. Winds blow constantly on Jupiter, whipping white clouds around the surface of this planet. It is believed that Jupiter consists of a rocky metallic core surrounded by a thick layer of ice.

Saturn is the second largest planet and it is orbited by 20 moons. The distinctive rings that surround Saturn have intrigued people for many years. These rings are probably composed of particles of ice. The atmosphere of Saturn is composed of hydrogen and helium. The temperature on Saturn is much colder than the temperature on Jupiter. As strong winds blow across this planet, storm systems are forming constantly. A day on Saturn is about 17 hours, and a year is about 29 times longer than on earth.

Uranus has an atmosphere composed of mostly hydrogen and helium. The density of Uranus is less dense than water, and it is surrounded by rings similar to those around Saturn. An interesting feature of Uranus involves its axis of rotation. Unlike the other eight planets, Uranus does not rotate in a uniform direction. A day on Uranus is about 13 hours, but a year is equivalent to 84 earth years.

Neptune shows little or no surface marking and is almost identical to Uranus. A day on Neptune is 16 hours, and a year is 165 earth years. Neptune has an icy, rocky surface and one large moon. Its atmosphere is like that of Uranus.

Pluto is an icy, rocky planet located the farthest from the sun of all nine planets. One year on Pluto is about 248 earth years, and a day is only 6 hours long. More research needs to be done on Pluto, because much information about this cold planet is speculation.

PLANET UNSCRAMBLE—VOCABULARY ACTIVITY ON
A SPACED-OUT FAMILY

Directions

Read *A Spaced-Out Family* and unscramble the words to arrive at the answer.

1. _____ (resretrtlai) The earthlike planets are called the _____ planets.

2. _____ (arusun) The planet that does not rotate in a uniform direction is _____.

3. _____ (yrcuemr) The planet closest to the sun is _____.

4. _____ (toulp) The planet the greatest distance from the sun is _____.

5. _____ (natsur) The planet with the icy rings around it is called _____.

6. _____ (itnogrne) The gas that makes up the greatest percentage of the earth is _____.

7. _____ (evsun) Sulfuric acid makes up the clouds of the planet _____.

8. _____ (sertcar) A great deal of _____, volcanoes, and mountains are found on the surface of Mars.

9. _____ (insdw) Jupiter has clouds of ammonia and methane, and constant _____ occur on this planet.

10. _____ (moecst) _____ are bright objects with glowing tails that travel in long and narrow orbits.

© 1994 by The Center for Applied Research in Education

10–2 BRINGING THE SOLAR SYSTEM DOWN TO EARTH
Activity on the Size of Our Solar System

Objectives

Students will develop their scaled-down model of the solar system.

Teacher Notes

Math skills are required in figuring the distances and diameters. Younger students may be given an already completed chart to do this activity. Older students can mathematically figure the distances and diameters and fill in the chart for themselves. The class should be divided into groups of four or five. Parts A and B (mathematical computations) of the lab activity should be done indoors. Part C of the activity will be done outdoors on the second day. The best solar system creation can be awarded a numerical grade or some other award.

BRINGING THE SOLAR SYSTEM DOWN TO EARTH
Activity on the Size of Our Solar System

Materials

Charts 1 and 2

Metric measuring apparatus for length in meters

Pencil

Outdoor materials such as stones, twigs, etc.

Large open outdoor area

Calculator

Part A: Calculating the scaled-down diameter of the planets

1. Look at Chart 1, which gives the diameter of the planets and the sun in kilometers.

2. The sun is 1,380,000 km in diameter. You will assign the sun a diameter value of 1.

3. To get the diameter value of Mercury, divide 1,380,000 km by 4989. The answer would be 277. Place this number in the part of the chart marked "# times smaller than the sun." Repeat this procedure for the other eight planets. For instance, Venus would be 1,380,000 km divided by 12,392 km. Record this value in Chart 1.

4. For the last column in Chart 1, you will assign a scaled-down value for each of the planets. Begin with the sun and assign the sun a value of 1 meter (1000 mm). Calculate the value of the planets by dividing 1000 by the number of times smaller you calculated that planet to be than the sun. For instance, Mercury will be calculated by dividing 1000 by 277. The answer will be 3.6 mm. This will be entered in the chart. Do this for each of the planets.

5. When the chart is complete, the last column will represent the diameter your group will use to represent each planet in the activity.

BRINGING THE SOLAR SYSTEM DOWN TO EARTH (continued)

10–2 CHART 1

Object	Diameter (km)	# Times Smaller than Sun	Scaled-Down Diameter (mm)
Sun	1,380,000	————	1000 mm
Mercury	4989	277	3.6 mm
Venus	12,392		
Earth	12,757		
Mars	6759		
Jupiter	142,749		
Saturn	120,862		
Uranus	51,499		
Neptune	44,579		
Pluto	2414		

Part B: Figuring the scaled-down distance of the planets from the sun

1. Study Chart 2, which lists the distance of the planets from the sun in millions of miles. Your group will convert these distances to astronomical units (AU). 1 AU is the distance of the earth from the sun. This means that 93 million miles is equivalent to 1 AU. In Chart 2 you will see the number 1 under AU for earth. To find the astronomical unit for the other eight planets, you should divide each planet's distance from the sun by 93 million. For instance, Venus is 0.7 AU. To arrive at that figure, the distance of Venus from the sun, 67.27 million miles, is divided by 93 million. You will record 0.7 in Chart 2 under AU. Follow this procedure for the remaining planets.

BRINGING THE SOLAR SYSTEM DOWN TO EARTH *(continued)*

2. In the last column of Chart 2, you will calculate the relative distance from the sun by assigning a value of 1000 mm (1 meter) for the distance of the earth from the sun—1 AU. Place 1000 mm in the last column on Chart 2. The distance from Venus to the Sun will be 700 mm.

   Do this for the remainder of the planets.

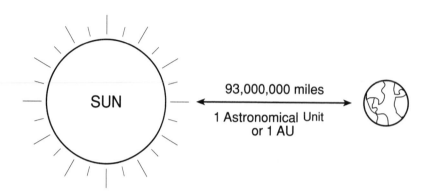

10–2 CHART 2

Planet Name	Distance from Sun (in millions of miles)	AU Equivalent (astronomical unit)	Scaled-Down Diameter in mm
Mercury	36		
Venus	67.27	0.7	700
Earth	93	1	1000
Mars	141.7		
Jupiter	483.9		
Saturn	887.1		
Uranus	1783.98		
Neptune	2795.5		
Pluto	3675.3		

Part C: Creation of Scaled-Down Model

1. Each group will take completed Charts 1 and 2 and a meter stick or metric tape measure outdoors.

2. Each group will use the data in the last column of Chart 1 to devise the appropriate diameter of the sun and the nine planets in millimeters. Rocks, twigs, straw, etc., can be used to build each planet and the sun.

3. The sun should be at one end of the model, and the planets should be placed in the proper order away from the sun. To determine the appropriate distance of each planet from the sun, use the meter stick and information from the last column of Chart 2. Measure the appropriate meters or millimeters for the distance of each planet from the sun.

4. Your group will create the sun and the planets in the appropriate scaled-down diameter and at the appropriate distance from the sun. Make the planets by using rocks, twigs, straws, etc., to form the outline of each planet in the appropriate size.

5. At the conclusion of your solar system model, the teacher will inspect your creation.

6. Each group should view the solar system created by other groups.

7. The best solar system will receive a special award.

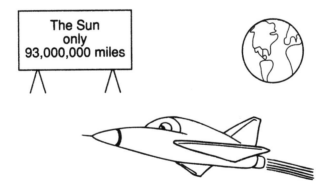

10–3 ASTONISHING PLANETARY DISCOVERY
Project on the Composition of the Planets

Objectives

Students will evaluate information about the nine planets in our solar system and synthesize an imaginary creature that can exist on a planet other than earth. Upon realization that no other planet can support life as we know it, students will understand the need for responsible stewardship toward our planet, earth.

Teacher Notes

This activity can be adapted for all grade levels. You can require students to build models of their creature, draw pictures or diagrams, describe it in writing, etc. The ability level and age of the student can dictate the approach you use. This activity can be taken further by integrating math skills for older students. It is best done in cooperative learning groups. Oral presentations are recommended when each group has completed a description of a creature.

Write the name of the eight planets except earth on eight different slips of paper. Put these in a paper bag. Divide students into groups of three or four. A member of each group will select one slip of paper from the paper bag to begin the activity. The slip of paper will indicate the planet the group will research.

Consult your media center for resource materials available on these planets.

ASTONISHING PLANETARY DISCOVERY
Project on the Compostion of the Planets

Introduction

Read *A Spaced-Out Family* before doing this activity. This will give you some background on our solar system and its planets. Read the following scenario:

Congratulations! Your team has been selected to work on a NASA space project. This project will require your space exploration team to examine the physical and environmental conditions on one of the eight planets other than earth. This mission is of vital importance because environmental projections indicate that the atmosphere of the earth is reaching toxic levels. Scientists project that the toxicity level will increase to an extent that one day human life will be unable to survive. At this time, environmentalists on earth are trying to halt our spiral toward destruction, but there are no guarantees that it is not too late. NASA and the governmental heads of all the countries of the world have elected to expand the research done on the planets in our solar system. It is the goal of this mission to uncover a planet that may be able to support a future form of life. Your exploration team will head the mission to one of the eight planets.

Your team will conduct detailed research on a planet. Upon completion of this research, your team will use this research information to design a creature that could exist on that planet. You are one of eight teams around the world researching each planet in detail. Each exploration team will randomly select a slip of paper that denotes which planet the team has been assigned.

Each team will decide what characteristics a creature must have to exist on the designated planet. Access to library materials written by space experts will be provided to aid in this decision. After your team has conducted adequate research on the planet, the designs for the perfect creature should be made and detailed drawing and written description of the creature should be provided. This information will be submitted to a team of world-renowned genetic engineers. They will then genetically design and genetically engineer this creature. The creature will be stored in a special environment until it is transported and released on the planet for which it was designed. In the future, each creature will be transported to its designated planet and monitored for 1 year.

At the conclusion of the year, NASA and the heads of the government will determine which creature was best suited for its planet. The team will be given a special award and their planet will be designated as the planet we will look to for future research.

Good luck in your voyage. Remember, good library research is extremely important.

Materials

The introduction, *A Spaced-Out Family*
Library materials and resource material on planets and adaptations for survival
Poster board and markers

Procedure

1. Draw a slip of paper from the paper bag that the teacher provides. This paper will indicate the planet your team will research.

2. Use the library resource materials and complete the Scientist Worksheet on your designated planet.

3. Take the information you gathered on the worksheet, and come up with a design for a creature that could best survive on that planet. A written description of its characteristics should be given, with an explanation for each characteristic. In addition, a drawing or a model of the creature should be made. This written description and picture will serve as the design given to the scientists for genetic engineering.

4. After completion of the creature design, your team will present its project to the rest of the class (who will represent NASA and the heads of the government). At the conclusion of the presentations, the class and the teacher will decide on the best-adapted creature.

Scientist Worksheet on the Planets

Exploration team members:

_____

_____

Planet explored: _____

Distance from the sun: _____

Diameter of the planet: _____

Distance from the earth: _____

Composition of the atmosphere (gases and their percentages): _____

_____

Temperature range: Low _____ to High _____

    Average temperature: _____

    Do seasonal temperatures exist? _____

    Average humidity (if any): _____

    Average barometric pressure: _____

Describe the surface terrain:

_____

_____

_____

Gravity on this planet compared with earth: _____

Storms or other climatic conditions that might exist:

_____

Period of one revolution around the sun (length of a year): _____

Period of one rotation on the planet's axis (length of a day): _____

Is there evidence of volcanoes? _____

Scientist Worksheet on the Planets *(continued)*

Number of satellites that orbit your planet: _____

Is there evidence of wind on your planet? _____ Explain how much: _____

_____

Describe the interior of your planet. Indicate the layers and what composes each layer:

_____

_____

_____

Special features and interesting information about your planet not included in the material above:

_____

_____

_____

_____

_____

_____

Information on Your Creature

Describe in detail the special features of your creature:

_____

_____

_____

_____

_____

_____

Scientist Worksheet on the Planets *(continued)*

What will your creature eat on your planet?

_____

_____

Describe how your creature will metabolize its food source for energy:

_____

_____

Describe the process of respiration for your creature:

_____

_____

List some dangers the creature will face on the planet:

_____

_____

Explain the adaptations of your creature which will help it deal with the following factors:

Temperature extremes: _____

Food intake: _____

Gravity: _____

Atmospheric conditions: _____

Loneliness and recreation: _____

Climatic conditions: _____

Dangers the creature may encounter on the planet: _____

How old will your creature be if it was 1 year old when taken to the planet and retrieved 10 earth years later? _____

Evaluation Sheet for the Best Creature

(Students and teacher can use)

Originality and creativity (20 points):   _____

Research (40 points):   _____

Organization and design (10 points):   _____

Illustration of creature (10 points):   _____

Oral presentation (20 points):   _____

Total (100 points)   _____

LESSON 11: STARS

11–1 STARLIGHT, STAR BRIGHT
Content on Stars

Where Are We?

What are stars, and how were they formed? The night sky is filled with sparkling lights, some bright and boldly twinkling, others faint and difficult to see. How many stars are there? Of what are they composed?

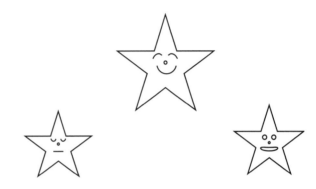

Galileo answered some of our questions when he determined that our sun and its nine planets are only a small part of a huge system, the galaxy we call the Milky Way. As a member of this galaxy, it is very difficult for us to get an idea about how the entire system looks. However, in our position we can see that the stars in or near the constellation Sagittarius are the brightest stars around us. The faintest stars are in the opposite part of the sky near Auriga and Cassiopeia. The brightness we see near Sagittarius is due to the large number of stars in that area of the sky. This has led us to believe that the center of the galaxy is in that direction.

We now know that our solar system is near the edge of the Milky Way, a huge galaxy that is about 100,000 light years in diameter. (A light year is the distance light travels in a year, which is 5 trillion, 878 billion miles.) The Milky Way has a spiral shape, and its stars are arranged in long, curved spiral arms. The entire galactic system revolves around a center at a rate of 612,000 miles per hour (mph). Even at this speed, it takes our sun and its planets 220 million years to make one entire trip around the galaxy.

Bright Stars and Black Holes

There are billions of stars in the Milky Way, and no two of them are exactly the same. Some stars appear bright to us, yet others are very dim; some are blue, and others are yellow. Some of the brightest stars in the heavens are novas, stars that are giving off enormous amounts of mass in a huge explosion of light and energy. The word nova means "new star." Early nova observers believed that they were

133

witnessing the birth of a star. Novae typically flare brightly for a few days and then recede to their original brightness. Novae may be shedding mass before dying of old age.

A supernova is an even more spectacular event. A supernova is a star that actually blows itself apart. Supernovae flare up millions of time brighter than the sun and can be seen over enormous distances. Only three supernova sightings have been recorded in the last 1000 years. In Chinese and Japanese literature of A.D. 1054, writers recorded a supernova event that could still be seen 2 years later. The remains of this explosion can now be seen as the Crab Nebula.

The ultimate star is a black hole. Black holes begin their existence as regular stars. Eventually the stars burn up all of their nuclear fuel and begin collapsing on themselves. The star matter becomes condensed into such a small volume that atomic structure no longer exists. The gravity on this dead star is incredibly strong, and nothing, not even light, can escape. Actually, the question of a particle escaping a black hole does not arise because there is nothing inside the structure. The particles themselves are reduced to zero diameter by the excessive gravitational forces; in other words, there are no particles in black holes. The radius of a black hole is extremely small; a black hole with the mass of our sun has a radius of 1.9 miles. Astronomers estimate that there are at least 1 million black holes in our galaxy.

Stardust

Nebulae (Latin for "clouds") are vast clouds of cosmic dust. Some nebulae form swirling, bubbling shapes that eventually condense into new stars. Other nebulae are bright remnants of supernovae, like the Crab Nebula. The Great Nebula is the only spiral nebula in the night sky that is visible to the naked eye; it is found in the constellation Orion, as is the Horse's Head Nebula. The latter is dark because there are no nearby stars to illuminate it. Dark nebulae are huge clouds of matter that have not yet formed into stars. Nebulae vary in size from as small as our solar system to thousands of light years in width.

Brightness and Distance

When you look carefully at the starry sky, some stars appear very bright to your unaided eye, whereas others appear faint. Astronomers want to know not how bright stars look, but how bright they actually are. Sirius, the brightest star in the sky, appears about four times as bright as the star Rigel. But to compare the light radiated by these two stars, luminosity must be known. Luminosity of a star is the total amount of energy radiated into space every second. This can be determined by multiplying the amount of light received on earth by the distance of the star from earth. When the luminosity of Sirius and Rigel are compared, Rigel is 2000 times more luminous than Sirius. Sirius appears brighter because it is 90 times closer to us than Rigel.

Two thousand years ago, astronomers used the magnitude system to compare star brightness. The Greek astronomer Hipparchus divided the stars in the sky into six magnitudes of brightness: First-magnitude stars were the brightest and sixth-magnitude stars were the faintest. There are about 20 first-magnitude stars in the sky, 50 second-magnitude stars, 150 third-magnitude stars, 450 fourth-magnitude stars, 1350 fifth-magnitude stars, and 4000 sixth-magnitude stars. Modern astronomers have extended this system to include all bright objects as well as objects too dim for Hipparchus to see. The brighter a celestial body, the lower its magnitude on the magnitude scale. A star of the first magnitude is about 2.5 times brighter than a star of the second magnitude. Thus a first-magnitude star is 6.4 times brighter than a third-magnitude star, 16 times brighter than a fourth-magnitude star, and 40 times brighter than a fifth-magnitude star.

The apparent magnitude of a star depends not only on its brightness but also on its distance from earth. To compare the brightness of two bodies, you must compare their absolute magnitudes. The absolute magnitude of a body is defined as the apparent magnitude that body would have had if it were situated at 10 parsecs from earth, a distance of about 3 light years. Thus, we can see that the brightest star in the sky, Sirius, is really less bright than Rigel (see Chart 1).

CHART 1. THE MAGNITUDES OF SOME FAMILIAR OBJECTS IN THE SKY

Star	Location	Apparent Magnitude	Absolute Magnitude	Distance in Light Years
Rigel	Orion	+0.11	−7.0	660
Sirius	Canis Major	−1.45	+1.41	8.64
Canopus	Carina	−0.73	+0.16	190

In astronomy, distances between objects are so great that they cannot be measured by conventional methods. The light year (l.y.) represents the distance light can travel in a vacuum in 1 year, or 9×10^{12} kilometers.

STAR PUZZLE—VOCABULARY PUZZLE ON STARLIGHT, STAR BRIGHT

Directions

Complete the following puzzle using terms from *Starlight, Star Bright.*

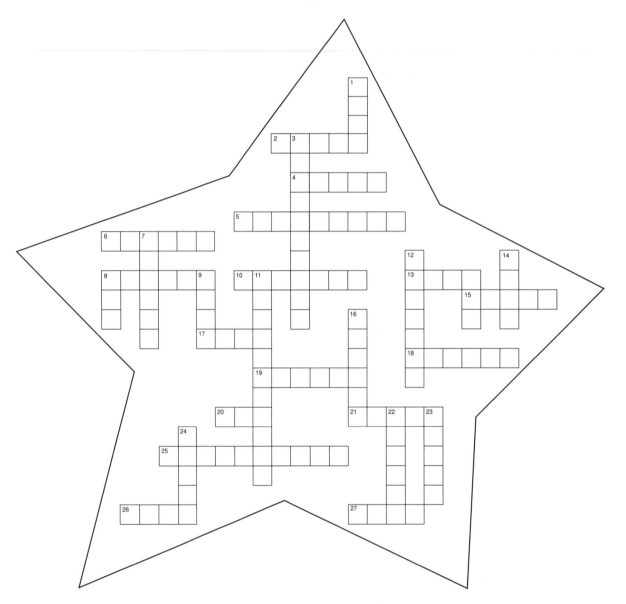

STAR PUZZLE *(continued)*

Across

2. Light cannot escape from the gravitational pull of a _____ hole.

4. Our galaxy is the _____ Way.

5. The brighter a star, the lower its _____ on the magnitude scale.

6. There are about 50 _____ magnitude stars.

8. The solar _____ is on the edge of the Milky Way.

10. _____ was an early astronomer who determined that our solar system is only a small part of the Milky Way.

13. In a black _____, matter is so dense that atomic structure collapses.

15. The distance light can travel in 2 years is two light _____.

17. Sirius is the brightest _____ in the sky.

18. The Milky Way has a _____ shape.

19. The Crab _____ is a remnant from a supernova.

20. Modern astronomers can see stars too _____ for Hipparchus.

21. A parsec is 3.626 light _____.

25. The astronomer _____ divided the stars into six magnitudes of brightness.

26. Stars burn nuclear _____.

27. Rigel is a _____ in the constellation Orion.

Down

1. The Horse's Head Nebula is _____ because there are no stars close by to provide illumination.

3. The _____ of a star is the total amount of energy radiated into space each second.

7. Nebulae are formed from clouds of _____ dust.

8. The Greeks divided the stars into _____ magnitudes of brightness.

9. A black hole with the sun's _____ has a radius of only 1.9 miles.

11. Scientists who study the heavenly bodies are _____.

12. In _____ and Japanese literature from A.D. 1054, a supernova event was recorded.

14. The _____ Nebula is a remnant from a supernova.

16. Our _____ is 100,000 light years in diameter.

22. The faintest stars are near the constellations Cassiopeia and _____.

23. Our _____ system consists of one star and nine planets.

24. _____ is 660 light years from earth.

11–2 STAR CHAMBER
Class Project on Constellations

Objectives

Students will use computational, graphing, and measuring techniques to re-create the positions of constellations.

Teacher Notes

In this activity, students are creating a large bag that can be inflated with air. If space is a problem, the size of the bag can be varied, as long as it is large enough for a few students to enter the bag and lie on their backs. Directions in the "Procedure" section enable students to create a bag that can hold 10 or 15 students.

Star charts for autumn and winter are provided. Enlarge pages to 11 by 17 inches.

STAR CHAMBER ACTIVITY
Class Project on Constellations

Constellations Are Star Patterns

For thousands of years, humans have seen patterns formed by stars in the night sky. The arrangement of the stars in the sky has been credited with determining the course of events on earth. Early astronomers who could "read" stars were important members of the community.

We know today that patterns seen between stars have no influence on our lives, and that visualizing constellations is just one way of studying the arrangement of heavenly bodies. Whether stars are viewed with the naked eye, with a low-power telescope, or with a stronger telescope, they can be beautiful and fascinating. One of the most famous star patterns, or constellations, is Ursa Major (the Great Bear), whose "tail" is known as the Big Dipper. Two stars in the Great Bear are alpha and beta Ursae Majoris; these are called the pointer stars because they point to Polaris, the North Star. The North Star indicates the position of the north celestial pole, the point around which all the heavens seem to rotate. Polaris is also the last star in the "tail" of Ursa Minor (the Little Bear).

A King, a Queen, and a Dragon

Several other easily identifiable constellations are near Polaris. Cepheus (Cepheus, the Monarch) is a circumpolar constellation, which means that it is near the north pole. It and Ursa Major are in exactly opposite directions from Polaris. Draco (the Dragon) is made up of fairly faint stars that form a long path between the tails of the Big and Little Dippers and then curve northeast around the bowl of the Little Dipper before winding southwest to form the easily recognizable, quadrilateral Dragon's Head. Cassiopeia (named for Cassiopeia, the Queen in Greek mythology) is easily recognizable because if forms a wide-spread W in the sky. It is the same distance from Polaris as Ursa Major.

A Dog, a Horse, and a Servant

Aquarius (the Water Carrier) is a faint but wide constellation. Its most prominent feature is the Water Jar, a group of four stars that form a Y. In ancient times, people saw the water jar as being inverted so that water poured into the mouth of the Southern Fish (Pisces). Pegasus (the Flying Horse) is most famous for the so-called Great Square of Pegasus, formed by four stars. One of these stars actually belongs to the constellation Andromeda. Beta-Pegasi is one of the largest stars known; if it were in the sun's location, its size would extend beyond the orbit of Venus.

Canis Major (the Great Dog) includes Sirius, the brightest star in the sky. The Little Dog, or Canis Minor, forms an equilateral triangle with Sirius and one of the stars in Orion. Orion is generally believed to be the most beautiful and imposing constellations in the heavens. Four bright stars form a large rectangle, and three smaller, evenly spaced stars within the rectangle form the belt. No other constellation has so many bright stars. Orion contains two nebulae. One of these, the Great Nebula, can be seen with the naked eye. It is a diffuse nebula, a great cloud of dust 26 light years in diameter and 1625 light years

STARS OF AUTUMN

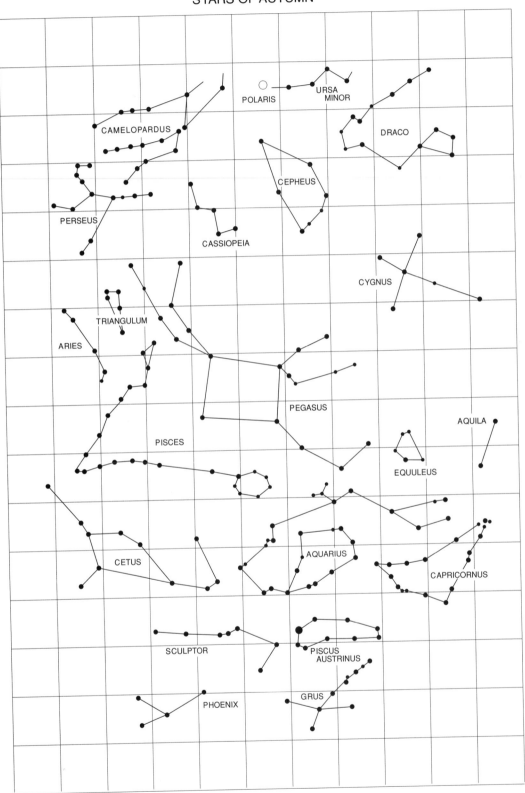

STAR CHAMBER ACTIVITY *(continued)*

STARS OF WINTER

from earth. The other nebula in Orion is the Horse's Head Nebula, a dark cloud silhouetted against a glowing cloud of cosmic dust. Long photographic exposures are required to reveal this beautiful object.

In this lab activity, you will recreate some of the constellations and form a star chamber for viewing them.

Materials

Star chart enlarged to 11″ × 17″

A sheet of black plastic, 80 feet by 40 feet

Wide masking tape

Narrow masking tape

Ice pick or knife

Meter sticks or measuring tapes

Large fan

Procedure

1. Spread out the black plastic. You will create constellations on one half of the plastic. When you are finished making the constellations, fold the plastic in half.

2 Use masking tape to create 4 foot by 4 foot grids on half of the black plastic (see Figure A).

3. Each little star chart grid represents one 4 foot by 4 foot grid on the plastic. Using a knife or ice pick, recreate on the plastic the constellation patterns depicted on the star chart.

4. For example,

   a. On the "Stars of Autumn" Star Chart, find the constellation Cassiopeia.

   b. On the Star Chart, it falls within the fifth grid from the left and the fourth and fifth grids from the top.

   c. Find the corresponding grids on the plastic, and punch holes to recreate the Cassiopeia design.

   d. Do not try to connect the stars with cuts in the plastic.

5. Fold the plastic in half. With the wide masking tape, tape two sides together. Tape part of the third side, leaving enough room for the fan and for students to enter the star chamber. The fourth side is formed by the fold (see Figure B).

6. Place the fan in the open area and turn it on. After the bag is inflated with air, enter and lie down on your backs. Constellations should be visible in the chamber.

7. Use the chamber to memorize constellations, or as a place to read and study astronomy.

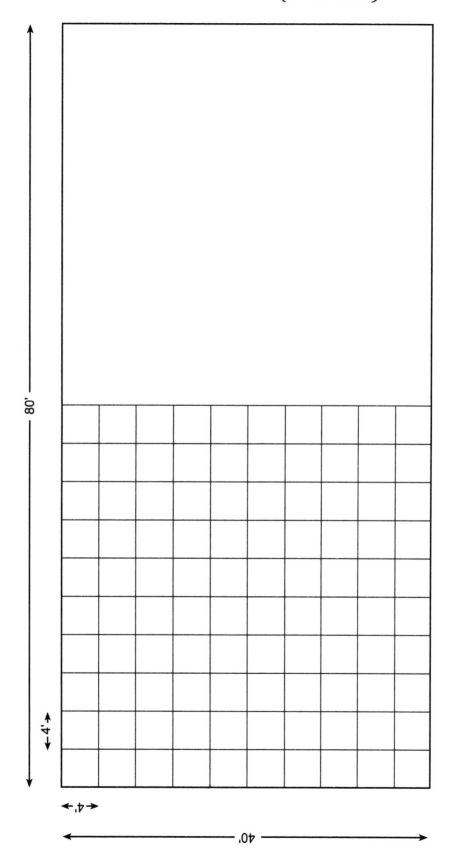

FIGURE A. Black plastic with masking tape grid.

STAR CHAMBER ACTIVITY *(continued)*

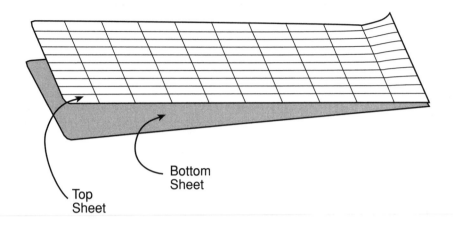

Top
Sheet

Bottom
Sheet

FIGURE B. Fold the plastic in half and tape the sides.

Conclusions

1. What is Polaris? Why does locating Polaris help lost people find their way home?

2. Why do we study constellations?

3. Look at the star patterns created in the Star Chamber. See if you can create your own constellation. Draw it and give it a name.

4. Fill in the blanks with the following words. Put the corresponding letter in the space to the left of each number.

<table>
<tr><td>a. Sirius</td><td>b. Orion</td><td>c. Ursa Major</td></tr>
<tr><td>d. Draco</td><td>e. Andromeda</td><td>f. Cassiopeia</td></tr>
<tr><td>g. Pegasus</td><td>h. Cepheus</td><td></td></tr>
</table>

_____ 1. ___ is a constellation that contains the Great Nebula, M 31.

_____ 2. The Big Dipper is the tail of ___.

_____ 3. Canis Major includes ___, the brightest star in the sky.

_____ 4. ___ is believed by many to be the most beautiful constellation in the sky.

_____ 5. ___ has more bright stars than any other constellation.

_____ 6. ___ is a long constellation that winds between the Big and Little Dippers.

_____ 7. ___ forms a wide W across the sky.

_____ 8. ___ contains the Horse's Head Nebula, one of the dark nebulas.

_____ 9. The pointer stars in ___ point to the North Star.

_____ 10. Beta-Pegasi, one of the largest stars known, is in the constellation ___.

LESSON 12: THE MOON

12–1 THE MAN IN THE MOON
Content on the Moon's Surface

Moon Tales

Have you ever seen the man in the moon? Since it is the largest object in our night sky, the moon has been the source of wonder and speculation for centuries. Legends and stories about the moon, its possible inhabitants, and its influence on earth abound. For example, farmers fear the "red moon," which legend says begins after Easter and continues through part of April and May and represents a period of time in which young plants can be reddened. The only proven influences of the moon on earth are of a gravitational nature and produce ocean tides.

An ancient German folk story explains that there was a man who was outcast to the moon because he had stolen cabbages from poor people. Nearly all countries have a similar legend or story about a thief who was sent to the moon for punishment. This thief acquired the power to influence people's behavior on earth, leading to the word *lunatic* (from the word *lunar*) as a description of those who behaved strangely because they had been exposed to moonlight.

In the second century B.C., Lucian of Samosata wrote two widely read books about his "trips" to the moon. Lucian met the "moonites" on these trips, whom he described as large and hairless except for beards that hung down below their knees. Moonites had the unique ability to pluck out their eyes when they needed to see around corners. A typical moonite evening meal consisted of the fumes produced by roasting frogs, accompanied by a drink of water obtained by melting the hailstones that grew on household vines.

In 1638, Bishop Francis Godwin wrote *The Man in the Moon,* the story of a traveler who was accidentally carried to the moon by his flock of trained birds. Godwin wrote about the reduced gravity of the moon, even though Newton had not yet formulated his theory of gravitational attraction. The "lunars" who lived on Godwin's moon had the ability to jump long distances and always spoke in song.

Craters and Maria

If you try, you can see facial features on the moon's surface. When the moon is full, dark areas look like a person's eyes and mouth, and light areas define a nose. These light and dark areas are created by changes that have occurred to the moon's surface over millions of years. Some of these changes were caused by meteor impacts that produced craters.

In 1647, Hinelius of Danzig published the first good map of the moon, and he named many of the features that he could see with his early telescope. Later the astronomer Riccioli started naming features after great men, a custom that has persisted until the present. When Galileo viewed the moon, he thought that the smooth, dark areas were seas, and he therefore named them Maria (plural of *mare,* meaning "seas"). The largest "sea" is Mare Serenitatis, whose diameter is 430 miles. We now know that these are smooth parts of the landscape covered with a dark dust (see Figure A).

FIGURE A. The moon.

The moon is marked with about 30,000 large craters and countless small ones. Clavier is a huge crater with a diameter of 146 miles. Tycho and Copernicus are equally impressive craters. Light-colored streaks radiating from craters are called rays. The origin of lunar craters has long captured the attention of selenographers, scientists who study the moon's physical features. An early theory was that craters are extinct volcanoes and that the seas are beds of lava. But this theory fell into disfavor for many reasons, one of which was the central peak found inside each crater. The American geologist G. K. Gilbert first suggested that craters are formed from meteorite impacts. This meteoritic hypothesis was easy to demonstrate because similar craters are formed by falling raindrops on a muddy or sandy surface. Earlier in the moon's history, meteoroids were much more numerous in our solar system, and consequently meteoritic impacts were more frequent and of greater intensity. Earth probably received a similar bombardment, but the processes of erosion and deposition that exist on earth because of its atmosphere have erased most earth craters.

Lunar craters are almost all round, suggesting that they did not arise from the direct effects of a solid impact. Many meteorites must have struck the lunar surface from low angles, and such an impact would have produced an elliptical crater. It is believed that the tremendous kinetic energy of a moving meteorite was converted to heat energy, raising the temperature of the meteorite and its surrounding area to millions of degrees and vaporizing the meteorite and surrounding rock material. This enormous heat resulted in an explosion, blowing out the crater and dispersing the contents as tiny fragments far over the surrounding surface. The force of the explosion threw rock out to form a rim, but below the center of the exploding mass a peak remained, which is characteristic of explosions (see Figure B). The crater rays are believed to be streaks of rock fragments shot outward from the meteoritic explosion. Such explosion particles could travel hundreds of miles since the moon has a small force of gravity and no atmosphere.

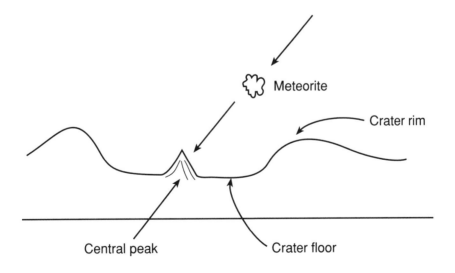

FIGURE B. Cross section of a crater.

Across the lunar surface are millions of stones embedded in a layer of dust. The dust is of a fine texture in the Swamp of Putrefaction at the foot of the Apennines, mountains where the *Apollo 15* landed. It is somewhat coarser at the *Apollo 14* landing site in the Ocean of Storms. Under the carpet of dust is a layer of broken rocks that varies from 2 to 20 meters in depth.

The six *Apollo* missions brought back to earth 2200 lunar rock samples, weighing 400 kilograms (882 pounds). Most of the elements found in these rocks are original to the moon's formation 4.6 billion years ago. Oxygen is the most abundant element on the moon's surface, as on earth. The presence of a few elements can be ascribed to meteorites (especially iron) and solar wind. There are 75 varities of minerals on the moon, as opposed to more than 2000 on earth. Three of these minerals had never been seen on earth before: tranquillitite, phroxyferroite, and armalcolite (which has since been discovered in the diamond mines of South Africa).

LUNAR MESSAGE CREATION—VOCABULARY ACTIVITY ON
THE MAN IN THE MOON

Fill in the blanks using the clues provided.

1. ☐ — —
2. — — — ☐ — — —
3. ☐ — — — — —
4. — — — ☐
5. — — — — ☐ — — — — —
6. — — ☐ — — — — —
7. — — — ☐ — — —
8. — — ☐ — —
9. — — ☐ — —
10. ☐ — — —
11. ☐ — — —
12. — — ☐ —

13. — ☐ —
14. — — ☐ —

15. — — ☐ — — — — —
16. ☐ — — — — —
17. — — — — — ☐ — — —
18. — — ☐ — — —
19. — — — — ☐ — — — —

Clues

1. *Mare* means _____.

2. Falling meteors have a lot of _____ energy.

3. Godwin wrote a book about fictional moon inhabitants that he called _____.

4. Legends say that the man in the moon is a _____ who was exiled for punishment.

5. The largest sea on the moon is Mare _____.

6. In the second century B.C., Lucian wrote about meeting _____ on his two lunar trips.

7. Meteors striking the moon's surface at a low _____ will produce an ellipitical crater.

8. Galileo named dark areas on the moon _____.

9. At one time, astronomers believed that the dark areas on the moon were made of _____.

10. Inside a meteor crater, there is a central _____.

11. The kinetic energy of a meteor is changed to _____ energy on impact.

12. Lines leading away from craters are called _____.

13. The edge of a crater is the _____.

14. The maria are covered with a layer of dark _____.

15. Craters were once believed to be old _____.

16. _____ means "crazy due to exposure to moonlight."

17. _____ is a large crater.

18. The moon has a small force of _____ compared to the earth.

19. The heat energy produced by a meteor impact is capable of _____ the meteor and surrounding rock.

12–2 MOON MADNESS
Lab on Lunar Craters

Objectives

Students will create craters and study their shapes, examine crater rays, and determine the relative ages of craters.

Teacher Notes

Peas and beans are only one type of material that can be used to form craters. Any small objects that are available in different shapes will do as well. Sand can be used in place of flour. This is a good activity for outdoors.

Moon Madness
Lab on Lunar Craters

Introduction

The moon's landscape is remarkably different from any landscape on earth. Seen from our planet, there are two major types of lunar landscapes, one dark and the other lighter. The light areas are called highlands or continents and the dark areas are called maria (Latin word for seas). The name *maria* is somewhat misleading because there are no seas on the moon.

Most of the geographic features of the moon are associated with circular depressions. The most conspicuous depression is the crater Copernicus, named for the famous astronomer. Copernicus Crater is 92 km wide and is composed of a depression with a central peak and walls that appear to be a series of terraces. The outside rim of Copernicus is light colored and is believed to be made of material thrown out of the crater. This rock is called the ejecta blanket and it forms deposits of white material called rays.

Some features are found only on maria, such as mare ridges. These wrinkled ridges are several kilometers wide and hundreds of kilometers long. Chain craters are rows of small craters that are only a few kilometers wide. They are found everywhere—in the maria, inside larger craters, and in the highlands. Rilles are another unusual landscape feature of the moon. They are ridges generally thought to be bounded by faults.

The surface material of the maria is soil that is crumbly but firm. The craters were once believed to have been formed from volcanoes but are now known to be due to meteor impacts. There are a few meteor craters on earth, and they have the same general shape as the craters on the moon. With a width of only 1.6 km, Meteor Crater in Arizona is small compared to some lunar craters but has many traits similar to those on the moon, including a rim and rays.

Materials

White flour
Whole wheat flour
Kidney beans
Peas
Butterbeans
Aluminum pans or pie plates
Ruler
Paper and pencil

Procedure

1. Pour 2 to 3 inches of white flour in your aluminum pan.

2. Sprinkle a thin layer of whole wheat flour on top of the white flour. This represents the moon's surface.

MOON MADNESS *(continued)*

3. The peas and beans represent meteors of different sizes and shapes. (One person should be the thrower for each lab group. Always throw with about the same amount of force.) Throw a pea into the pie plate from directly above the plate with enough force to make a crater. Leave the pea in place. Squat beside the plate and throw another pea into the flour, leaving it in place.

4. Repeat these two throws with two butterbeans and then with two kidney beans.

5. Measure the diameter of each crater in three directions so that you know the shape of each crater produced. Record your data in Table 1. Also describe and sketch each crater to answer question 1 in the "Conclusions" section.

6. Remove the peas and beans very carefully, without disturbing the craters. Observe the craters and answer question 5 in "Conclusions."

Conclusions

TABLE 1. CRATER MEASUREMENTS

	Pea from above	*Pea from squat*	*Butterbean from above*	*Butterbean from squat*	*Kidney bean from above*	*Kidney bean from squat*
1st						
2nd						
3rd						

1. Describe and draw the craters formed by the following throws. Use the back of this sheet if you need more space.

   a. pea from above

   b. pea from an angle

   c. butterbean from above

    d. butterbean from an angle

    e. kidney bean from above

    f. kidney bean from an angle

2. Which craters were formed by peas/beans with the lowest angle of impact, those thrown from above or those thrown from an angle?

3. Were all of the craters the same size and shape? Explain your answer.

4. Why was it important for one student in a lab group to be the one who throws?

5. After all the beans and peas were removed, could you tell which crater was the oldest (formed first) and which was the youngest (formed last)? How could you tell?

6. The craters on the moon are all round. Do you think they were formed by the impact of a meteor striking the moon's surface? Explain your answer.

7. Do the craters created in flour have rays? If so, how were these formed?

Lesson 13: Space Travel

13–1 THE SPACE SHUTTLE
Content on Space Travel

Early Flight

The United States manned space flight program has evolved through a series of increasingly complex steps. In May of 1961, Astronaut Alan B. Shepard, Jr. was launched from Cape Canaveral in the first U.S. manned space flight. His suborbital mission lasted 15 minutes as he traveled 116 miles high into space. In February of 1962, John H. Glenn, Jr. became the first American to orbit earth, circling it three times in *Friendship 7*. Glenn's craft was about 95 feet tall and used RP-1 (refined kerosene) and liquid oxygen for fuel. The *Gemini* spacecraft that followed this experimental effort consisted of a two-part ship: a reentry module containing a life support cabin, and an adapter module. The adapter module is made of two separate sections so that the *Gemini* actually had three parts. Only the reentry module returned to earth, where it crash landed into an unoccupied location in the sea. During the *Gemini 11* mission, a record altitude of 853 miles was reached. The *Gemini* ships were 108 feet tall and used UDMH (unsymmetrical dimethylhydrazine) and nitrogen tetroxide for fuel.

Reusable Spacecraft

The space shuttle is the first reusable manned space craft developed in the United States. The shuttle can take off like a rocket, orbit earth like a spaceship, and land like an airplane. It was designed to deliver heavy payloads, such as satellites, or repair objects already orbiting earth. Each space shuttle has three components: two solid rocket boosters, an external tank, and a winged orbiter. In the solid rockets, the propellant is a mixture of aluminum powder, aluminum perchorate powder, and iron oxide catalyst held together by a polymer binder. This fuel produces a thrust of 3.1 million pounds for the first few seconds and is burned out completely in 2 minutes. Liquid oxygen (140,000 gallons) and liquid nitrogen (380,000 gallons) are stored in the fuel tanks. These tanks feed into the main engines during the 8-minute ascent into orbit; then they are jettisoned. The fuel tanks are the only disposable part of the space shuttle.

The orbiter has a size and shape similar to a DC-9 jetliner. An orbiter is designed to last for about 100 flights. The first orbiter, *Enterprise,* was designed for atmospheric flight tests. Since that time, five other orbiters have been built: *Columbia, Challenger, Discovery, Atlantis,* and *Endeavour.* (The *Challenger* and

155

crew were lost in an accident in 1986.) Each orbiter is covered with a special silicon-based insulation in the form of 100-square-inch tiles. These light-weight tiles can survive temperatures of up to 1260 degrees Celsius, and they protect the orbiter during reentry into the earth's atmosphere.

The space shuttle can carry a two- to eight-person crew. Space flight no longer requires intensively trained, physically perfect astronauts. Scientists and technicians now fly along with the pilot and crew. The low-acceleration launch and low-deceleration reentry produce forces that normal, healthy people can tolerate (1.5 to 3 g). Astronauts live in a two-floor, pressurized cabin in the nose section of the shuttle. The top floor consists of the flight deck and a work area. The bottom floor houses living quarters, galley, and bathrooms. The cabin is maintained with microgravity, a condition that seems weightless because the astronauts are in free-fall all the time.

Problems in Space Travel

Microgravity produces special problems for travelers. Food and beverage particles cannot be allowed to escape and float around the craft. Food trays have clasps that hold dishes in place. Food can be warmed in the convection oven, but no refrigerator is carried to space because of its weight. Most food is preserved by dehydration. Astronauts choose from 70 different food items and 20 beverages to maintain a 3000-calorie/day diet.

Because the shuttle cabin is small, people are close together and microbes find plenty of opportunity to grow. To prevent bacterial infection, dirty clothes are sealed in airtight plastic bags. Sponge baths are the only form of bathing permitted, to minimize water droplets floating in the shuttle. Men shave with shaving cream and water so that loose whiskers cannot be set floating. Toilets are similar to gravity toilets but depend on air to force wastes into plastic bags.

Astronauts sleep in "sleeping cocoons" in a bunk area. Since there is no gravity on the ship, there is no up or down, and the crew can sleep in any position. Crew members exercise to maintain muscle strength. One of the special problems of weightlessness is mineral loss from bones due to lack of force exerted on the bones. Some astronauts suffer from space adaptation syndrome, a form of motion sickness.

The Travelers

Shuttle crew members include the commander and pilot, who are responsible for the safety of the crew and the success of the mission. In addition, the coordinator plans the crew activities, keeps track of consumable usage, and performs experiments. Payload specialists are often technicians or scientists who have specialized duties on board.

A typical shuttle flight lasts from 2 to 10 days, but in the future people will be able to stay in space for weeks. After delivering its payload and performing experiments, the orbiter reenters the atmosphere and lands. Landing speed is about 216 miles per hour. The orbiter is immediately "safed" by a ground crew by draining dangerous propellants from the fuel tanks. This crew also prepares the shuttle for storage until the next flight.

LANDING SPACECRAFT—VOCABULARY ACTIVITY ON *THE SPACE SHUTTLE*

Directions

Draw a circle around the shuttle that *cannot* land on the air strip.

1

Byrd

Glenn

Shepard

Astronauts

2

Friendship

Gemini

Sputnik

Manned U.S. Spacecraft

3

External tank

Orbiters

Adapter module

Parts of Space Shuttle

4

Challenger

Friendship

Atlantis

Orbiters

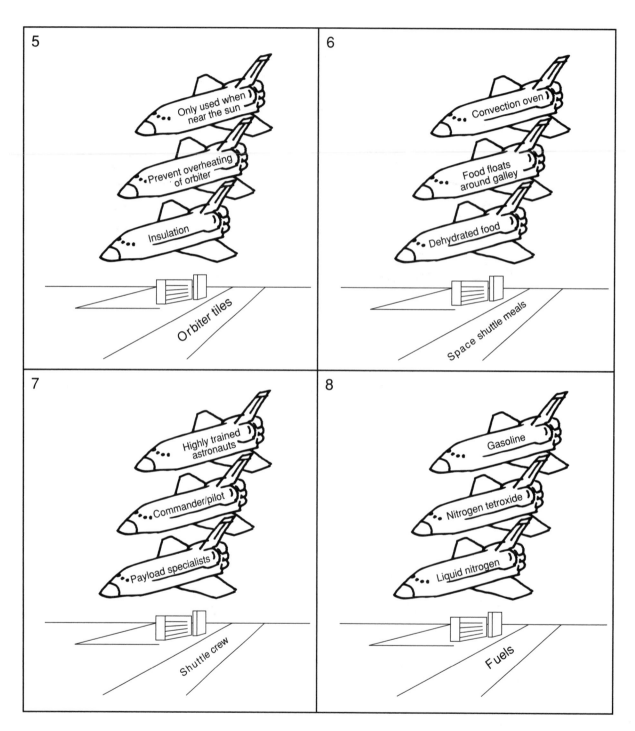

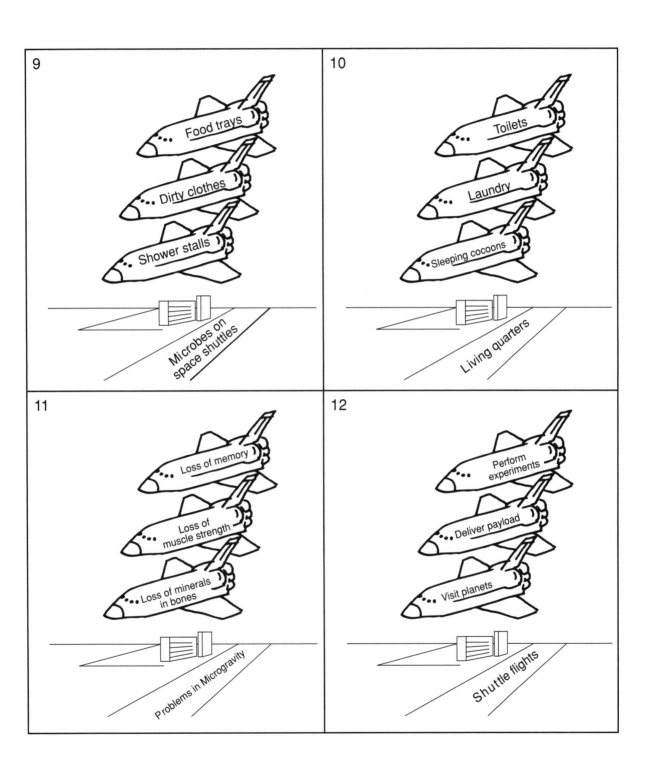

13–2 DESIGN A SPACECRAFT
Lab on Designing an Original Space Vehicle

Objectives

Students will design an original spacecraft that can

a. Travel in space

b. Land on the moon

c. Depart from the moon

d. Land on Mars

e. Depart from Mars

f. Return to earth and land

Students will describe the needs of the crew that is, things or conditions, that are necessary for the crew during space travel, and will design their living quarters.

Teacher Notes

Students may want to have a competition for the best spacecraft. Students, teachers, or parents might be asked to act as judges.

Students can extend this activity by doing research in the library on spacecraft, the moon, and Mars. If you want to study all of the planets with this unit, ask students to design spacecraft that can visit Mercury, Venus, Jupiter, Saturn, Uranus, Neptune, and Pluto.

Design a Spacecraft

Lab on Designing an Original Space Vehicle

Introduction

Space travel in the future will take humans to places they only dream about today. As the space program advances, more and more people will be able to enjoy the experience of space flight. Ships will become more comfortable and faster.

The fuels of the future can only be guessed today. Solar energy seems like a viable option for flights near the sun. A solar wind (made of charged particles) blows from the sun and may be another source of spaceship energy. Nuclear energy and solid rocket fuel are two methods that we now use, and they may still be viable fuel choices in the futures.

The moon is our most likely place to visit. Traveling to the moon will require special considerations for the crew and ship. Visits to Mars may even be an option one day. See Table 1 for a description of characteristics of the moon and Mars.

TABLE 1. CHARACTERISTICS OF MOON AND MARS

Characteristic	Moon	Mars
Distance from earth	239,000 miles	48,600,000 miles
Diameter	1/4 earth's diameter	1/2 earth's diameter
Gravity	1/6 earth's gravity	1/3 earth's gravity
Atmosphere	None	Thin carbon dioxide 1% air pressure of earth
Day length	28 earth days	24 hours, 37 minutes
Trip time	3 days	1.88 earth years
Communication time	2.6-sec. round trip	10- to 41-minute round trip

In this lab activity, you will design a spacecraft that will allow a crew of your choice to travel to the moon and then on to Mars. Consider what type of fuel will be needed, the shape and size of the spacecraft, special design features that protect it from heat and cold, supplies the crew will need, and environmental hazards or special problems that will be encountered along the way. Draw an illustration of the inside and outside of your craft. Make a model of this spacecraft using various art supplies.

Materials

Art supplies (paper, scissors, glue, modeling clay, aluminun foil, etc.)
Spacecraft Worksheet

Design a Spacecraft *(continued)*

SPACECRAFT WORKSHEET

Fuel used by your spacecraft	Reason/explanation
Shape and size of craft	Reason/explanation
Special environmental protective devices	
Crew size	
Crew requirements	
Supplies required by crew	
Other necessary supplies	

Illustrations

Sketch of interior	Sketch of exterior

SECTION 4

Chemistry

LESSON 14: FATS

14–1 FAT FOODS
Content on the Structure and Role of Fat

Concentrated Energy

Fats and oils, also called lipids, are an essential part of everyone's diet. About 95% of the fats in our foods and in our bodies are made of triglycerides, although some are phospholipids and sterols. Triglycerides are the form of lipid in which the body stores excess fat.

Lipids serve several important roles in the body. Fat is concentrated food energy that delivers twice as much energy as the same amount of carbohydrate. Fat surrounds and pads all the vital organs, protecting them from injury and temperature variations. Cell membranes contain fat. Some essential nutrients, such as linoleic acid and vitamins A, D, E, and K, are soluble in fat and are found in fatty foods. Fat is the component of food that gives it aroma and flavor.

Triglycerides

Chemically, the majority of lipids in animals are triglycerides, molecules formed of three fatty acids and a glycerol. Fatty acids are chains of carbohydrates, and glycerol is a three-carbon alcohol. The general formula for a triglyceride is

$$
\begin{array}{c}
\text{CH} - \text{O} - \underset{\underset{\text{O}}{\|}}{\text{C}} - \text{R} \\[2mm]
| \\[1mm]
\text{CH} - \text{O} - \underset{\underset{\text{O}}{\|}}{\text{C}} - \text{R} \\[2mm]
| \\[1mm]
\text{CH} - \text{O} - \underset{\underset{\text{O}}{\|}}{\text{C}} - \text{R}
\end{array}
$$

R in the formula stands for "radical group" and represents a variety of hydrocarbon variations in the fatty acid. Fatty acids differ primarily in two ways: chain length and degree of saturation.

Chain length affects solubility in water. Shorter fatty acid chains are more soluble than longer ones. *Saturation* refers to the chemical structure of the fatty acid and reflects the number of hydrogens in the chain. If every available bond for carbon is holding a hydrogen atom, the chain is said to be saturated, or filled with hydrogen atoms. Many animal fats are saturated. If there is a hydrogen missing, then the fatty acid is unsaturated, and if two or more hydrogens are missing, it is polyunsaturated. Most polyunsaturated lipids are found in plants, where they form the protective coating on leaves and the skin of seeds.

A saturated fatty acid chain.

```
     H   H   H   H   H   H
     |   |   |   |   |   |
     C – C – C – C – C – C – H
     |   |   |   |   |   |
     H   H   H   H   H   H
```

An unsaturated fatty acid chain.

```
     H   H   H   H   H   H
     |   |   |   |   |   |
     C – C = C – C – C – C – H
     |           |   |   |
     H           H   H   H
```

The presence of unsaturated fatty acids in lipids affects the temperature at which the fats melt. A high degree of unsaturation causes a fat to be liquid at room temperature. The more saturated a fat, the firmer its texture. Therefore, animal fats tend to be solid at room temperature and plant fats or oils tend to be liquid. Hydrogenation (adding hydrogens) of liquid fats causes them to become firmer. Some margarine manufacturers hydrogenate their liquid product to produce a firmer, more spreadable food.

For years scientists have advised consumers to select vegetable oils and to avoid eating saturated fat like butter, tropical oil, and the fats in meats because such foods are most likely to lead to high blood cholesterol and heart disease. However, recent research indicates that the process of hydrogenating peanut oils creates an artificial class of fats called trans fatty acids. Trans fatty acids can raise blood cholesterol levels, even though the vegetable oil itself contains no cholesterol. Therefore, hydrogenated vegetable oils may be as unhealthy as saturated fats.

Phospholipids

Phospholipids, another form of fats are important compounds that play a key role in cell membrane structure. Phospholipids are amphipathic; that is, one end is attracted to water molecules and the other end is attracted to organic molecules like lipids. The lipophilic (lipid-loving) end of a phospholipid is the long fatty acid chain. The hydrophilic, (water-loving) end is the phosphate end which has a positive and a negative charge. Because of this amphipathetic nature, phospholipids tend to form bilayers in which the fatty acids are forced together and the hydrophilic groups are exposed (see Figure A). The basic structure of a cell membrane is the phospholipid bilayer.

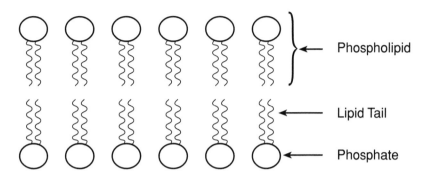

FIGURE A. Phospholipid bilayer.

Sterols

One of the sterols is cholesterol, which has many functions in the body. It is part of bile acids and is necessary in the digestion of fats. Cholesterol is involved in the formation of sex hormones, and it is important in the structure of brain and nerve tissue. Even though many tissues require cholesterol, it causes problems when it forms deposits in arteries, constricting the flow of blood.

Because Americans consume a large amount of fat in their diets, they often suffer from obesity and atherosclerosis (a condition in which blood vessels become clogged with deposits of fatty substances such as cholesterol). To protect themselves from the killer disease atherosclerosis, many people reduce the amount of cholesterol they take into their bodies. The amount of cholesterol circulating in the blood can be used to forecast heart and artery disease. Blood cholesterol is made primarily from saturated fats. To lower your blood cholesterol, you might attempt the following three strategies: reduce total fat intake, increase the proportion of polyunsaturated fat relative to saturated fat, and reduce cholesterol intake.

FAT WORDS—VOCABULARY CROSSWORD PUZZLE ON
FAT FOODS

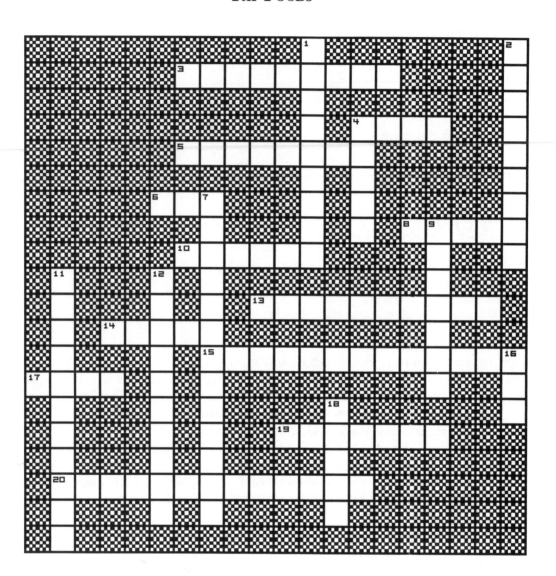

© 1994 by The Center for Applied Research in Education

Across

3. Linoleic acid and vitamins are essential ___.

4. Fat ___ organs and protects them for injury.

5. ___ is one component of triglycerides.

6. ___ and oil are also called lipids.

8. Cholesterol is a component of ___ tissue.

10. ___ are a form of concentrated energy and give food its flavor and aroma.

13. The length of a fatty acid chain affects its ___ in water.

14. ___ acids are chains of carbohydrates.

15. ___ are a type of food that supply half as much energy as fat.

17. ___ acids are important in digestion of fats.

19. All cell membranes are made of a ___ of phospholipids.

20. ___ of liquid fats causes them to become firm.

Down

1. Lipids are an important structural part of cell ___.

2. Hydrogenation means adding ___ to a chain of carbon atoms.

4. ___ lipids are usually oils.

7. Most of the fat in our bodies is in the form of ___.

9. A ___ group represents several hydrocarbon variations.

11. ___ molecules are attracted to water on one end and to lipids on the other end.

12. ___ reflects the number of hydrogens on a fatty acid chain.

16. Cholesterol is important in the formation of ___ hormones.

18. Cholesterol in the ___ can contribute to arteriosclerosis.

Word List: Fats

AMPHIPATHIC	FATTY	PADS
BILE	GLYCEROL	PLANT
BILAYER	HYDROGENATION	RADICAL
BLOOD	HYDROGENS	SATURATION
BRAIN	LIPIDS	SEX
CARBOHYDRATES	MEMBRANES	SOLUBILITY
FAT	NUTRIENTS	TRIGLYCERIDES

14–2 FAT IN FOOD
Activity that Compares the Fat Content of Meats

Objectives

Students will isolate fat in food, determine the percentage of fat in food, and compare the fat content of foods.

Teacher Notes

In this lab, students compare the fat content of lean ground beef (round or chuck) to regular, more fatty ground beef. Chicken and fish could be substituted for either of the beef samples or added for additional comparison.

Meat samples are boiled to separate the fat from the protein. Fat floats on top of the water and can be removed easily.

Samples of 100 grams are used to make calculations of fat percentage more convenient. However, any size sample can be used. The following formula helps calculate percent fat:

$$\frac{\text{Grams of fat}}{\text{Grams of sample}} \times 100 = \text{percent fat}$$

FAT IN FOOD
Activity that Compares the Fat Content of Meats

Introduction

In 1900, people were eating about 125 grams of fat per day; in 1972, fat intake was up to about 160 grams per day. By 1975, fat intake was down to 147 grams per day. Nutritionists hope that this reduction in dietary fat is due to efforts by the health industry to demonstrate the relationship between fat intake and cardiovascular disease and cancer.

U.S. citizens probably take in more fat than citizens of any other country, often eating 40 to 50% of their calories as fat. Nine-tenths of this fat comes from three groups of food: fats and oils; meat, poultry, and fish; and dairy products. All meats contain fat, but some contain more than others. Leaner cuts of meat contain about 3 grams of fat per ounce, medium cuts of meat contain about 5.5 grams of fat per ounce, and high-fat meats contain about 8 grams per ounce. One gram of fat contains 45 calories.

Meats that are considered lean are chicken or turkey without skin, leg of lamb, and fish. Meats in the medium fat groups include ground round steak, liver, heart, and kidney. High-fat meats are ground hamburger, steak, cold cuts, and hot dogs.

Consumers often think of meat as a source of protein, but analysis of meat's content shows that it often contains more fat than protein. For example, a quarter pound of hamburger contains 28 grams of protein and 23 grams of fat. Protein provides 4 calories per gram and fat provides 9 calories per gram, making the protein contribution of a hamburger 112 calories and the fat contribution 207 calories.

Prelab Questions

1. Compare the amount of fat Americans have included in their diets in the years since 1900.

2. Why do you think Americans are eating less fat now than they did 20 years ago?

3. Why do you think Americans eat more fat than citizens of other countries?

4. What are some lean meats? What are some fat meats?

5. How many protein calories and fat calories do you get from a quarter pound of hamburger?

Materials

100 grams lean ground chuck
100 grams ground beef
Two 600-ml beakers
100-ml graduated cylinder
Dropper
Water
Bunsen burner with ring stand or hot plate
Balances

FAT FOOD *(continued)*

Procedure

1. Label your beakers 1 and 2.

2. Weigh 100 grams of lean beef and put it in beaker 1.

3. Weigh 100 grams of ground beef and put it in beaker 2.

4. Cook both samples in 400 ml of water for 10 minutes.

5. Carefully pour the fat layer into 100-ml graduated cylinders. Use a dropper to remove all traces of fat.

6. Measure and record the volume of fat in the graduated cylinders and record in the data table.

7. One milliliter of fat has a mass of about 1 gram. Therefore, the volume of fat in your graduated cylinder is the approximate percentage of fat in your 100-gram sample. Record your percentage of fat in the data table.

Data and Analysis

1. Record results in the data table.

DATA TABLE

Volumes and percentages of fat in meat samples

Sample number	Type meat	Vol. of fat	% of fat

2. Which type of meat contains the most fat per gram?

3. What are some health problems associated with high fat intake?

4. What is the purpose of cooking the meat sample?

5. If you used 100 grams of skinless chicken in this experiment, how do you think it would compare to the fat in beef?

LESSON 15: SURFACE TENSION OF WATER

15–1 WALKING ON THE WATER
Content on the Surface Tension of Water

When Water Has a Thick Skin

How do some bugs stride across the top of a pond without sinking or even getting their feet wet? A concept called surface tension gives us the answer to that question. The word *tension* means "tightening force." Surface tension is the pulling together of the surface of a liquid by the attraction from the molecules inside the liquid. This property is displayed by a liquid when its surface acts like a stretched elastic membrane or a skin.

This skin forms on the surface of a liquid such as water due to the force of the molecules in the liquid. Molecules in the middle of the liquid are attracted and pulled on equally by surrounding molecules. Molecules found on the surface of the liquid are pulled in a sideward and downward direction by the other molecules. The upward pull on the surface molecules is produced by air molecules rather than other liquid molecules. The air molecules have a much weaker attraction than the liquid molecules; therefore, the pull is much greater inward than upward. These inward intermolecular forces are like chemical bonds tugging at the surface molecules. This tugging action causes the surface molecules to be pulled downward and squeezed together, creating the tight skin that allows the pond critters to walk on the water.

Cohesion and Adhesion

Surface tension depends mainly on the forces of attraction between the particles within the given liquid but also on the gas, solid, and liquid that contact it. The attraction of liquid molecules to themselves that keeps the liquid together is called cohesion. The attraction of the liquid molecules to the molecules of other surfaces is called adhesion. The adhesion of water molecules to glass molecules is greater than the cohesion of water molecules to each other. This causes the water to be attracted to the glass, and this is seen as water rising up the sides of the glass to form a concave surface. These molecules are being pulled up the sides of the glass by attraction of the molecules of the glass.

When cohesion of a liquid is greater than the adhesion of the neighboring substance, the liquid will adopt a shape as near spherical as gravity will allow. This is seen in raindrops. Water droplets are nearly spherical because the

173

cohesion of the water molecules is greater than the adhesion of the water molecules to the air molecules. The downward pull of gravity prevents the raindrops from being perfect spheres.

Breaking Through the Skin

The property of surface tension is also important in a simple activity such as washing dirt off your hands. If you wash your hands with water, the water will tend to roll off in drops. Your skin produces oily molecules that do not break the water's surface tension. These oily (greaselike) molecules are joined together in long chains that repel the water, and your hands remain dirty. But there are ways to reduce the surface tension of water to get to the dirt on your hands. The application of soap during the washing process is the easiest way to accomplish this feat.

Soap and other detergents weaken the surface tension of water. This weakening occurs because the molecules of the soap or detergent move between the molecules of water and weaken the cohesion of the water molecules from each other. Substances that reduce surface tension are called surfactants (surface-active agents). Surfactants increase the spreading and wetting properties of a liquid. A surfactant has molecules shaped like a tadpole. The surfactant molecule has a long, fatty tail which is hydrophobic (water insoluble) and a small electrically charged head which is hydrophilic (water soluble). The charge of a surfactant can be either negative (anion) or positive (cation). Most of the domestic detergents today are anionic and are very efficient in cleaning glass containers. Since the surface of glass normally carries a slightly negative charge, anionic detergents can clean the glass without binding to it. Cationic surfactants will be so strongly attracted to the glass that a thin layer adheres to the glass, with the long hydrophobic (fatty) chain outward, making the glass look greasy. On the other hand, cationic surfactants are more useful in washing plastic containers than anionic surfactants because the plastic has a slightly positive charge on the surface. This is the reverse of what occurs with glass.

In the cleaning process, the surfactant molecules tend to concentrate on the surface layer of the water due to the hydrophobic portion of the molecule moving away from the interior of the water. This allows the water to wet the normally nonwettable surface. Some of the cleaning power of the surfactant results from the enhanced ability of water to wet the normally hydrophobic surface and lift off the dirt.

In summary, the strong surface tension of water provides a skin for insects to stroll across. If you were to drop some soap or detergent near that insect, the insect would sink into the pond due to the reduction of surface tension and destruction of the water skin. If it were not for the ability of cleaning materials to reduce the surface tension of water, removal of dirt and grease would be a much more complicated task.

WATER WORD FIND—VOCABULARY ACTIVITY ON
WALKING ON THE WATER

Directions

Fill in the blanks with the correct answer. Each of the answers appears in the Word Find Puzzle that follows. Circle these words in the puzzle to make sure you chose the correct terms.

1. The attraction of water molecules to other water molecules holds the liquid together. This attraction is called _____.

2. _____ is a cleaning substance that weakens the surface tension of water.

3. A molecule with a positive charge is also called a(n) _____.

4. Cationic detergents do a better job cleaning _____ containers than anionic detergents.

5. Water-soluble substances are called _____ substances.

6. Water-insoluble substances are called _____ substances.

7. _____ is the force that keeps raindrops from being perfectly spherical.

8. _____ is the attraction of molecules in a liquid to the molecules of another substance such as a container.

9. Cationic detergents leave a thin, greasy film on _____ containers.

10. Another name for a surface cleaning agent is a _____.

11. A molecule with a negative charge is called a(n) _____.

12. The surface of water often resembles a tight _____ because of the inward pulling force exerted on the surface molecules.

13. Because of adhesion, water poured in a container will have a _____ shape to its surface.

14. Due to cohesion of water molecules, water will tend to assume a nearly _____ shape unless acted on by gravity.

15. The force exerted on surface water by _____ molecules is always less than the force exerted by the internal water molecules.

16. Detergents and soaps will tend to _____ the surface tension of a liquid.

17. Substances that tend to avoid water and will not dissolve in water are called _____ substances.

VOCABULARY ACTIVITY ON WALKING ON THE WATER *(continued)*

Directions

Locate the answers to statements 1 through 17. Find these words vertically, horizontally, diagonally, backward, or forward. Circle each word as you locate it in the puzzle.

```
K  P  R  C  R  Y  T  I  V  A  R  G  V  R  I  G  H  K
M  C  S  O  B  L  D  H  Q  M  D  R  R  T  L  L  N  T
O  O  T  H  F  G  P  Q  Y  F  K  C  G  B  J  A  O  R
J  N  U  E  H  K  P  S  R  D  V  B  E  F  E  S  I  S
F  C  B  S  A  E  O  L  S  L  R  N  L  G  L  S  S  N
T  A  L  I  R  A  C  A  O  U  B  O  D  T  B  K  E  O
Z  V  U  O  P  I  A  C  K  V  M  I  P  F  U  T  H  I
M  E  K  N  T  T  N  I  Z  N  T  N  E  H  L  V  D  T
J  V  D  S  B  I  B  R  D  D  U  A  F  E  O  L  A  A
K  D  A  C  K  M  F  E  N  E  K  A  E  W  S  B  M  C
R  L  B  S  L  Q  J  H  D  K  R  I  A  M  N  J  I  K
P  R  H  Y  D  R  O  P  H  I  L  I  C  I  I  J  S  C
S  M  D  B  R  L  V  S  T  N  A  T  C  A  F  R  U  S
```

15–2 SURFACE TENSION
Lab on the Effect of Detergents on the Surface Tension of Water

Objectives

Students will demonstrate the property of surface tension in pure water and in water to which detergent has been added.

Teacher Notes

In Part 1, you can substitute other materials for gem clips. Thumbtacks, small nails, and pennies are a few possible substitutions. You will want to emphasize that the cup should be filled up to the rim with water before beginning this activity. Be sure to have plenty of paper towels available for overflows.

In Part 2, you can use various materials to construct the water bug. Pipe cleaners for legs, a straw for the body, and candle wax on the feet work well. Let the students be inventive in designing their water bugs instead of dictating the specific materials they should use. When each student group has completed the design for their bug, you might consider having them present their bug to the class. A special competition could be held among each of the bugs in a large tub of water to see whose bug stays on top of the water the longest without sinking. A special prize or grade could be given to the winning group.

SURFACE TENSION

Lab on the Effect of Detergents on the Surface Tension of Water

Introduction

Like all forms of matter, water consists of molecules. Water molecules are attracted to one another by a force called cohesion. The molecules in the middle of a container of water have molecular forces exerted on them by water molecules on all sides. Molecules on the surface of the container have molecular forces exerted on them by water molecules underneath and air molecules above them. The force of attraction produced by air molecules is much weaker than the force exerted by water molecules. The water molecules beneath the surface exert an inward-pulling force on the surface of the water. This inward pull, due to the cohesion of the water molecules, forms a tightness on the surface of the water. This skinlike texture or surface tension allows water to dome above the top of a glass when water is added slowly.

Certain conditions can lower the surface tension of water and break the skin. An increase in temperature will lower surface tension, because the density of the vapor above a liquid increases as the liquid gets hotter. These vapor molecules have a stronger attraction for the surface molecules in the liquid, and the tightness of the surface skin of the water is decreased.

Addition of substances such as soap and detergent (known as surfactants) can reduce the surface tension by increasing the spreading and wetting properties of water. These surfactant molecules look like a tadpole. The tail of a surfactant molecule is composed of a fatty material that prevents it from dissolving in water but allows it to stick to greases, oils, and fats. This property of being insoluble in water makes it hydrophobic (meaning "fear of water"). The head of the surfactant molecule is hydrophilic ("water loving") because it is water soluble. The surfactant molecules possess the ability to break the surface tension of water and allow water to contact the dirt molecules on materials being cleaned. Dirt contains grease and oil. Detergents enable water to penetrate the air spaces in washing to make dirt removal easier. This surface-skin-breaking ability of surfactants forms the basis for the cleaning industry.

Surface tension also allows some insects, commonly called water striders, to walk on the surface of ponds and rivers. Hypothetically, any object whose density is greater than water will sink when placed in a body of water. What property allows these insects to stride across the water even though their density is significantly greater than that of water? Once again, surface tension accounts for this feat.

Small hairs are located on each of the water strider's feet. These hairs are equipped with a special material that prevents water from wetting them. This inability of water to wet these hairs allows the water strider to rest on the surface of the water. What would happen to the water strider if it tried to walk on the surface of a pond that laundry detergent had polluted? Would it sink or could it still stride freely? In Part 2 of this lab, you will examine that possibility.

Prelab Questions

1. Define surface tension.

2. Name two factors that lower surface tension. Explain the reason behind each.

3. Explain why water striders can stay on top of the water.

4. Define cohesion.

5. What is a surfactant? Discuss the effect it has on water and cleaning.

Materials for Part 1

Four small clear plastic cups
Water
Hand mitts for the hot glassware
Two boxes of gem clips per group
Dishwashing liquid detergent (a few drops per group)
Paper towels
Hot plate and a large beaker
Black pen for labeling

Part 1—Procedure

1. Label the four cups A, B, C, and D.

2. Place a beaker of water on the hot plate and heat it on High until the water has begun to reach the boiling stage.

3. While you are waiting for the water to boil, fill Cup A to the brim with tap water from the faucet. Do the same for Cup B. Be sure the water level on each of these cups is exactly to the rim of the cup without spilling over the side.

4. Drop one gem clip at a time carefully into Cup A until you see the water begin to seep over the side of the cup. Count the number of gem clips it takes to cause this to occur. Record this number in Chart 1, and describe the shape of the dome of water building on top of the cup.

5. Now add five drops of dishwashing detergent to Cup B and allow about a minute for it to disperse in the water. Repeat the process you used with Cup A. Count the number of gem clips required to cause the water to seep over the side of the cup. Record this in Chart 1, and describe the dome of water building on top of the cup.

6. Fill Cups C and D to the top with the water you have been heating on the hot plate. Be very careful not to burn yourself with the hot water or the hot container. Make sure you get the water level to the rim as you did with Cups A and B.

7. Add five drops of dishwashing detergent to Cup D and allow about a minute for it to disperse in the water.

8. Add gem clips to Cup C until water overflows. Describe the dome. Record this in Chart 1. Repeat this process for Cup D and record your results in the chart. (See Figure A for the proper set-up of the four cups.)

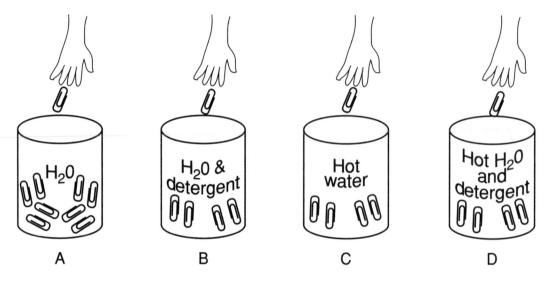

FIGURE A

CHART 1

Cup	# gem clips added	description of dome appearance
A		
B		
C		
D		

Postlab Questions

1. Which container had the least surface tension? Explain why.

2. Which container had the greatest surface tension? Explain why.

3. What effect does heat have on surface tension?

4. What effect do detergents have on surface tension?

5. Why was a dome able to form on top of the containers of water?

SURFACE TENSION *(continued)*

Part 2—Making a Water Strider

Materials for Part 2

The list of materials is left up to the teacher, but the following are some suggestions.

Drinking straws	Pipe cleaners
Glue	Thin wire
Hot glue	Popsicle sticks
Candle wax	Matches
Garbage bag ties	Lard or other types of grease
Toothpicks	Cardboard
A bowl of water	Five drops of liquid detergent

Procedure for Part 2

1. Form groups of two.

2. Look at Figure B. This represents a water strider. Your group will design your own water strider. It must have six legs, a central body, and two antennae.

3. You may use any of the materials to perform this task. But your finished product must be able to stand on top of the water. This may require some trial-and-error construction on your part.

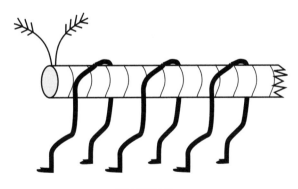

FIGURE B

4. Remember, the feet of this insect are coated with a waxy substance that prevents it from getting wet. You will want to use some candle wax or other fatty material on the feet of your insect to accomplish this.

5. Test your water strider in the bowl of water to check your design.

6. Once you have completed this creature and it is able float, call the teacher over to demonstrate its ability to stand on water. The teacher will place his or her initials beside your sketch of the insect to verify that you achieved this feat.

7. Remove your strider from the bowl. Add five drops of detergent to the bowl and wait 1 minute. Place the strider back in the bowl of water. Observe what happens.

8. Answer the postlab questions, and then be prepared to show your creation to your classmates when each group is finished.

Postlab Questions

1. In the box provided, draw a sketch of your water strider. On the back of this sheet, list the materials you used to design this creature and your reasons for this design.

2. Why did you place a fatty substance on the feet of the insect?

3. What would have happened if you had not added the fatty substance to the feet of the water strider?

4. What happened when the strider was placed in water with detergent?

5. Explain why this occurred.

6. Now answer the question "What effect would adding detergent to a pond have on the water striders in the pond?"

LESSON 16: HAIR CHEMISTRY

16–1 HAIR CARE CHEMISTRY
Content on the Chemical Nature of Hair and Hair Products

Hairy Bodies

As mammals, the bodies of humans are covered with hair. Hair serves various functions. The long hair that grows on top of our head helps us conserve body heat. The hair that forms our eyebrows keeps sweat out of our eyes, and eyelash hairs keep particles out of our eyes. Pubic and armpit hairs help trap body odors, a function that was important in early humans' society. Human hair is also an important expression of personality. In some cultures, the length and condition of hair indicate social status.

Hair's Structure

Hair is composed of the hard form of keratin, a protein. This is the same protein that, in the soft form, creates the calluses on our hands and feet. Like all proteins, keratin is composed of the elements hydrogen, oxygen, carbon, nitrogen, phosphorous, and sulfur. Keratin has more sulfur than any other protein. The presence of sulfur in a protein allows it to form cross links, a characteristic that gives a protein strength. Because keratin can form extensive cross links, hair is chemically and biologically resistant to decay and decomposition. Hair is also indigestible.

Layers of Hair

Hair has three parts: the cuticle, the cortex, and the medulla.

The Cuticle. The protective covering on the outside of a hair shaft is the cuticle. It is arranged in overlapping scales along the length of the hair (see Figure A). One function of the cuticle is to protect the inner cortex. At the ends of hair, there is no cuticle and the cortex is exposed to air. This causes the cortex to dry and the ends of the hair to split. Cuticle scales give hair strength and flexibility. One hair can support 5 to 7 ounces of weight.

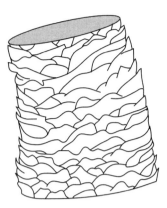

FIGURE A. The cuticle is composed of overlapping scales.

Cuticle scales vary with different types of hair. Some hair is very porous because it has loose, open scales; other hair has close, tight scales. Hair with porous scales is easier to treat because chemicals can easily reach the cortex. On the other hand, hair with tight scales is somewhat resistant to treatment. Cuticle scales also function as traps that hold oil produced by cells on the scalp. This oil gives hair its natural luster. Unfortunately, the cuticle scales also trap dust or dirt.

The Cortex. Beneath the cuticle scales is the cortex, the layer of hair that composes 75 to 90% of each strand. This layer is composed of millions of protein fibers arranged in a parallel fashion. Occasional twists in the fibers add to hair's strength. The color of hair is due to the presence of pigment granules in the cortex. These granules are originally in cells that produce melanin, our body's color molecule. As the hair lengthens and melanocytes die, granules of melanin are left in the cortex.

The Medulla. The innermost layer of hair is the medulla. It is only two to four cells thick and is often filled with soft keratin. The role of the medulla is not clear.

Changing the Bonds Within Hair

Chemical services by cosmetologists primarily alter the cortex of the hair. Permanent waves, permanent colors, and hair straightening are achieved with chemicals that penetrate the cuticle layer. There are two types of bonds that connect the protein fibers in the cortex: hydrogen bonds and sulfur bonds. Hydrogen bonds are weak bonds formed by the attraction of negative charges (anions) and positive charges (cations). Even though these bonds are weak, there are thousands of them within the cortex. Sulfur bonds are stronger than hydrogen bonds and are formed between two different parts of a protein. Hydrogen bonds and sulfur bonds give hair its natural shape: straight, wavy, curly, or kinky.

Basic Chemicals Penetrate Hair

The cuticle of hair can be penetrated and bonds in the cortex can be broken by chemicals that are very basic (alkaline). The pH scale is used to represent the acidity or alkalinity of a substance. This scale is from 1 to 14, and 7 is the neutral point. Substances with a pH below 7 are acidic, and those with a pH above 7 are basic (see Table 1).

TABLE 1
pH Scale

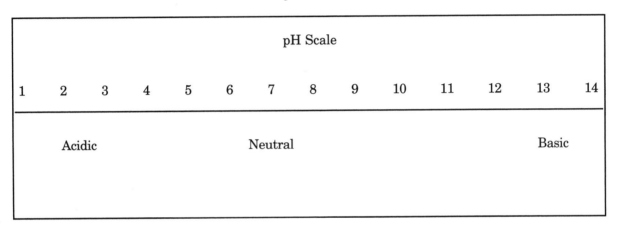

Many foods are acidic: Coffee has a pH near 6, cola has a pH near 5, and vinegar has a pH of about 4. Substances with a pH in the 1 to 3 range are considered to be strong acids; those with a pH in the 4 to 7 range are mild acids. Strong bases are those in the 10 to 14 range, and mild bases are in the 7 to 10 range. Some cleaners and antacids are mild bases. Hair is damaged at a pH below 3 or above 10. Table 2 summarizes how products with various pH's affect hair.

TABLE 2
Effects of Various pH Levels on Hair

pH	Hair Treatment	Effect on Hair
1–3	None made at this pH level	Could dissolve hair
3–6	Neutralizers, antidandruff shampoos, conditioners, lightening agents	Have an astringent (shrinking) effect, harden cuticle
7–10	Semipermanent colors, soap shampoos, permanent waving solutions	Remove oil, swell and soften hair
10–14	Depilatories	Hair swells up to 10 times original size; may dissolve

Basic Permanent Wave and Hair Relaxer Solutions

Ammonium thioglycolate, a permanent waving solution, is made of thioglycollic acid and ammonia and has a pH of 9. Sodium hydroxide, another base, is used as a hair relaxer. These basic hair solutions break sulfur bonds in the hair's cortex. Mild acids (like acetic acid, citric acid, and tartaric acid) and oxidizers (such as hydrogen peroxide and bleach) reform sulfur bonds in the cortex (see Figure B).

Hair before treatment	*Hair wrapped around cylinder; base breaks sulfur bonds by adding H*	*Acid causes sulfur bonds to reform and give hair new shape*

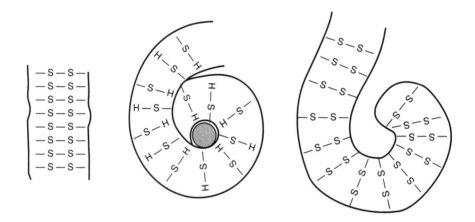

FIGURE B. Sulfur bonds are broken, hair is reshaped, and sulfur bonds are reformed to produce permanent curls.

Acidic Hair Colors

Temporary hair colors, or rinses, are mildly acidic and leave the hair in good condition. The effect of an acid on hair is to harden the cuticle, so no color enters the hair cortex. Only a small amount of color is absorbed on the hair surface. Since rinses are water soluble, the color left on the cuticle is easily rinsed out upon washing.

Mildly Basic Temporary Hair Colors

Semipermanent hair colors are mildly alkaline and cause the cuticle to swell somewhat, allowing a limited number of large, tinted hair color molecules to enter the cortex. Once inside the cortex, the alkaline solution is washed off the hair, and color molecules are trapped. However, since shampoos are mildly alkaline, some swelling of the cuticle takes place with every shampoo, and some color escapes.

Basic Permanent Hair Colors

Permanent hair colors use small, colorless molecules that can pass easily into the cortex. Once inside, a developer such as hydrogen peroxide combines the small, colorless molecules into giant, colored molecules. These large molecules are trapped in the cortex. They are stable and insoluble, giving hair a permanent color. Therefore, permanent hair colors cannot be shampooed out of the hair. Since permanent hair colors do not combine with the hydrogen and sulfur bonds in the cortex, these are still free for various other hair treatments.

Conditioners

Hair that has undergone several chemical treatments may have a damaged cuticle. Consequently, hair may look dry and be hard to manage. In this case, preconditioners can be applied to the hair that even out the cuticle and add oil. Many preconditioners and conditioners are made of protein fillers plus lanolin or cholesterol. Lanolin (a fat from sheep's wool) and cholesterol replace the lost, natural oil produced by the scalp. Protein fillers are made from cheap, waste protein such as scrap leather, animal hooves, and turkey feathers. These protein sources are chopped and cooked under pressure in a strong alkaline solution. They are then neutralized with an acid to a pH of 7. The resulting solution is almost pure protein. These protein molecules have positive and negative charges on them, just like the protein molecules that make up hair. The negatively charged filler proteins bond to the positively charged hair proteins, and the positively charged filler proteins bond to the negatively charged hair proteins so that the conditioner joins with the hair.

Hair Chemists

Today, the hair care industry is growing in importance in our economy. Millions of dollars are spent annually on hair and its care. The beauty and barber industries employ thousands of workers, who must be knowledgeable about the effects of chemicals on hair as well as the skin.

A Tri-ing and Hairy Experience—Vocabulary Activity on *Hair Care Chemistry*

Introduction

Dr. Colorfast, a professor at a prominent cosmetology school, likes to give his tests in an original manner. He takes a full-size mannequin and cuts a puzzle in the hair on the back of the mannequin's head. He then tapes the clues and word choices to the mannequin's back.

Directions

Read puzzle clues 1 through 15 and find a vocabulary word that matches one of the clues. The letter next to the correct vocabulary word answer corresponds to a letter in the triangle. Place the number of the clue above this letter on the triangle. Repeat this until all 15 blocks have been filled in with numbers.

You can check to see if you have the correct answers by adding the numbers on the HUMAN side of the triangle and entering that number in the box above this word. Do the same thing for the numbers on the SPLIT side of the triangle and for the numbers on the COVER side. If all of your choices are correct and you have added correctly, the three boxes will contain the same number.

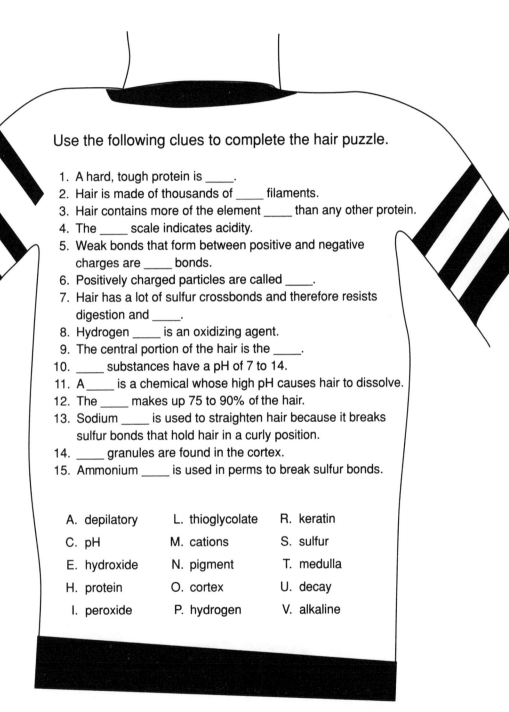

Use the following clues to complete the hair puzzle.

1. A hard, tough protein is ____.
2. Hair is made of thousands of ____ filaments.
3. Hair contains more of the element ____ than any other protein.
4. The ____ scale indicates acidity.
5. Weak bonds that form between positive and negative charges are ____ bonds.
6. Positively charged particles are called ____.
7. Hair has a lot of sulfur crossbonds and therefore resists digestion and ____.
8. Hydrogen ____ is an oxidizing agent.
9. The central portion of the hair is the ____.
10. ____ substances have a pH of 7 to 14.
11. A ____ is a chemical whose high pH causes hair to dissolve.
12. The ____ makes up 75 to 90% of the hair.
13. Sodium ____ is used to straighten hair because it breaks sulfur bonds that hold hair in a curly position.
14. ____ granules are found in the cortex.
15. Ammonium ____ is used in perms to break sulfur bonds.

A. depilatory	L. thioglycolate	R. keratin
C. pH	M. cations	S. sulfur
E. hydroxide	N. pigment	T. medulla
H. protein	O. cortex	U. decay
I. peroxide	P. hydrogen	V. alkaline

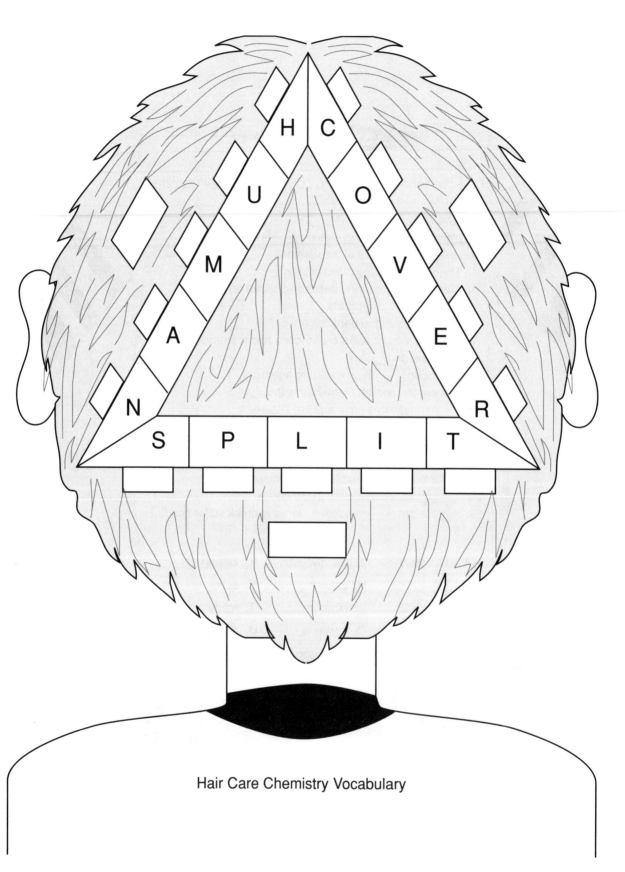

Hair Care Chemistry Vocabulary

16–2 HOMEMADE PERMS
Hair Chemistry Activity

Objectives

Students will demonstrate the effects of different solutions on hair. In addition, they will observe untreated and treated hair under the microscope.

Teacher Notes

A week or two before this lab, ask a local cosmetologist or the cosmetology department in your school to save you some long hair (2 to 5 inches). Hair samples should be bundled together with a rubber band for easy handling by students.

HOMEMADE HAIR PERMS
Hair Chemistry Activity

Introduction

Most of the permanent treatments for hair must affect the inner layer of the hair, the cortex. That means that the outside protective layer, the cuticle, must be opened so that hair chemicals can enter and alter the arrangement of the sulfur and hydrogen bonds.

All proteins are composed of chains of amino acids. There are 20 amino acids, some of which are positively charged, some negatively charged, and some neutral. The amino acid cysteine will form a strong sulfur bond with other cysteines in nearby proteins. These bonds are extremely durable and give hair its strength.

Hair is a fiber protein, which consists of thousands of polypeptide chains twisted around each other into long fibers. Sulfur bonds link the fibers together. Other fiber proteins are animal hair, natural silk, and the horns of some animals.

In this lab, you will expose hair to sodium hydroxide, a strong base, and acetic acid, a mild acid, to demonstrate the procedure for breaking and reforming sulfur bonds. This mimics the process of creating a permanent wave in hair.

Materials

Lab apron	Rubber bands
Goggles	Vinegar
Hair sample	
Pencil	
20 ml NaOH (pH 12 to 14)	
20 ml acetic acid	
Clock or timer	
Microscope, slide, and coverslip	
Hair dryer	

Procedure

1. Put on goggles and lab apron.

2. Take one strand of hair and make a wet-mount slide by placing the hair and a drop of water on the slide, and place a coverslip on top. Observe on low, medium, and high power. Sketch what you see in the "Conclusions" section.

3. Wrap the hair around a pencil and secure with rubber bands. Submerge in NaOH.

4. After 15 minutes, rinse the sample with water and carefully remove one strand of hair to examine under the microscope. Wash your hands after handling NaOH. Sketch, and return the sample to the NaOH.

HOMEMADE HAIR PERMS *(continued)*

5. Repeat step 4 after another 15 minutes.

6. Remove the hair sample from NaOH and rinse it in vinegar to neutralize. Dry with a hair dryer for 10 minutes. Unroll the hair.

Data and Conclusions

1. Sketch of hair

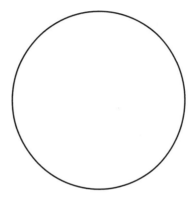

2. Hair after 15 minutes in NaOH

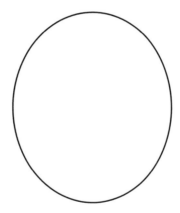

3. Hair after 30 minutes in NaOH

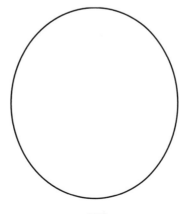

4. Hair after 10 minutes of drying

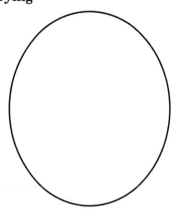

5. Why does NaOH break the sulfur bonds in hair?

6. What is the purpose of the acetic acid?

7. Did your samples become permanently curled?

LESSON 17: ANTHOCYANINS

17-1 NATURE'S INDICATORS
Content on Anthocyanins

Plant Pigments

What makes some cabbages purple or red? What makes the blue iris flower blue? Where do beets and radishes get their deep red hue? Certain flowers, fruits, and vegetables have a special pigment to give them this coloration. Anthocyanin is the water-soluble pigment that is responsible for the brilliant colorations seen in certain plants.

Anthocyanins are used by industry to color soft drinks and other acid solutions. These pigments can produce colors in soft drinks and acid solutions based on the pH of the solution.

Perhaps you might have forgotten what is meant by pH. It is the measure of the acidity or alkalinity of a substance. The pH scale ranges from 0 to 14, with pH 7 being neutral. Any pH reading less than seven on the scale is considered an acid, while readings greater than 7 represent bases (alkalines).

Acids and Bases

Let's briefly review the difference between acids and bases. Acids are a special group of chemical substances that taste sour and react with some metals to produce hydrogen gas. All acids contain hydrogen. The hydrogen is given off by the acid when it reacts with certain metals. It is the hydrogen in the acid that gives acids their unique properties. Some common acids include acetic acid or vinegar, lactic acid in sour milk, carbonic acid in carbonated beverages, and hydrochloric acid in the digestive juice in the stomach. Some chemical formulas are H_3BO_3 for boric acid in eyewash, H_2CO_3 for carbonic acid in soda water, and CH_3COOH for acetic acid.

Bases are chemical compounds that taste bitter, feel slippery, and contain hydroxide (OH^-) ions. When some metals are placed in water, they produce a base and hydrogen gas. All bases contain hydrogen and oxygen atoms. The hydrogen and oxygen are combined in a polyatomic ion called a hydroxyl ion (OH^-). Bases are compounds of metals in combination with a hydroxyl ion. Soap and milk of magnesia are two common bases. Magnesium hydroxide ($MgOH^-$) is milk of magnesia, while potassium hydroxide is a component of many soaps (KOH).

Anthocyanins and pH

What relationship do anthocyanins in plants have with acids and bases in the science laboratory? Anthocyanins serve as natural indicators of acidity and alkalinity. An indicator develops a characteristic color at a certain pH because of the way it reacts with other substances. The addition or removal of hydrogen ions from an anthocyanin molecule alters the molecular structure of this pigment. The alteration causes light to be absorbed at various wavelengths, giving rise to variable colors. Synthetic indicators used in the laboratory today are litmus paper, methyl red, and phenolphthalein. They do the same job as the natural indicators but at greater expense to the consumer.

If the acidity in the environment of an anthocyanin pigment increases, the pH is lowered due to an increase in hydrogen ions. The more hydrogen ions that are added to the anthocyanin molecules, the more acidic the solution being tested and the lower the pH number. Remember, 1 is the strongest acid and 6 is the weakest. When the number of hydrogen ions is decreased on the anthocyanin pigment, the pH rises. The higher the pH above 7, the more alkaline the solution. Remember, 8 is a weak base, while 14 is a very strong base.

Red Cabbages, Acids, and Bases

Anthocyanins are easy to obtain from plants because they are water soluble. Red cabbage, *Brassica oleracea,* is often used as an indicator. The red cabbage can be heated in water and the pigment will merge into the water. This liquid can be used as a pH indicator in the lab. The indicator will appear red in the presence of a strong acid (pH 1 to 3), violet in a weak acid (pH 4 to 6), blue-green in alkaline solution (pH 8 to 10), and yellow in a strong alkaline (over 12).

PETAL PICKIN'—VOCABULARY ACTIVITY ON
NATURE'S INDICATORS

Directions

Match the flower with the pot that can best be used to extract the anthocyanin pigment. The words on one of the flowers will best correspond to the words on the cooking pot in each series of pictures. Circle the flower that best suits each pot.

17–2 THE CABBAGE PATCH INDICATORS
AND THE PETAL PAPERS

Lab on Using Anthocyanins to Determine the Acidity of Substances

Objectives

In Part 1, students will extract anthocyanin from cabbage leaves or poinsettias and use this liquid extract to test for acids and bases. In Part 2, students will make indicator test paper from flower petals (such as poinsettias) and use these to test for acids and bases.

Teacher Notes

These two labs will require at least two class periods. Try to complete Part 1 the first day and begin Part 2 on day two.

Be sure to collect all the materials you need ahead of time. Students should be cautioned to be very careful when handling the drain cleaner since it is caustic to the skin. Some suggestions for the five items you might require the class to test are apple juice, shampoos, baking powder, garden fertilizer, soil, ammonia water, Sprite® or 7-Up®, and limewater.

The recipe for making up the eight solutions for the test tubes is as follows:

Prepare enough of each of the eight solutions and the five teacher choice solutions for each lab group to have at least 10 ml of each (enough for Part 1 and Part 2).

Place your prepared solutions in a labeled beaker, with the name of the contents on the outside of the beaker.

Beaker 1—The juice of pitted lemons freshly squeezed

Beaker 2—White vinegar

Beaker 3—Boric acid (2 grams of boric acid per 200 ml of water) *CAUTION:* USE CARE WHEN MIXING THIS.

Beaker 4—Water (distilled water is recommended)

Beaker 5—Sodium bicarbonate (2 grams of sodium bicarbonate per 200 ml of water)

Beaker 6—Borax (2 grams of borax per 200 ml of water. *CAUTION:* USE CARE WHEN MIXING THIS.

Beaker 7—Washing soda, 2 grams of sodium carbonate per 200 ml of water)

Beaker 8—Sodium hydroxide (2 grams of solid drain cleaner Drano® in 200 ml of water) *CAUTION:* SODIUM HYDROXIDE IS CAUSTIC AND CAN CAUSE SEVERE BURNS.

Part 2 requires the use of ethanol if you want the process to be done quickly. If you are willing to boil the petals for 20 to 30 minutes in water, you can avoid the use of ethanol. If you choose to use the ethanol, caution students not to have any open flames around this flammable alcohol. The flowers used in this part should be dark colored to obtain good results. Flowers such as the blue iris, purple dahlia, and purple hollyhock often give good results. If poinsettias are in season at the time of this lab, the red varieties work well. You may have to repeat the wetting and drying of the strips of paper several times to get a dark color. A microwave oven and plate can be used instead of a conventional oven and cookie sheet to hasten the drying process.

If time is a factor, you may want to demonstrate the anthocyanin removal process to the class instead of having them perform this task. You could then provide the class with some extract and students could perform the experimentation.

Poinsettias can be used for both Parts 1 and 2 if this is more convenient.

CABBAGE PATCH INDICATORS AND THE PETAL PAPERS
Lab on Using Anthocyanins to Determine the Acidity of Substances

Introduction

Indicators are types of organic compounds that will alter colors at various pH's. Indicators will usually change from dark colors in acid solutions to lighter colors in alkaline solutions.

Indicators can be complex organic dyes that are synthesized in the laboratory. But this does not have to be the case. Many flowers contain the pigment anthocyanin. Anthocyanin is a natural indicator that can be extracted from plants with water and/or alcohol. In acidic solutions, anthocyanins appear red and turn blue-green and finally yellow in basic solutions. The darker the color of acid plus indicator, the stronger the acid.

Acids produce hydrogen ions (H^+) in the water, while bases produce hydroxide (OH^-) ions. The anthocyanins that readily accept more hydrogen ions are strong acids. The anthocyanins that readily lose hydrogen ions are the strong bases.

Litmus paper is a synthetic indicator that turns red litmus blue in the presence of bases. Phenolphthalein turns colorless in acids but pink in the presence of bases. Many more synthetic indicators exist. But the homemade version will serve the same function as the more expensive synthetic variety.

Prelab Questions

1. Why can substances such as ketchup or chocolate not be tested in this way?

2. What is an indicator?

3. What is the difference between a natural and a synthetic indicator?

4. Explain the connection between hydrogen ions and acids, and hydroxyl ions and bases.

5. Describe the color change as you go from acids to bases.

Materials

Part 1

Lemons to squeeze	White vinegar	Boric acid
Water	Sodium bicarbonate	Borax
Washing soda solution	Drain cleaner	13 test tubes
Hot plate or stove	Red cabbage (or a poinsettia plant)	
Graduated cylinder	Stirring rod	

Part 2

All the materials used in Part 1 (except the red cabbage) and the following:

Flower petals of dark-colored flowers (poinsettias are recommended)
Paper towels   Scissors   Oven or fruit dryer (or microwave)
Ethanol   Hot plate   White typing paper
                                    Cookie sheet or pan

Procedure

Part 1—The Cabbage Patch Indicators (or Poinsettia Indicators)

1. Shred some cabbage into a large beaker. Add 80 ml of water to the cabbage. Gently heat the cabbage on the Bunsen burner, hot plate, or a stove top until it boils. Continue heating the cabbage until the solution turns a deep purple. Poinsettias may be used instead of cabbage to extract the reddish-colored anthocyanin pigment.

2. Allow the solution to cool, filter out the decolored leaves, and place the indicator solution in clean beakers.

3. Gather eight clean test tubes and get 5 ml of each of the eight solutions the teacher has prepared for you.

   Label test tube 1, pH 2. Place 5 ml of freshly squeezed lemon juice in this test tube.

   Label test tube 2, pH 3. Place 5 ml of white vinegar in the test tube.

   Label test tube 3, pH 5. Place 5 ml of boric acid solution in the test tube. (*CAUTION:* Boric acid can be corrosive to the skin.)

   Label test tube 4, pH 7. Place 5 ml of distilled water in the test tube.

   Label test tube 5, pH 8. Place 5 ml of sodium bicarbonate solution in the test tube.

   Label test tube 6, pH 9. Place 5 ml of borax solution in the test tube. (*CAUTION:* Borax can be toxic to the skin.)

   Label test tube 7, pH 12. Place 5 ml of washing soda solution in the test tube.

   Label test tube 8, pH 14. Carefully add 5 ml of drain cleaner solution to this test tube. (*CAUTION:* Drain cleaner can be caustic to the skin. Use extreme caution when handling this solution. Gloves may need to be worn. If you spill some on your hands or clothing, wash them immediately in cold water and inform the teacher.)

DATA CHART 1

Name of substance	pH of substance	Color of the solution after mixing
Lemon juice		
White vinegar		
Boric acid		
Water		
Sodium bicarbonate		
Borax		
Washing soda solution		
Drain cleaner		
TEACHER CHOICE SECTION		

4. Once these eight test tubes have been prepared, add about 2 to 3 ml of cabbage indicator (or poinsettia indicator) to each test tube. Mix the solutions gently with a stirring rod. You should begin to notice a distinct color change ranging from dark red to yellow. Indicate on Chart 1 the color of each test tube. This will now serve as your standard for comparison. Leave the test tubes set up throughout the activity to use as a comparison.

Now test five substances your teacher selects. Place five additional test tubes in a test tube rack and put 5 ml of each solution you are given in each test tube. Write the name of the solutions the teacher provides in the blank sections on the chart. Test each solution and write down the color each turned when 2 ml of cabbage juice (or poinsettia juice) was added to 5 ml of the chosen substances. On the chart, indicate the pH of the substances by comparing them with the control test tubes.

Postlab Questions

1. Of the five new substances, which was the strongest acid?

2. Of the five new substances, which was the strongest base?

3. Describe the color differences among the following: strong acids, weak acids, neutral, weak bases, and strong bases.

4. What does the word *caustic* mean?

5. How can you find out if your results were accurate?

Part 2—The Petal Papers

Procedure

1. Obtain a few colored flowers. Dark colors such as the blue iris, purple dahlia, purple hollyhock, roses, and petunias generally work best. Poinsettias are recommended.

2. Place about 25 ml of ethanol in a small beaker, and add 10 to 15 petals from your dark-colored flower.

3. After checking to be sure there are no open flames in the room, place the beaker on a hot plate. Gently heat the beaker and petals until the color has faded from the petals. This generally will take about 5 to 10 minutes. Stir the petals frequently while they are being heated. *CAUTION:* ALCOHOLS SUCH AS ETHANOL ARE FLAMMABLE. THIS IS WHY ALL FLAMES MUST BE EXTINGUISHED WHILE ALCOHOL IS BEING USED. If you choose not to use alcohol and use only water, the heating will take from 20 to 30 minutes to remove the anthocyanin pigment from the plant.

4. Remove the faded petals from the beaker. The remaining colored liquid is the indicator liquid you use to make your test papers.

© 1994 by The Center for Applied Research in Education

5. Place a sheet of white paper towel on a cookie sheet or metal pan. Wet the paper towel with the indicator liquid you prepared. Place this in an oven or fruit dryer until the liquid has dried. If a microwave is available, you can place the saturated paper towel on a plate and heat for 2 to 3 minutes to dry the paper.

6. Add more indicator liquid to the dried paper towel and place it back in the oven (or microwave) to dry. This is done to darken the color. You may even want to repeat this a third time if the color is still not dark enough.

7. Once the paper is completely dry, cut the paper towel into small strips. You may want to cut the top of the strip into the shape of flower petals to hold onto when you dip the strips into solutions. Cut out about 30 or 40 strips from the paper towel.

8. Refer back to Procedure 3 in Part 1 of this activity. Set up eight test tubes as you did in that procedure. Label them exactly as before. Place a piece of white typing paper in front of the eight test tubes and dip one paper petal strip into each test tube. Place the strip on the white paper in front of each of the eight test tubes. Underneath each strip, write the pH of the contents of the test tube you tested each time. This will give you a calibration chart. Complete Chart 2 by indicating the color of each strip of paper after it was dipped.

9. Obtain five more test tubes and test the five substances you tested in Part 1 with the cabbage juice. Dip one strip in each solution of that substance. Compare the color with the calibration strips. In Chart 2, write in what color the strip turned and what you believe to be the pH of each substance.

Postlab Questions

1. How did the results for the pH of the five substances compare in Parts 1 and 2?

2. Indicate whether you think the cabbage test or the petal paper test is more accurate in testing acidity and alkalinity. Explain your answer.

3. What is meant by the term *calibration*?

CHART 2

Name of substance	pH of substance	Color of the petal paper after dipping
Lemon juice		
White vinegar		
Boric acid		
Water		
Sodium bicarbonate		
Borax		
Sodium carbonate		
Drain cleaner		
TEACHER CHOICE SECTION		

SECTION 5

Biology

LESSON 18: THE BLUEPRINT OF LIFE

18–1 THE BLUEPRINT OF LIFE
Content on DNA

Why Do You Look Like That?

Hair on our head grows up to 25 inches, but hair on our eyebrows grows only an inch or less. Why?

Humans have five fingers on each hand instead of six. Why?

Cats have tails that twitch back and forth when they are angry. Why?

Dogwood leaves always have smooth edges. Why?

People rarely grow over 6-1/2 feet tall. Why?

How do our bodies know just what to do? We are not surprised that all people have two arms and two legs, but how did the developing fetus "know" to grow two arms and two legs?

The Answers Are in the Nucleus

Our bodies, and the bodies of all living things, are made of cells. A cell is a tiny living structure that contains a set of directions for what to do, when to do it, and how much of it to do. All of these directions are tightly packed in the cell's nucleus, a large, dark structure in the cell. Inside the nucleus are long, thin strands of chromatin, a molecule made of deoxyribonucleic acid, or DNA. The chromatin is made up of little units called nucleotides, which are composed of a nucleic acid, a sugar, and a phosphate group (see Figure A).

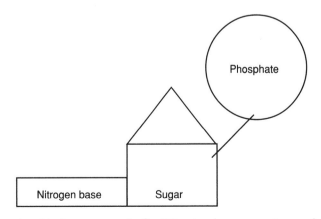

FIGURE A. A DNA nucleotide is composed of a Nitrogen base, a sugar, and a phosphate group.

Let's take a close look at the DNA inside of a cell's nucleus. If we had a magic microscope, we could see that a strand of chromatin is made of two strands of DNA that are arranged in a spiral shape, or double helix (see Figure B).

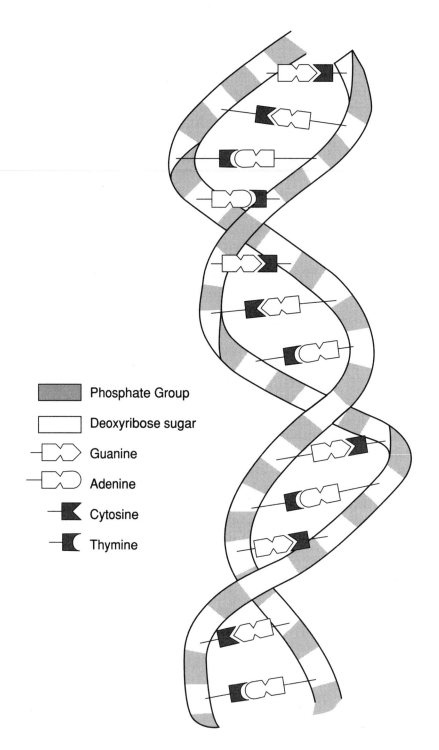

FIGURE B. DNA is a double helix.

A Molecule That Has a Familiar Shape

If we could take a strand of chromatin and straighten it out so that the helix shape is gone, it would look like a ladder (see Figure C). The outside parts of the ladder are made of alternating sugar (s) and phosphate (P) molecules. The sugar in a DNA molecule is deoxyribose.

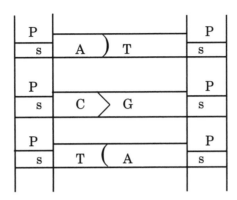

FIGURE C. A strand of DNA looks like a ladder.

The rungs of the DNA ladder are made of pairs of nitrogen bases. There are only four nitrogen bases in any DNA molecule: thymine, adenine, guanine, and cytosine. Thymine and adenine fit together like two puzzle pieces, and guanine and cytosine fit together. Because of this special fit, thymine never pairs with anything but adenine, and guanine never pairs with anything but cytosine.

The DNA Code

How does DNA direct the cell and tell it exactly what to do? The sequence of the Nitrogen bases in a DNA strand forms a code. This code determines which protein will be made. Proteins, important molecules that make up most of a living thing, are composed of strings of amino acids. A triplet, the sequence of three nucleotides on the DNA strand, codes for a particular amino acid.

Protein Synthesizers

The parts of the cell that make products, like ribosomes, are out in the cytoplasm. Ribosomes assemble proteins. DNA is in the nucleus and is too large to leave the nucleus through pores in the nuclear membrane. Therefore, DNA has to send a message to a ribosome to tell it what kind of protein to assemble. The messenger that DNA makes and sends is called messenger ribonucleic acid, or mRNA. mRNA is very similar to DNA but differs from DNA in three ways: It is single stranded and can leave the nucleus by passing through the nuclear pores; the sugar that is found in RNA is ribose instead of deoxyribose; and RNA does not have any of the nitrogen base, thymine. Instead, it has uracil. Uracil can pair with adenine.

DNA's Message

To make a messenger, the DNA molecule in the cell's nucleus spreads out in a V formation. RNA nucleotides floating around in the nucleus line up along one side of the open DNA. They arrange themselves so that adenine can pair with uracil and guanine can pair with cytosine (see Figure D).

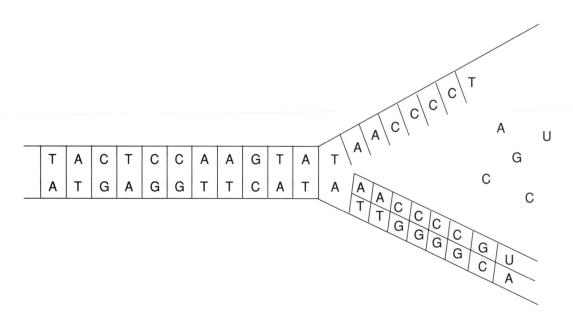

FIGURE D. A strand of DNA opens, and RNA nucleotides form an mRNA strand.

When the mRNA strand is complete, it leaves the nucleus and enters the cell's cytoplasm, where it attaches to a ribosome. Within the cytoplasm are all the parts necessary for the construction of a new protein. Amino acids, the sub-units of proteins, are floating around in the cytoplasm. The purpose of mRNA is to arrange amino acids in the correct order to make a particular protein. There are 22 different amino acids, and their arrangement in a protein is of vital importance. Just one mistake in amino acid sequencing can produce a defective protein.

Codons and Anticodons

On the mRNA, three nucleotides that correspond to a particular amino acid are called a codon. The mRNA is carrying the correct sequence of codons needed to make a protein. The problem is that something needs to deliver the correct amino acids to their spot on the mRNA. This something is a special form of RNA called transfer RNA, or tRNA. There are 22 amino acids and 22 tRNAs. On the tRNA, the spot that matches or base pairs with the mRNA's codon is called the anticodon.

DNA CONCEPT MAP—VOCABULARY ACTIVITY ON
THE BLUEPRINT OF LIFE

Directions

Fill in the blanks in the concept map.

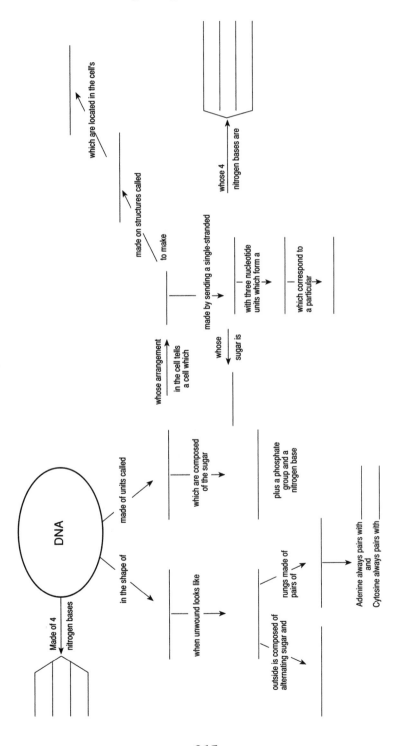

18–2 RECIPE FOR PROTEINS
DNA Modeling Activity

Objectives

Students will learn the steps of translation and transcription. In addition, they will make a paper model of a short polypeptide.

Teacher Notes

Give each lab group a strip of paper numbered 1, 2, 3, 4, 5, or 6 that represents a strand of DNA.

1. TACCGAACAACACCATAATTTATC

4. TACTTTGTTCCATTAAAACAAATC

2. TACACACCATAAAAACGAAAAATT

5. TACTAAAAACGAACATAAAAAATT

3. TACCCAACAAAATTTCGACCAACT

6. TACCCCTAATTTGTTACACCAACT

When students have completed the exercise, they will have created the following polypeptide chains:

1. Initiation–alanine–cysteine–cysteine–glycine–isoleucine–lysine–termination

2. Initiation–cysteine–glycine–isoleucine–phenylalanine–alanine–phenylalanine–termination

3. Initiation–glycine–cysteine–phenylalanine–lysine–alanine–glycine–termination

4. Initiation–lysine–glutamine–glycine–aspargine–phenylalanine–valine–termination

5. Initiation–isoleucine–phenylalanine–alanine–cysteine–isoleucine–phenylalanine–termination

6. Initiation–glycine–isoleucine–lysine–glutamine–cysteine–glycine–termination

RECIPE FOR PROTEINS
DNA Modeling Activity

Introduction

DNA is a molecule made of units called nucleotides. Each nucleotide contains one of the four nitrogenous bases. The sequence of these bases determines what protein will be made.

In this activity you will make a model of DNA, mRNA, and a short protein.

Materials

Scissors   Glue
Construction paper (2 sheets)   Ruler
Three strips of construction paper   Components handout
Nitrogen base cutouts

Procedure

A. Create a double strand of DNA using the nitrogen base cutouts.

1. Make a nucleus out of construction paper that is 30 cm wide.

2. Use the sequence given to you by your teacher as the left hand strand. Cut out the appropriate bases, glue them to a strip of paper, and place them in the nucleus.

3. Use the nitrogen base cutouts to form a strand of DNA that will match the strand given to you by the teacher, and glue this to another strip of paper and place in your nucleus. Arrange the two strands so that there is some space between them. This is your complete, double strand of DNA.

4. Make a strand of messenger RNA that corresponds to the left-hand strand of DNA (the strand from your teacher). Glue to a third strip of paper and place this strand of messenger RNA out in the cytoplasm. Do not glue it to the construction paper at this time.

B. To make a short protein do the following:

1. Cut out the tRNAs, amino acids, and ribosome from the Components Handout.

2. Use your strand of mRNA to determine the anticodons you will need on tRNAs. Put the correct anticodons in the square part of all six tRNAs.

3. Put the name of each amino acid in the blank and attach the amino acid to its appropriate tRNA. See Table 1 for a list of amino acids and the codons with which they pair.

4. Glue the ribosome out in the cytoplasm of your cell.

5. Lay the strip of mRNA in the ribosome so that the left side of the mRNA is in the ribosome and the right side is sticking out.

6. Match each tRNA with its correct amino acid.

7. Match the first mRNA codon to the correct anticodon on one of the tRNAs.

8. Match the second mRNA codon to the correct anticodon on one of the tRNAs. Match the other six mRNA codons to correct anticodon in the same manner.

9. Attach the amino acids together to form a short amino acid chain; glue to your construction paper cell in the cytoplasm.

10. You have created a model of a short polypeptide. Long polypeptides form proteins.

Conclusions

1. What determines which proteins a cell will make?

2. What is the function of a ribosome?

3. What is the function of a tRNA?

4. Why is it important that amino acids be assembled in a particular sequence?

5. DNA is in the nucleus and ribosomes are in the cytoplasm. Explain how DNA sends a message about protein synthesis to the ribosomes.

© 1994 by The Center for Applied Research in Education

TABLE 1
Amino Acids and Codons

Amino Acid	RNA Codons
Alanine	GCU, GCC, GCA, GCG
Arginine	AGA, AGG, CGU, CGC, CGA, CGG
Asparagine	AAU, AAC
Aspartic Acid	GAU, GAC
Cysteine	UGU, UGC
Glutamic Acid	GAA, GAG
Glutamine	CAA, CAG
Glycine	GGU, GGC, GGA, GGG
Histidine	CAU, CAC
Isoleucine	AUU, AUC, AUA
Leucine	UUA, UUG, CUU, CUC, CUA, CUG
Lysine	AAA, AAG
Methionine (Initiation)	AUG, GUG
Phenylalanine	UUU, UCC
Proline	CCU, CCC, CCA, CCG
Serine	UCU, UCC, UCA, UCG, AGU, AGC
Threonine	ACU, ACC, ACA, ACG
Tryptophan	UGG
Tyrosinse	UAU, UAC
Valine	GUU, GUC, GUA, GUG
Termination	UAA, UAG, UGA

Components Handout

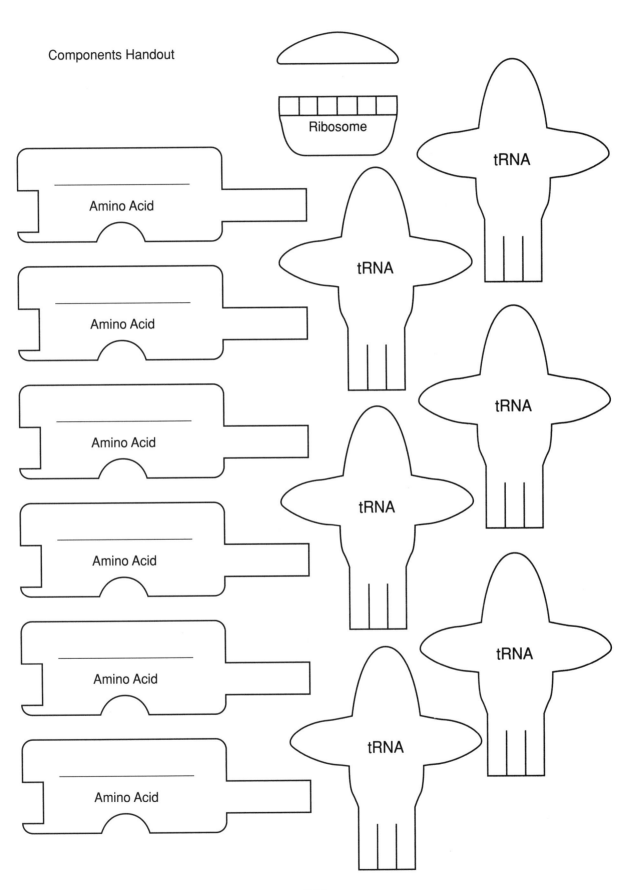

Nitrogen Base Cutouts

LESSON 19: THE BASIC UNIT OF LIFE

19–1 THE BASIC UNIT OF LIFE
Content on Cells

A Celebration: Meeting the Cell

Everyone begins life as a single cell. The single fertilized ovum eventually grows into an adult composed of trillions of cells. Cells are constantly dying and being replaced in the human body. Some cells, such as the skin cells, die every 60 seconds and are replaced by cellular division to keep the cell number constant in the body. Cytologists (scientists who study cells) have compiled much information about the anatomy (structure) and physiology (function) of the cell.

The English naturalist Robert Hooke coined the word *cell* in 1665. He arrived at this name from the Latin word *cella,* which means "small containers." Hooke observed cork cells under the microscope and described them as resembling small honeycombs. Due to the poor quality of microscope lenses in that day, Hooke described only the outer casing of the cell without considering the importance of the material inside the cell. In 1831, the scientist Robert Brown made the first exciting observation about what went on inside a cell. Later in the seventeenth century, a scientist, Matthias Schleiden, recognized that the protoplasm and the nucleus were vital parts of the cell. In this same year an anatomist, Theodor Schwann, recognized the importance of a cell wall or membrane in protecting the contents of a cell. Over the next three centuries, the invention of the electron microscope and improved sectioning and staining techniques led to continued expansion of knowledge about the content of a cell.

All cells have certain basic components that enable them to carry out life processes. These components allow the cell to make specialized contributions to the functioning of the body. Some structures that are common to almost all cells are the outer membrane, cytoplasm, and organelles (structures within the cell with a specific function).

The Ins and Outs of the Cell

The outer membrane, called the plasma membrane (plasmalemma), is made of a double layer of phospholipids. The plasmalemma separates the cell's internal fluid and external fluid environment, receives communication from other cells, transports substances, and plays a role in the immunity of the cell. This membrane protects the organelles of the cell and is selectively permeable to materials

221

that enter and exit. *Selectively permeable* means that the membrane can choose which materials it will permit to enter and exit the cell based on the composition and size of the materials. Some smaller particles, such as oxygen and carbon dioxide, can enter and exit the cell by the process of diffusion. Diffusion is the movement of molecules from a place of greater concentration to a place of lesser concentration. This requires no energy expenditure by the cell and is called passive transport. Larger particles, such as glucose and sodium ions, require energy to make their way across the cell membrane (active transport). Phagocytosis and pinocytosis are two more mechanisms that allow transport of materials across the cell membrane. Phagocytosis represents the taking in of bacteria and foreign bodies into the cell and then storing these in vacuoles until they are digested and passed out of the cell (exocytosis). Pinocytosis involves the ingestion of fluid by inward movement of part of the membrane.

The cytoplasm of the cell is the jellylike material inside the cell membrane. It is made up of proteins, water, minerals, organelles, and inclusions. An organelle is a living permanent structure vital to the life of the cell. Inclusions are a nonliving accumulation of cell products such as fat globules and waste products. Also within the cell membrane is the cytoskeleton, a network of protein filaments that act like flexible scaffolding to maintain the cellular shape and provide the cell with the ability to move.

Cilia and flagella are motile processes that protrude from the cell. Cilia look like small hairs on the surface of a cell. In the respiratory tract, cilia can propel fluid material such as mucus upward as coughing clears the congested lungs. Flagella are motile protrusions of a cell that provide cellular locomotion. The motile tail of a spermatozoan cell is an example of a flagellum that allows the sperm to travel toward the egg for fertilization.

Cellular Organelles

The nucleus of the cell is the largest of the cell structures. It governs all the activities of the cell since it dictates protein synthesis within the cell. The nucleus contains nucleoplasm and is bounded by a double-layered nuclear envelope. Genetic material in the form of DNA molecules is found in the nucleus packaged in bundles of chromosomes. The DNA, in combination with proteins called histones, forms the material chromatin. The nucleus will also contain a nucleolus, a structure that controls the synthesis of some of the cell's RNA (ribonucleic acid). Some of the RNA is used to make ribosomes, which function in protein synthesis.

The endoplasmic reticulum is a series of canals that forms intricate connecting links between the plasma membrane and the nuclear membrane. They serve as a miniature circulatory system for the cell as proteins move through these canals. There are two types of endoplasmic reticulum (sometimes referred to as ER): rough and smooth. The rough ER is given this name because it has ribosomes that line the outer surface of the membrane of the ER. The ribosomes on the ER synthesize proteins and then transport these proteins to the Golgi apparatus. Cells such as lymphocytes contain large quantities of rough ER because of their role in antibody formation and production of protein for export. The smooth ER does not contain ribosomes and is involved in the synthesis of

© 1994 by The Center for Applied Research in Education

lipids and carbohydrates. Much smooth ER is found in cells that specialize in lipid formation, such as steroid hormone production. The testes and corpus luteum contain large quantities of smooth ER.

The structures on rough ER that engage in protein synthesis are called ribosomes. A cell may have thousands of ribosomes both attached to the ER and scattered throughout the cytoplasm. Ribosomes are the "protein factories" of the cell and contain RNA and enzymes to perform this function.

Located near the nucleus are a series of membrane-bound, complex stacks of interconnecting membranes called the Golgi apparatus. This apparatus functions to synthesize large carbohydrate molecules and then combine them with proteins to form compounds called glycoproteins, which are then secreted out of the cell. The major role of the Golgi apparatus is to transport and release secretory material from the cell. Large amounts of Golgi apparatus are located in liver cells that secrete proteins, plasma cells that secrete antibodies, and bone cells that secrete substances used in their formation.

Most cells have a powerhouse organelle to generate energy from sugars and fatty acids. These powerhouse organelles are called mitochondria. The mitochondria have a double membrane, with an inner membrane folded into extensions called cristae. These organelles synthesize ATP (adenosine triphosphate) from ADP (adenosine diphosphate) to provide the energy for the cell. The number of mitochondria in a cell will vary depending on the metabolic activity of the cell. The higher the cellular metabolism, the greater the number of mitochondria in the cell. Muscle cells have a large number of mitochondria because of the energy demands of the muscles. Liver cells do much more work than sperm cells. One liver cell will have 40 mitochondria to every 1 mitochondrion found in a sperm cell. Mitochondria also function in cellular respiration.

The membrane-bound organelle within the cell that contains digestive enzymes is the lysosome. The enzymes within the lysosome can dispose of bacteria or other foreign material that enters a cell. Because of the strength of these enzymes in destroying foreign material, lysosomes are referred to as "suicide sacs," "digestive bags," and "cellular garbage disposals." White blood cells contain a large number of lysosomes since they function as the scavenger cells of the body by engulfing bacteria and destroying them.

Centrosomes are organelles that are located close to the nucleus. They contain a pair of centrioles that appear as two cylinders located at right angles to each other. The major role of the centrioles is in cell division, and they become prominent during mitosis.

The storage chambers of the cell are called vacuoles. Since they contain mostly water, they are often referred to as "water bubbles" of the cell. They are fewer in number in animal cells than in plant cells.

Special Cells

Cells have evolved in numerous ways to fulfill specific tasks within organisms. An enormous degree of chemical variability can exist within a single cell. In complex animals such as humans, cells have become specialized in one type of function only. In simple animals such as a paramecium, a cell must be able to carry out wide ranges of functions to be self-sufficient.

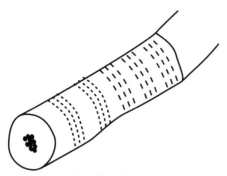

Cardiac Cells

Red Blood Cell

White Blood Cells

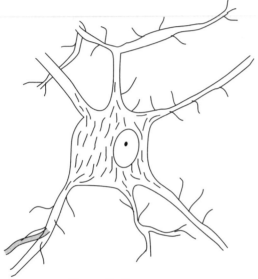

Nerve Cell

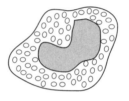

Monocyte

Eosinophil

Lymphocyte

Basophil

Smooth Muscle

Neutrophil

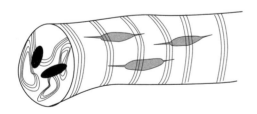

Striated Muscle

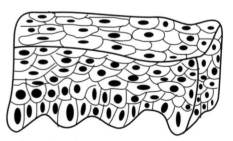

Stratified squamous epithelium
in mouth lining

FIGURE A

Human cells can be classified in a variety of ways based on function and appearance. One of the most common means of classification groups cells into four principal tissue types. Tissues are groups of cells with a common function. The four tissues are epithelial, connective, muscular, and nervous. (See Figure A for a diagram of some human cells.)

Specialized Cell and Tissue Types

Epithelial tissue consists of cells that line surfaces of organs in the body and compose the secretory cells of the glands. Epithelial cells do not have blood vessels (they are avascular), and some may have cilia. They replace themselves by mitosis at a high rate. These cells serve as a protective mechanism against invasion of bacteria and a buffer against injury. Epithelial cells compose the surface of the skin and the lining of the mouth, esophagus, and vagina. The sweat glands, salivary glands, pituitary glands, and thyroid gland are some more examples of the location of glandular epithelial tissue.

Connective tissue is the most widespread and abundant tissue in the body. Connective tissue has the most variety of the four forms of basic tissues. Some examples of connective tissue are bone, cartilage, blood, and adipose (fat).

Connective tissue is made of cells that provide support, flexibility, transport, and defense. Red blood cells are a component of connective tissue that functions solely to carry oxygen and carbon dioxide around the body to where it can be used or exhaled. The red blood cell (erythrocyte) possesses a nucleus and all the other major organelles in its immature state, but it pushes out its nucleus and disintegrates its organelles when it becomes mature. At maturity a red blood cell has only a cell membrane, hemoglobin (pigment for carrying oxygen), and a few enzymes. White blood cells called leucocytes serve as the body's defense against microorganisms. They possess a nucleus and a large number of lysosomes.

Muscle cells are specialized for contraction to produce movement of the body. They possess a plasma membrane (sarcolemma), ER (sarcoplasmic reticulum), large numbers of mitochondria, and protoplasm (sarcoplasm).

Adipose cells (fat cells) are among the largest connective tissue cells in the body. They have a nucleus that is pushed to one side of the cell. The rest of the adipose cell is composed of a thin area of cytoplasm containing the organelles. The rest of the cellular space is composed of a large fat droplet that makes up 95% of the cell.

Nervous tissue is adapted to collecting and transmitting information. Nerve cells vary in size and function. The nerve cell (called a neuron) has a cell body (soma) that contains a nucleus. The neuron also has cell processes called dendrites (which conduct impulses to the soma) and an axon (which conducts impulses away from the soma). Some nerve cells can be more than 3 feet long, so they can carry messages from the spinal cord down to the extremities of the body. The human brain which contains about 100 billion neurons (about the same number of stars in our galaxy).

Cells of common function make up our body tissues. Groups of tissues, in turn, make up the organs of the body. Organs of common function make up organ systems. Groups of organ systems make up the organism. Underlying this organizational structure of an organism is the basic unit of structure we call the cell.

The Tri-ing Cell Puzzle—Vocabulary Puzzle on
The Basic Unit of Life

Directions

Read puzzle clues 1 through 15. Find the word that matches the clue from the "Choices" section. The letter next to the correct answer will correspond to the letter on the triangle. Place the number of the clue above this letter on the triangle. Repeat until all 15 blocks are filled with numbers.

You can check to see if you have the correct answers by adding up the numbers on the FOCUS side of the triangle and entering that number in the box above this word. Do the same for the numbers on the BREAK side of the triangle. Record this number in the box above the word *break*. Finally, add up the numbers on the LIGHT side of the triangle, and record this number in the box above the word *light*. If you have selected all correct choices and added correctly, you will find that these three boxes will all contain the same number.

Clues

1. _____ are groups of cells with a common function.

2. _____ are cells that are made in the bone marrow and transport oxygen throughout the body.

3. The _____ contains the chromatin material and is the director of the cell.

4. _____ are found on rough endoplasmic reticulum.

5. _____ have a cell body, dendrites, and an axon.

6. The higher the metabolic requirements of the cell, the more _____ you find in that cell to provide energy.

7. _____ are the cellular garbage disposal units.

8. _____ are organelles that play a major role in cell division.

9. _____ are canals that connect the plasma and nuclear membrane. They can be granular or agranular in appearance.

10. _____ are protrusions from the epithelial cells that can propel particles or instigate movement of the cell itself.

11. _____ is composed of cells that make tissues that line organs and surfaces and act in a protective function.

12. _____ are related to the secretory activity of the cell. They also synthesize glycoproteins.

13. Osteoclasts and osteoblasts are examples of _____.

14. _____ are specialized for contraction and production of body movements.

15. _____ make up adipose tissue.

Choices

A. Lysosomes
B. Cilia
C. Nucleus
E. Ribosomes
F. Centrosomes
G. Endoplasmic reticula
H. Golgi apparatus
I. Mitochondria

K. Nerve cells
L. Erythrocytes
O. Fat cells
R. Muscle cells
S. Tissues
T. Epithelium
U. Bone cells

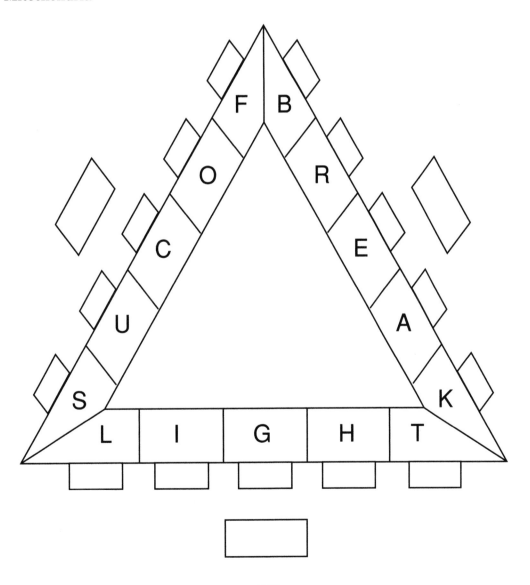

19–2 HANGING OUT WITH CELL MODELS
Project on Construction of Cell Mobiles

Objectives

Students will construct a three-dimensional mobile of the cell and its organelles.

Teacher Notes

This can be done by students individually or in groups of two. You may choose to have students work on these in class or as an out-of-class assignment. The mobile should contain all of the cell parts required, with each organelle properly labeled. An oral presentation and description of the mobile should be given by each student at the conclusion of the project. You may choose to ask one question of each student about the cell. A grading outline follows.

Evaluation Sheet for Cell Project

All cell parts included in the project	20
Neatness and time spent on construction	20
Proper representation and design of the organelles	25
Mobile is properly balanced and ready to be hung from ceiling	10
A label for each organelle is provided	10
Oral presentation of mobile and ability to answer questions from the teacher	15
Total	100

HANGING OUT WITH CELL MODELS
Project on Construction of Cell Mobiles

Materials

Hot glue gun	Poster board	Construction paper	Markers or crayons
Scissors	String	Elmer's® glue	Cardboard
Ruler	Black marker	Pattern page of organelles	Tape measure

Optional materials: Selected by teacher, such as pipe cleaners, toothpicks, etc.

Directions

1. Divide into groups of two.

2. You will construct a cell mobile that contains the following organelles:

Cell membrane	Nucleus	Smooth endoplasmic reticulum
Golgi apparatus	Nucleolus	Chromatin
Vacuole	Ribosomes	Rough endoplasmic reticulum
Mitochondria	Lysosome	

3. A suggested design for the mobile is as follows:

A. Cut a circle (12 to 18 inches in diameter) out of a piece of stiff cardboard.

B. Measure the circumference (distance around the outside of the circle) with a tape measure.

C. To construct your cell membrane, obtain a piece of colored construction paper, and draw a circular cell border equal to the circumference of the cardboard circle and about 2 inches in width. Use your scissors to cut the cell membrane out of the construction paper.

D. Use the hot glue gun and apply a thin layer of glue around the circumference (outside) of the cardboard circle. Wrap the cell membrane around the circle by centering the cardboard circle in the middle of the cell membrane. Press the cell membrane firmly in place. (Be careful with the hot glue.) When you complete this step, the cell membrane will extend the same distance above the cardboard as below it. The cardboard circle represents the cytoplasm of the cell.

E. Using the sharp end of a pair of scissors, place a hole in the top of the center of the cardboard circle. Thread a piece of string through the hole and tie a large knot on the underside of the cardboard to keep the string from being pulled back through the hole. This string will be tied from the ceiling after the organelles are all added.

Pattern Page of Organelles

Mitochondria

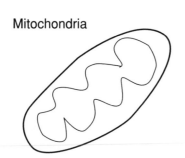

Vacuole

Lysosome

Ribosomes

Nucleus

Golgi apparatus

Nucleolus

Chromatin

Rough Endoplasmic
Reticulum

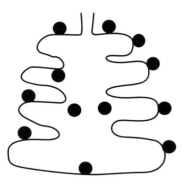

Smooth Endoplasmic
Reticulum

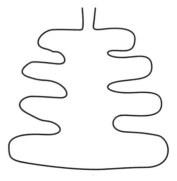

F. The other organelles can be made of poster board and then colored with markers or crayons. The organelles should be colored on both sides. The nucleus should be made first. Use the pattern page of organelles as a guide for your construction. These patterns are not drawn to scale for the mobile. You should use these only as a guide and experiment with appropriate sizes on your mobile.

G. Punch a hole in the top of each organelle and tie a string through it. The other end of the string will be threaded up through the cardboard circle and tied with a knot on the top of the circle, so the organelle is dangling down. The nucleus should be suspended from the center of the cardboard circle. The nucleolus can be made by using a piece of construction paper cut into a small circle and then pasted on both sides of the nucleus. The chromatin material can be cut out of construction paper and pasted on the nucleus as well.

H. Arrange the remainder of the organelles anywhere inside the cell membrane border keeping the mobile balanced. Balance can be achieved by varying the length of the strings supporting each organelle or rearranging the position of various organelles.

I. Hot glue the names of each organelle to the suspended string. Remember to glue the name to each side of the string.

J. Once all steps are completed and the strings are firmly attached and balance has been achieved, suspend the main string from the ceiling. See Figure A for an example of how the completed mobile will look.

K. Each group will present its cell mobile to the rest of the class and should be prepared to answer questions from the teacher on organelle function. The teacher will ask each student the function of one of the organelles on the mobile or some fact about the organelle.

L. The teacher will give you a list of criteria for grading this project.

Extensions and Variations

Students may design their organelles out of materials such as pipe cleaners, styrofoam, toothpicks, beads, etc. The sheet of organelle patterns can be used as a reference.

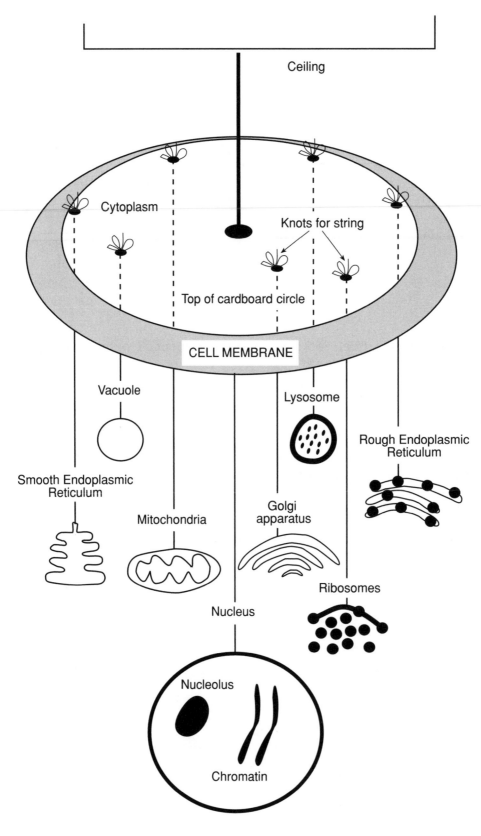

Ceiling

Cytoplasm

Knots for string

Top of cardboard circle

CELL MEMBRANE

Vacuole

Lysosome

Rough Endoplasmic
Reticulum

Smooth Endoplasmic
Reticulum

Mitochondria

Golgi
apparatus

Ribosomes

Nucleus

Nucleolus

Chromatin

FIGURE A

19–3 CELL TREK
Review Board Game on the Cell

Objectives

Students will learn the organelles and their function in an animal cell.

Teacher Notes

Before beginning the game for the first time, the Student Cell Worksheet should be duplicated on the copy machine so each participant in the game has a copy. The Cell Trek game boards (labeled Cell Trek) should be duplicated so one board is available for every four students. You should also duplicate the Cell Part Worksheet (one sheet per group). Each cell part on the worksheet should be cut out with scissors and placed in a white envelope labeled Cell Organelles.

Questions 1 through 69 should be duplicated on the copy machine (one set for each group) and cut apart into 69 separate cards. Place these questions in an envelope or manila folder marked Cell Trek Questions.

To protect the game board, glue it on cardboard and have it laminated. Multiple boards and worksheets can be made to give every group of students a board and a cell part worksheet.

A die is needed to determine the number of times a person moves on the board, and any object can represent the marker each player moves. Two to four students can play this game. Assign a student to ask the questions and give out the organelles.

As an incentive, you may want to award extra test points to the winner of each group.

CELL TREK—REVIEW BOARD GAME ON THE CELL

Directions

Cell Trek can be played by two to four persons. One person must serve as the question giver and/or distributor of the organelles.

Materials

One die

Cell Trek Game Board (one board per two to four players)

A marker of any type for each player

One Student Cell Worksheet (19-4) for each player

The student who will serve as the question giver should gather these materials:

Envelope of organelles cut out from the Cell Part Worksheet

Envelope of question cards

Purpose of the Game

Each student will try to collect cut-out organelles to place on his or her cell worksheet. Organelles are earned as students land on them on the game board and correctly answer a question about the cell. Each time students receive an organelle, they place it in the proper location on the worksheet. When someone lands on an organelle he or she has already collected, the turn goes on to the next player. The game is over when a player has collected all of the organelles during his or her cell trek adventures.

To Begin the Game

Each player should place his or her marker anywhere on the game board. Each person will roll the die. The person rolling the highest number will go first, followed by the next highest number, etc. To begin the game, the first player rolls the die. He or she moves the marker this number of spaces. If the player lands on an organelle, he or she can attain that organelle by correctly answering a question from the question giver. The question giver draws a question from the envelope and reads it aloud. If the player answers this question correctly, the question giver will remove that organelle from the organelle envelope and give it to the player. The player will place this organelle in the proper location on the Student Cell Worksheet. (*Note:* Answers are provided in parentheses at the bottom of each card.)

The game continues in this order. If a student fails to answer a question correctly, he or she does not receive an organelle but is not penalized. You will notice that the game board has some spaces that cause players to lose organelles or gain other players' organelles.

End of the Game

Once a player has completed the Cell Worksheet, the game is over and that player is declared the winner.

CELL TREK GAME BOARD

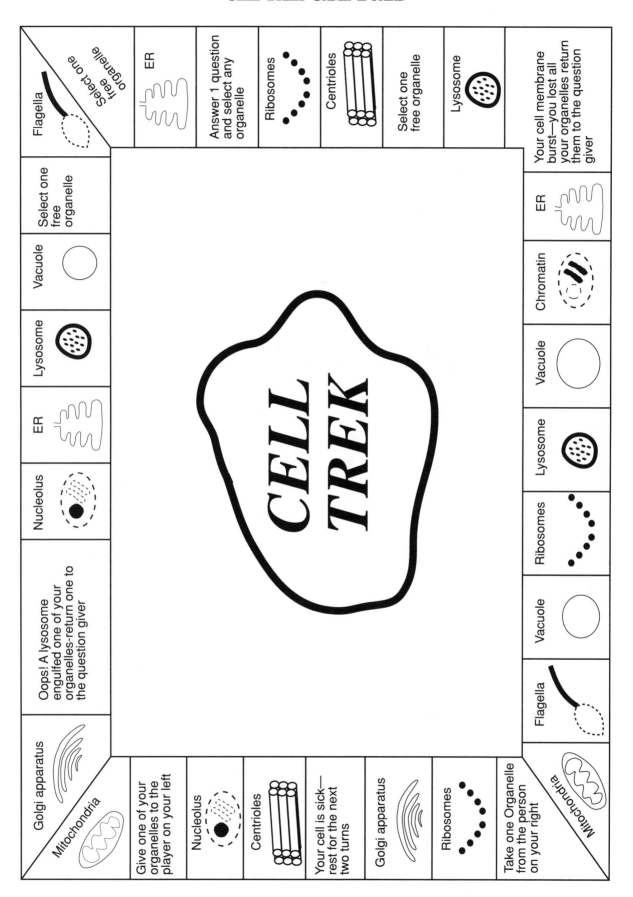

© 1994 by The Center for Applied Research in Education

235

STUDENT CELL WORKSHEET

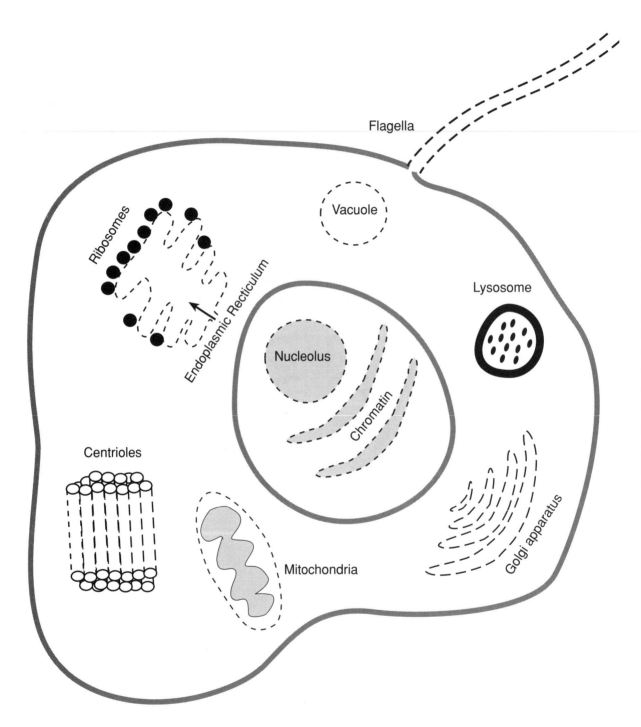

CELL PART WORKSHEET

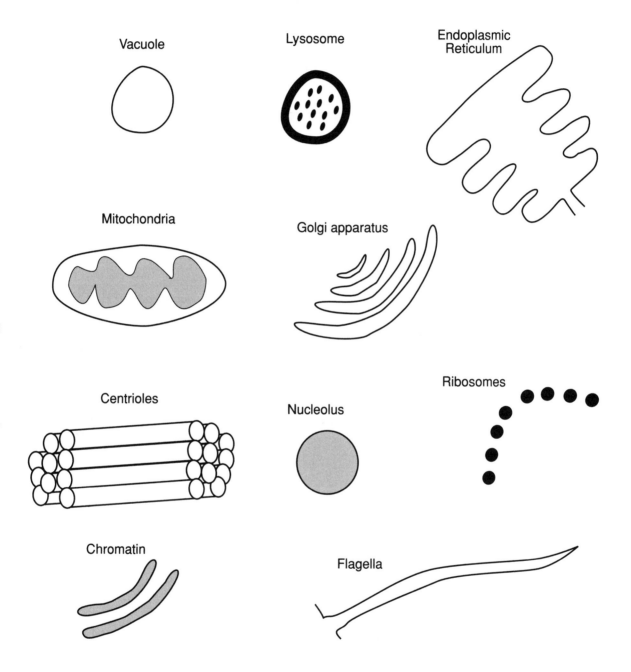

Vacuole

Lysosome

Endoplasmic Reticulum

Mitochondria

Golgi apparatus

Ribosomes

Centrioles

Nucleolus

Chromatin

Flagella

1 Leucocytes are also called _____ blood cells. (white)	**2** _____ is the organelle that transports and releases secretory material. (Golgi apparatus)	**3** A(n) _____ is a motile process on a spermatozoan. (flagellum)
4 A dendrite conducts impulses _____ the neuron's cell body. (toward)	**5** A _____ is a group of cells with a common function. (tissue)	**6** Name the pigment that carries oxygen. (hemoglobin)
7 DNA is the molecule in the nucleus that holds _____ information. (genetic)	**8** *Avascular* means that the tissue does not have _____. (blood vessels)	**9** Which organelle is known as the cellular garbage disposal? (lysosome)
10 What structure in the nucleus makes RNA? (nucleolus)	**11** A red blood cell is also called a(n) _____. (erythrocyte)	**12** Adipose cells are commonly called _____ cells. (fat)

13

_____ tissues are specially adapted to collect and transmit information.

(Nerve)

14

_____ cells may reach up to three feet in length.

(Nerve)

15

The plasma membrane is made of a double layer of _____.

(phospholipids)

16

What is the protoplasm of a muscle cell called?

(sarcoplasm)

17

In the immature stage, a _____ has a nucleus and organelles, but it loses them upon maturity.

(red blood cell)

18

_____ are networks of protein filaments that maintain the shape of a cell.

(Cytoskeleton)

19

_____ are groups of tissues with a common function.

(Organs)

20

The cells of this basic tissue type undergo rapid mitosis and replace themselves frequently: _____.

(epithelium)

21

Name the botanist that first described the workings inside the cell membrane.

(Robert Brown)

22

Nonliving accumulations of cell products like fat and waste in a cell are called _____.

(inclusions)

23

What projections on the respiratory tract help bring mucus out of the lungs when you cough during congestion?

(cilia)

24

The basic unit of structure of an organism is the _____.

(cell)

25 The plasmalemma is also called the _____. (plasma membrane)	**26** _____ is the powerhouse of the cell. (Mitochondria)	**27** _____ are also called "protein factories." (Ribosomes)
28 Which organelle is found in great abundance in muscle cells because of energy requirements? (mitochondria)	**29** The cell body of a neuron is the _____. (soma)	**30** Small, hairlike, motile projections on the cell are called _____. (cilia)
31 Which tissue type has cells that line and protect the surface of organs? (epithelial)	**32** What type of tissue is bone and cartilage? (connective)	**33** Which organelle is responsible for cellular respiration? (mitochondria)
34 What do ribosomes synthesize? (protein)	**35** What does smooth ER synthesize? (lipids and carbohydrates)	**36** ATP is a molecule in the cell that provides the cell with _____. (energy)

37 The inner membrane of mitochondria is folded into extensions called _____. (cristae)	**38** _____ is the ingestion of liquid into the cell with the help of the cell membrane. (Pinocytosis)	**39** Glands that produce steroids and other hormones will have a large amount of _____ ER. (smooth)
40 The miniature circulatory system of a cell is called the _____. (endoplasmic reticulum)	**41** _____ is the organelle that functions in cell division. [Centrosome (centriole)]	**42** The _____ is the network of canals that connects the plasma membrane to the nuclear membrane and transports materials. (endoplasmic reticulum)
43 An axon conducts nerve impulses _____ the cell body of a neuron. (away from)	**44** _____ is the organelle called the storage chamber of the cell. (Vacuole)	**45** These cells comprise the tissue type that produces movement in the body: _____. (muscle)
46 _____ cells compose the lining of the mouth, esophagus, and skin. (Epithelial)	**47** _____ tissue provides support, flexibility, transport, and defense for an organism. (Connective)	**48** Sarcolemma is the plasma membrane of a _____ cell. (muscle)

© 1994 by The Center for Applied Research in Education

49 _____ is the study of the structure of an organism. (Anatomy)	**50** Name the scientist who discovered the import-ance of the cell wall. (Theodor Schwann)	**51** Name the scientist who discovered that the protoplasm and nucleus are important parts of the cell. (Matthias Schleiden)
52 Exocytosis is the passage of material _____ the cell. (out of)	**53** _____ are living perm-anent structures with specialized functions vital to the cell. (Organelles)	**54** _____ transport across the plasma membrane requires no energy expenditure. (Passive)
55 The invention of this piece of equipment permitted viewing of cellular organelles: _____. (electron microscope)	**56** _____ is the taking in of bacteria and foreign bodies into a cell and storing them in the vacuole. (Phagocytosis)	**57** _____ is the term that describes how the plasma membrane allows only certain substances to enter and exit the cell. (Selective permeability)
58 These organelles are very abundant during mitosis: _____. [Centrosomes (centrioles)]	**59** White blood cells have a large number of these organelles because of their role as scavenger cells of the body: _____. (lysosomes)	**60** Which has more mito-chondria: a sperm cell, or liver cell? Explain why. (liver—because it needs more energy to meet its needs)

© 1994 by The Center for Applied Research in Education

61

_____ are scientists who study cells.

(Cytologists)

62

Another name for a nerve cell is a _____.

(neuron)

63

_____ was the scientist who coined the term *cell.*

(Robert Hooke)

64

_____ is the jellylike material inside the cell.

(Cytoplasm)

65

95% of adipose tissue is composed of _____.

(fat globules)

66

_____ is the study of the function of the cell.

(Physiology)

67

Which organelle are called "suicide sacs"?

(lysosomes)

68

What makes the ER rough?

(ribosomes)

69

_____ is the movement of molecules from a place of greater to lesser concentration.

(Diffusion)

LESSON 20: CHANGES AND ADAPTATIONS

20–1 CHANGING WITH THE TIMES
Content on Adaptations

Adaptations—Changes for the Better

Why do ducks have webbed feet while horses have hooves? Why do roses have thorns while trees have thick bark? Why do birds fly south for the cold winter months, and why do humans shiver when they are cold? These questions plagued scientists even before the nineteenth century. In 1809, the French naturalist Jean Lamarck first attempted to answer these questions. Lamarck stated that organisms recognize the need to acquire a trait that would adapt them to a changing environment. He gave the name *acquired characteristics* to these traits.

In 1859, Charles Darwin challenged this theory. Darwin refuted the explanation that organisms acquire special traits in response to the environment and then pass these traits on to their offspring. In his book, *The Origin of the Species,* Darwin wrote that the variations rather than the acquired characteristics are inherited by offspring. These variations (genetically controlled characteristics) that increase an organism's ability to survive long enough to produce offspring were later called adaptations. Darwin went on to say that individuals with adaptive traits have a greater chance than other individuals to survive and pass on their traits to their offspring. This statement summarized Darwin's new concept of natural selection.

Fit to Survive

Darwin explained that organisms produce more offspring than can possibly survive. Only some of these offspring will survive and reproduce. The organisms that survive will be the ones that are better equipped to function in the environment. Survival of organisms will involve competition among offspring for food, sunlight, space, etc. The organisms that have the favorable variations (adaptations) in a specific environment usually survive in great numbers. These variations are the traits that make an individual different from another individual of the same species. These variations are controlled by genes. These surviving organisms reproduce and make a new generation of better adapted individuals. Nature will, in turn, drop out any variations that harm or do not benefit a living organism. This explanation by Darwin is known today as survival of the fittest.

Darwin had no knowledge of modern genetics when he first proposed his theory. He could not offer an explanation of how variations (adaptations) are produced. He only knew they did exist. Today we know that mutations are the source of new traits that help living things survive. A mutation is any change in the DNA code of an organism that produces a different trait than what is expected. Adaptations are the result of this process. All mutations are not helpful, nor are they planned. Mutations are random changes in the chromosomes due to chance. The variation that results is not related to the present need of the organism in nature. The new trait coded on the genes of the chromosomes will either help, hurt, or not affect the new individual. If the trait increases the probability of survival, it will be retained and passed on to future offspring. Otherwise, the new trait will eventually be discarded by nature.

Mutant Manchester Moths

The concept of natural selection was illustrated in Manchester, England in the nineteenth century. Before 1850, a population of light-colored moths existed in this town, but by 1895 almost all the moths were dark in coloration. What caused the change from light to dark moths? The Industrial Revolution helps to explain this reversal of moth color. Soot from factories covered rocks and trees in the countryside during this period. When the light-colored moths landed on these now darkened surfaces, they were visible to predators that previously could not see them. This increased visibility caused more and more of the light moths to be eaten by predators. The relatively small number of dark moths that existed in Manchester at that time could hide themselves as they blended with the soot-covered structures. In turn, the dark moths survived and reproduced more moths like themselves. The light-colored moths did not live to reproduce as they had in the past. This resulted in a dominance of dark moths as the twentieth century approached.

To better understand natural selection, it is important to realize that it can only occur when a genetic variation is already present in the environment. Since dark moths already existed in small numbers in 1850, natural selection could proceed. The amount of time required for a complete reversal depends on the reproductive capabilities of an organism. Moths accomplished this reversal in less than 50 years, while organisms like bacteria can accomplish this in hours or days. This helps explain why some type of bacteria become resistant to particular antibiotics so quickly. Humans require hundreds or thousands of years to undergo an evolution of comparable magnitude.

Box Puzzle Adaptations

Vocabulary puzzle on *Changing with the Times*

Directions

After reading the clues, complete the puzzle by filling in the correct word in the box puzzle.

Clues

1. Variations in an organism are controlled by information in the _____ located on the chromosomes of an organism.

2. Offspring of an organism will engage in _____ for food and space, with the best-adapted individuals surviving this engagement.

3. A genetically controlled characteristic later known as an adaptation was called a _____ by Charles Darwin.

4. This is the scientist who proposed the theory of survival of the fittest.

5. The genetically controlled characteristics that increase an organism's chance for survival are called _____.

6. A change in the DNA code of an organism that produces a trait different from what was exp ected is called a(n) _____.

7. _____ _____ is also called survival of the fittest.

8. The scientist who believed that organisms recognize a need to acquire a trait that would adapt them to a changing environment, and thus acquire that trait in life, was _____.

9. The amount of time required for a species of organism to completely reverse a trait it possessed previously depends on the _____ capabilities of that species.

10. Nature will dispose of adaptations that are _____ or do not affect the ability of the organism to survive.

20–2 PLANT PRODUCTION
Project on Plant Adaptations

Objective

Students will create a plant that has adaptations that enable it to survive in a designated set of environmental conditions.

Teacher Notes

The teacher should cut 10 slips of paper and write a number from 1 through 10 on each slip of paper. The numbers should then be placed in a paper bag. The numbers in the bag correspond to the numbers found on Chart 1.

Possible Evaluation Scale

Correctness of information on the poster	20 points
Design and creativity of poster	20 points
Neatness and colorfulness of poster	15 points
Amount of research done	10 points
Information presented on Chart 1	20 points
Oral presentation and ability to explain the design of the plant	15 points
Total	100 points

PLANT PRODUCTION
Project on Plant Adaptations

Introduction

Animals are not the only organisms that possess special adaptations that enable them to survive. Plants are often equipped with special mechanisms for protection. Thorns (sharply pointed woody branches) on shrubs and prickles (pointed outgrowths of stems) on roses protect these plants from being consumed by herbivores. These protections are used by plants to puncture and scratch predators as a line of defense. Cacti have specialized leaves called spines to discourage grazing animals from dining on these fluid-filled delicacies in the dry desert environment.

Mushrooms, members of the fungi family, are sometimes equipped with poison to discourage animals from consuming them. Even though all mushrooms are not poisonous, only the most keen observer can distinguish a poisonous from a nonpoisonous species. The inability to make this determination discourages most animals from consuming mushrooms in the field.

Plants, such as nettles, have tips on the stems and leaves that break off when touched. These nettles release a hypodermic-size injection of fluid that causes stinging and swelling. Poison ivy is another plant that discourages predators by giving off an irritating sensation upon touch. A plant called milkweed protects itself from predators by giving off a terrible taste when being eaten by animals. These adaptations all work by offending the senses of predators.

Even such simple things as the thick, woody bark on trees is used to protect trees from injury and demise. Thick leaves (called succulents) on jade plants store food for later use if conditions become unfavorable for a time. Plants called insectivores (such as the pitcher plant) can obtain nutrients in boggy areas by eating insects to obtain the needed nitrogen for their diet, even though they can photosynthesize their food.

Plants like the pine tree have adapted to temperature extremes by having needles rather than leaves. These needles have a small surface area covered with a thick, water-resistant cuticle that is resistant to freezing. These needles can remain on the tree when the weather is cold. Jade plants (succulents) are not found in these cold environments because they are extremely susceptible to freezing. The jade plants are more commonly found in the subtropical desert.

Plants called epiphytes (such as orchids and bromeliads) exist in the tropical rain forest, where they obtain moisture and nutrients from the air. These plants have developed aerial roots and can live in tall trees.

These are only a few of the adaptations plants possess. Hopefully, this information will give you an idea of how to design your plant.

Materials

Poster board

Markers and crayons

Reference books on plants and adaptations

Reference books on biomes

PLANT PRODUCTION *(continued)*

Procedure

1. Select a partner to work with on this project.

2. Draw a number from the paper bag that the teacher provides. This number will correspond to the plant in Chart 1 you will be designing.

3. Read the information in the chart about your plant. Use the reference material provided to find information about adaptations a plant might develop that would enable it to survive under the conditions listed. Your plant should be able to protect itself from predators and disease, get adequate sunlight, adjust to temperature extremes, gather nutrients, and obtain water.

4. The project will be completed by thoroughly filling in Chart 2. After completing the chart you should draw, color, and name your special plant on a piece of poster board. This poster will be shown to the class and explained by you and your partner at a later date.

CHART 1

Plant #	Predators	Exposure to sunlight	Soil nutrients (good / fair / poor)	Temperature (degrees F)	Rainfall (inches)	Other information
1.	Insects	Open field with tall grass	Good	70–100	25	Fires
2.	Fungi	Full	Epiphyte - (soil not requried)	70–95	300	Air pollution
3.	Deer	Moderate	Poor	10–90	60	Soil erosion
4.	Bison	Extreme	Poor	40–70	10	Droughts
5.	Grazing animals	Great	Poor	–30 to 110	3	Droughts Fires
6.	Root parasites	Poor	Poor Little nitrogen	50–85	50	Boggy area
7.	Fungi and fish	Poor	Poor	40–90	N/A	Underwater plant
8.	Birds	Great	Fair	50–80	15	Wind erosion
9.	Vines that strangle trees	Moderate	Fair	–20 to 30	10	Freezing
10.	Caterpillar	Full	Good	30–80	60	Toxic waste dump nearby

Example of Plant Adaptation Project

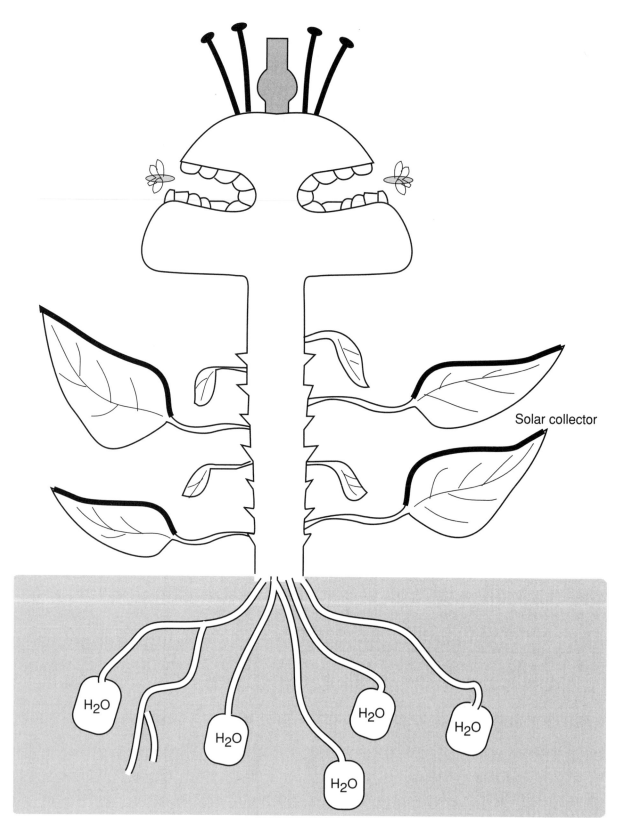

Solar collector

PLANT PRODUCTION *(continued)*

Chart 2

Your name: _____ Date: _____

Information given about your plant:

Plant #: _____ Predators: _____

Sunlight exposure: _____ Soil nutrients: _____

Temperature range: _____ Rainfall range: _____

Other special conditions listed: _____

_____

Name you gave your plant and the reason: _____

_____

Describe the following adaptations the plant you designed would possess to help it survive in the conditions you listed above:

Features of the stem: _____

_____

_____

Features of the leaves: _____

_____

_____

Features of the roots: _____

_____

_____

Average height of the plant as an adult: _____

Describe what will be the most difficult problem your plant will encounter for survival:

_____

What biome would be the most likely candidate to house one of the plants you designed?

_____ Explain your reason: _____

_____

Now write a scenario that describes how the special features ("Other information" category) would be accommodated in the environment:

20–3 MONSTROUS MUTATIONS
Lab on the Effect of Random Mutations on Animals' Survival Skills

Objectives

Students will demonstrate and evaluate how random mutations affect the survival skills of a species.

Teacher Notes

You may wish to make up your own mutations if the ones suggested in this activity are not compatible to the materials available in your school. You may also wish to vary the layout of the classroom or conduct this activity outdoors. Collection of the materials for the activity should begin prior to the day of the activity. In preparation for the activity, write the letters A through H on slips of paper (one letter per slip). These letters will correspond to the letters in Chart 1 in the "Procedure" section.

Figure A shows a suggested configuration for preparing the classroom for this activity. You should place a blanket in the center of the room. Three peanuts for each student should be placed on the blanket. Place plastic bowls with lids or tennis ball cans with lids in different locations around the room. These bowls or cans represent the storage locations for different groups. You should assign a group a home location, as in Figure A.

MONSTROUS MUTATIONS

Lab on the Effect of Random Mutations on Animals' Survival Skills

Introduction

The process of evolution involves changes in the genetic makeup of a population over a period of time. The production of the new genetic material results from alterations in the DNA of a developing organism. This random alteration of DNA from parent to offspring (called mutations) produces variable characteristics in offspring. These mutations are not related to the present needs of an organism but are merely the result of chance.

As a result of mutations, some organisms in a population will have a set of genes that are better suited to the current environmental conditions. These organisms will have a better chance of surviving and reproducing offspring. This is the manner in which the genes better suited to the environmental conditions are passed on to future generations.

Unfortunately, not all mutations are helpful. Some alterations of DNA result in characteristics that harm the organism or do not affect it at all. Lizards' ability to change color is an example of a beneficial mutation that was retained and passed on to future generations. A fawn born white instead of brown as the result of a mutation would probably not survive long enough to reproduce because of its inability to conceal itself from predators. Such harmful mutations do not remain in the population long enough to be passed on to future offspring.

The variable characteristics caused by mutations that are retained and passed on to future offspring are called adaptations. These adaptations can be structural, physiological, or behavioral. Some structural adaptations found in animals provide defense mechanisms for the organism. Antlers on deer, quills on porcupines, and venomous glands on rattlesnakes are a few examples of structural adaptations. A cat arching its back and an owl ruffling its feathers are examples of behavioral adaptations. A physiological adaptation in an organism is characterized by the reduction of the flow of warm blood to the skin in response to cold weather.

Why do organisms adapt? They do this in response to the need to obtain energy, nutrients, and water from the environment. Adaptations are necessary to protect animals from predators and ward off disease-causing organisms. These adaptations allow them to compete with other organisms for limited resources.

At the start of the activity, your teacher will have the room arranged like the picture in Figure A. A blanket in the center of the room and three peanuts on the blanket for each student will represent the food supply. Plastic bowls with lids will represent the location for food (peanut storage). The teacher will have the home location for each group marked as shown in Figure A.

Prelab Questions

1. What is a mutation?

2. Explain why mutations are random occurrences rather than planned alterations.

3. An opossum's ability to play dead when approached by a predator is an example of a _____ adaptation.

MONSTROUS MUTATIONS *(continued)*

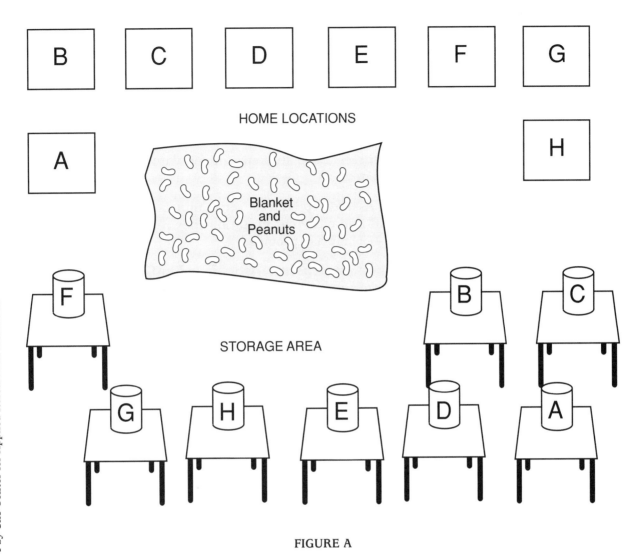

FIGURE A

4. A bird's ability to fly south when winter weather approaches is an example of a _____ adaptation.

5. The growth of a heavy coat of hair by an organism in response to cold temperatures is an example of a _____ adaptation.

6. On the back of this sheet, name five adaptations not mentioned in the "Introduction" section.

Materials

Nine dry peanuts in a shell (per group of three students)

Blanket for the peanuts

Table or desk

One potato chip or tennis ball can with a lid or plastic container with lid (per group of three students)

15 plastic knives

MONSTROUS MUTATIONS *(continued)*

Several rolls of duct tape

Three socks

Six pairs of goggles

Paper bag containing the letters A through H on slips of paper

Cotton

Stop watch

Procedure

1. Students should form groups of threes. Each student will simulate an animal that can only digest peanuts as its food source.

2. Unfortunately, random mutations have produced some unusual characteristics in recent offspring. Each group will find out what mutation they represent by selecting a letter from the paper bag the teacher has provided.

3. The letter drawn will correspond to the characteristics listed in Chart 1. This letter will also represent the letter of your group's home location and storage can. Figure A will help you locate these areas.

CHART 1

Letter drawn by groups	Characteristic produced by mutation
A	Long fingernails (produced by plastic knives taped to fingers with duct tape)
B	No fingers (produced by placing a sock over each hand and taping the hand closed)
C	Lack of peripheral vision (produced by putting on goggles and stuffing cotton in the sides to prevent viewing from the side)
D	Hands fused together in front of body (produced by placing hands together in front of body and taping them together)
E	Feet and ankles fused together (produced by taping the ankles tightly together with duct tape)
F	No arms (produced by taping the arms down to the side of the body with duct tape)
G	Arms fused together behind the back at the wrists (produced by placing arms behind the back and taping tightly at the wrists)
H	Blind (produced by using goggles taped over securely with duct tape)

4. Each group should attain the proper materials and prepare itself to represent the characteristic produced by the letter of the mutation selected from the paper bag. (See Figure B for an illustration of the mutations.)

FIGURE B

5. Each group should begin the activity at the specified location in Figure A. The goals of each group are to

   A. Gather the food (nine peanuts per group).

   B. Store the food for later use (place the nine peanuts in your letter-designated plastic container with lid or tall can with lid).

   C. Retrieve the food at a later time (remove the nine peanuts from the container and return with the peanuts to the home location).

   D. Process and consume the food (remove the peanuts from the nine shells and consume these peanuts).

6. To begin the activity, each group should position itself at its specified home location. The teacher will start the stop watch and each group will begin with food gathering. Group members should proceed to the blanket containing the peanuts and gather nine peanuts per group. These nine peanuts should then be transported to a plastic con-

tainer or tall can. The nine peanuts should be placed in the container and the lid placed securely on top. The three group members should return to their home location. At this point, the group will proceed back to the plastic container to retrieve its food. Once the group has removed all nine peanuts, it will return to the home location. The group will open the peanut shells and remove the contents. Each group member will consume the contents of three of the peanut shells. At the completion of this process, the amount of time required to achieve this will be recorded.

7. Each group will continue until the peanuts have been consumed and time has been recorded.

8. The teacher will write the times required for each group to complete the process on the chalkboard.

9. Groups will answer the postlab questions.

Postlab Questions

1. Which characteristic caused by mutation appeared to be the most detrimental to the survival of a species? Explain your answer.

2. Which characteristic caused by mutation appeared to have the least detrimental effect on an organism's ability to survive? Explain your answer.

3. What activity in nature is represented by placing peanuts in the plastic bowl?

4 Select an animal in nature and describe how it gathers, stores, retrieves, and processes its food.

5. Make up an adaptation that might result from a mutation that would enable the organism to achieve these goals.

6. Make up an adaptation that might result from a mutation that would prevent the organism from achieving these goals.

LESSON 21: TREE GROWTH

21–1 BARKING UP THE RIGHT TREE
Content on Trees

Judging a Tree by Its Bark

Think about this riddle: What obtains energy directly from the sun, has an automatic humidifier, manufactures its food, is powerful enough to support tons of weight, produces oxygen and water, and has a built-in thermostat? If you guessed "tree," you were right on target. A simplified definition of a tree is a woody plant with a trunk. This definition does not seem to take in the complexity of the internal structure of a tree.

Let's journey into the complex world of the tree for a minute. When you look at the giant oak tree, one of the first things you notice is the trunk. You can easily see that the trunk supports the branches and twigs and allows the leaves to be exposed to the sunlight. Scars and other imperfections on the tree can give you some indication about the history of the tree. Scars and broken branches on the tree can be caused by a variety of agents. Insects, wildlife, wind damage, fire, or even a vehicle might be the culprit. But what goes on inside the trunk? As you travel inside the trunk of the tree, you see cells (called xylem cells) that transport water and minerals and cells (called phloem cells) that transport food.

How "Wood" You Determine the Age of a Tree?

Xylem and phloem cells are added yearly by a tiny growth ring of cells just inside the bark called the cambium layer. The phloem is located on the outer edge of the cambium, while xylem is located inside the cambium. The part of the tree we know as wood is composed of thousands of dead xylem cells. In fact, *xylem* is the Greek word for "wood." Cambium produces xylem cells in the spring and the summer. Due to more favorable conditions, the xylem cells that form in the spring are usually larger than those formed in the summer. These spring and summer xylem cells are seen as alternating light (spring) and dark (summer) bands. The tree will add one light and one dark band each year. By counting the number of bands called growth rings, you can determine the age of the tree. The wider each ring, the greater the growth of the tree during that particular year. As time goes by, new xylem is formed, and the width of the trunk is increased.

Phloem cells are the innermost bark tissue, but they do not increase the width of the tree. Instead, the new phloem pushes the existing phloem against the outer tissues, crushing the older phloem cells.

Water Pipes and Food Factories

At the base of the tree, you find the roots. The roots serve to anchor the tree and absorb minerals and water from the ground. The root of a tree has amazing strength. It is estimated that a growing root that is 3 inches wide and 4 feet long can lift a 50-ton weight. The design of the root system varies from one tree type to another depending on the specific needs of the tree.

Extending from the branches, you observe the leaves. The leaves are the food factories of the tree. They convert water and carbon dioxide to glucose and oxygen through the process called photosynthesis. The leaves also rid themselves of excess water by transpiration, the evaporation of water from the leaves. It is believed that 99% of water drawn up the tree is transpired out through the leaves.

Pathogenic Invaders

Plants, like animals, are susceptible to attacks by other living organisms, which may live inside them or upon them. These parasitic organisms, which invade plant tissues and rob them of food or injure them in some manner, are called pathogens. The disturbances they bring about are called diseases. The principal agents responsible for many plant diseases are

1. Bacteria (an example is the bacterial blight of walnut)

2. Higher fungi (an example is the Dutch elm disease)

3. Parasitic flowering plants (an example is mistletoe on pines and oaks)

4. Animals (insects rob trees of nutrients and stunt their growth)

5. Viruses (an example is the tobacco mosaic virus)

6. Chemical agents (from atmospheric pollution or toxic chemicals in the soil)

Treatment of these diseases can be carried out in a variety of ways. Some of the principal methods include spraying and dusting for fungi and insects, soaking seeds in chemicals to kill bacteria, removing the infected trees from a field, destroying insects that carry bacteria and viruses, and introducing animals that feed on the pest organism into an area to destroy the pest (biological control method).

Tree-Mendous Benefits to Humans

Why are trees important to humans? The obvious reason is they make the oxygen we need to exist on earth. People plant a large variety of trees when landscaping their yard to provide shade from the summer sun and beauty to their lawn. Trees provide us with food in the form of many varieties of fruit. Trees provide us with wood products to build houses and furniture, and paper for schools and industry. They provide homes for animals such as birds and squirrels. Once trees die, they decompose into the soil and are reused by future plants and trees as vital nutrients and minerals. Even rotting logs can house insects and ants and become the den of certain animals. Trees play an important role in the energy cycle of the earth. If you remove the trees, you break the food chain and eventually the food web in the ecosystem. Organisms such as wood lice and forest bugs feed on materials from a tree. They are then preyed on by larger organisms and the cycle continues. Without the tree, the cycle never begins.

Trees also are used to make products important to humans. Paper is made from tree pulp. Pine sap is used to make resin, which is used for lacquers and adhesives. The neem, a native tree of Asia, is a powerful source for a new insecticide for the leaves of trees.

Trees serve a variety of useful functions for humans and the earth. As a responsible citizen of the earth, you should strive to protect our trees and help replenish those which are cut down for lumber.

WOOD YOU LEAVE HIM OUT ON A LIMB?—VOCABULARY ACTIVITY ON
BARKING UP THE RIGHT TREE

Directions

Read the word on the leaf, and circle the tree the leaf matches best.

Directions

Read the word on the leaf, and circle the tree the leaf matches best.

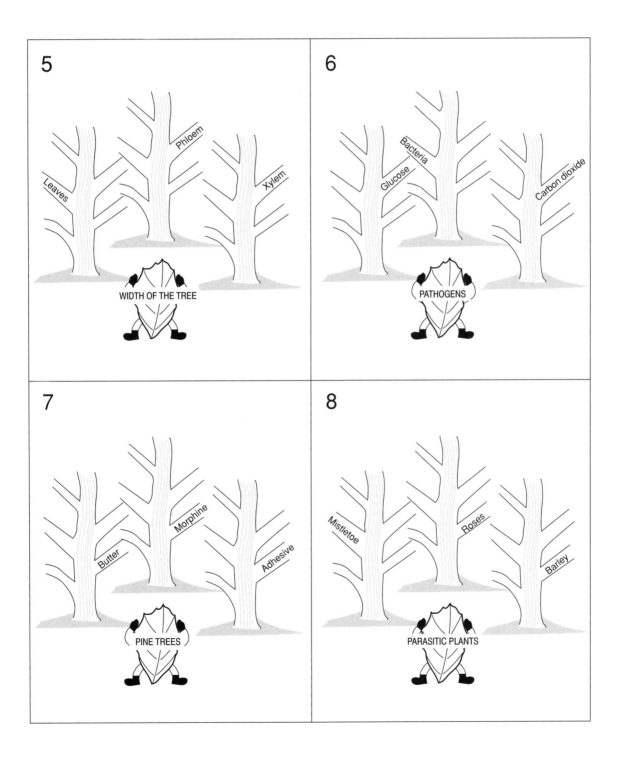

Directions

Read the word on the leaf, and circle the tree the leaf matches best.

21–2 A DEAD RINGER
Lab on Tree Growth Rings

Objectives

Students will determine the age of a tree from the growth rings in the stem of a sawed-off tree.

Teacher Notes

You can replace Figure B, which accompanies this lab, with actual samples of tree slices (obtained from a lumber company or sawmill). This will make the activity more realistic.

A DEAD RINGER
Lab on Tree Growth Rings

Introduction

You may have walked through the forest or even a neighbor's yard at some point and noticed a sawed-off tree trunk. If you examined it closely, you may have noticed a series of circular rings. The lightest part of the ring represents tree growth in the spring. The darkest part of the ring represents summer growth. The fall and winter do not add any new growth.

Wood is made up of tissues called xylem that transport water from the roots upward to the leaves. Xylem tissue is made from long, tube-shaped cells with side walls that have been thickened with a material called lignin. When the cells die, long, strong tubes thousands of cells long form. Thousands of these tubes are pushed together to make wood.

In the spring, the tree grows most rapidly and needs a great deal of water and minerals. For this reason, the xylem tubes are wide and thin walled. In the summer, growth slows and the xylem tubes are narrow and thick walled.

The growth rings can be counted to determine the age of the tree. When counting the rings, do not count the bark or the center. The number of rings will represent the age of the tree in years.

In years when water was plentiful, rings are large. Rings can also indicate disasters such as fires. Trees that have been exposed to fires will have black areas in their rings.

Prelab Questions

1. What is the difference between the light and dark growth rings?

2. What is the function of xylem?

3. What makes up wood?

4. What is lignin?

Materials

Figure A on measurement techniques
Drawings of the tree slices (Figure B)
Ruler (showing centimeters)
Chart 1 (the data table)

A Dead Ringer *(continued)*

Procedure

1. Obtain Figure B of the five slices of trees.

2. Obtain Chart 1 and complete it as you do the activities that follow.

3. Count the number of tree rings in tree slices A, B, C, D, and E. (Do not count the center or the bark of each slice.) Record the number of rings in Chart 1.

4. Take the ruler and measure the diameter across the tree stem (excluding the bark). Record this in the column "Diameter of tree" in Chart 1. See Figure A for the proper measurement technique.

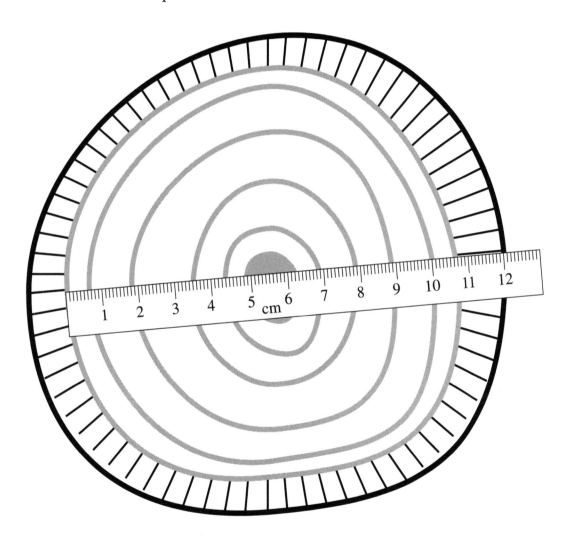

FIGURE A

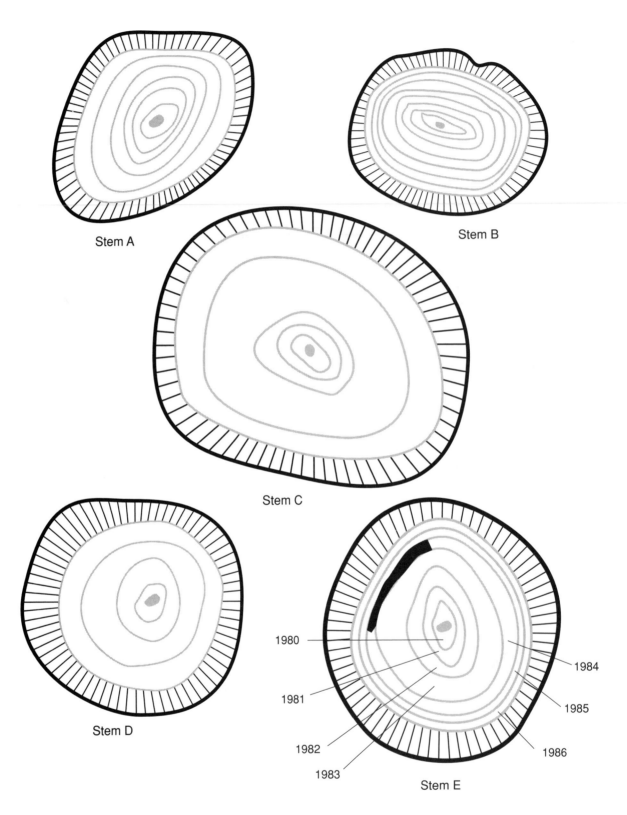

Stem A

Stem B

Stem C

Stem D

1980

1981

1982

1983

1984

1985

1986

Stem E

FIGURE B

A Dead Ringer *(continued)*

CHART 1

Data Table

Tree slice	Age of the tree when cut down	Diameter of tree (cm)
A		
B		
C		
D		
E		

Postlab Questions

1. Which stem was the oldest of the five stems?

2. Which stem was the youngest of the five stems?

3. Correlate the width of the stem with the age of the tree. In other words, are the wider stems necessarily older stems?

4. Which tree probably grew in the wettest area?

5. Which tree probably grew in the driest area?

6. Which stem has been exposed to a fire?

7. What year did the fire occur in the tree in number 6?

8. What year did Tree E have the most water?

9. What were the two driest years for Tree E?

21-3 LIFE STORY OF A TREE
Lab on the Vital Statistics of a Tree

Objectives

Students will learn the importance of trees to humans' existence on earth. In addition, they will learn to take the vital statistics of a tree.

Teacher Notes

When students select their trees, you will want to be sure that no two students have the same tree. If a student selects a tree with an usually wide circumference, another student may need to assist in the measurement. You can use a variety of field guides to help students identify the name of the tree.

LIFE STORY OF A TREE
Lab on the Vital Statistics of a Tree

Introduction

Over 10,000 years ago, before people began to farm, forests covered over half of the earth. Today that percentage has decreased to less than one third. As the number of humans has increased, billions of trees have been cut down to provide wood and land for farms and building structures. Different types of forests grow in different areas of the world depending on the climatic conditions.

Deciduous forests are characterized by trees that lose their leaves at certain times of the year. Oak trees and maple trees are often found in this type of forest. The leaves on the deciduous trees are wide and flat, and the wood is called hardwood. Many species of plants and animals use these trees for their habitat (home). In fact, a small oak forest can provide homes for over 4000 species of insects, plants, and birds.

Conifer forests consist of pine trees and fir trees. The leaves on the conifers are needle- or scalelike. Conifers do not lose their leaves and are referred to as evergreen trees. The wood obtained from a conifer is called softwood. Conifer forests that have grown naturally will contain of much more wildlife than conifer forests planted by humans.

The tropical rain forests grow near the equator and consist of evergreen trees. Over half of all the different kinds of animals and plants in the world live in the rain forests. The Amazon rain forest of South America is the largest tropical rain forest on earth. Over 41,000 species of insects can be found in a small patch of forest in South America.

The trees found in each type of forest have a significant role in the ecosystem. Humans depend on these trees for a variety of resources. Shelter, food, tools, fuel, paper, and wood are a few of the gifts trees give to humans. Trees also hold soil in place and help keep the air clean.

Fruit, coconuts, nuts, chocolate, cinnamon, spices, maple syrup, cork, rubber, medicines, and chewing gum are made from products produced by trees. Homes and furniture are made of wood, and wood is used primarily for fuel in some countries, such as India, to help prepare meals. Because of their fast growth patterns, conifer and eucalyptus trees are often used for wood to make paper. In fact, an edition of a daily newspaper can use wood from over 5000 trees. Trees not only provide humans with oxygen to breathe, but they clean pollutants out of the air by trapping dust in their leaves. The binding effect of the roots of trees helps hold soil in place and prevent washing away of the nutrients of the soil (erosion). Plants found in the tropical rain forests are used to make over 20% of our medicines.

Trees and forests are an important commodity to life on earth. With this in mind, it is essential to protect (conserve) trees. Every minute, an area of rain forest larger than the size of 15 football fields is destroyed for the purpose of clearing land for mining, logging, and farming. Not only are the tropical rain forests being destroyed, but forests in all parts of the world are being depleted (lowered in quantity) at an accelerated rate. Pollution, acid rain, fires, diseases, storms, and humans contribute to this depletion. Humans cut down trees to obtain wood for buildings and furniture and to clear land for buildings, industry, parking lots, farm land, etc.

Actions are presently being taken to save the tropical rain forests. National parks and reserves are being set aside where plants and animals can live safely. Removal of only the largest trees, rather than all the trees in an area (called selective logging), allows the forest to repair itself. Formation of extractive reserves, where people take out nuts, fruit, and rubber, has helped to control forest damage.

In the United States, forests are being restored by planting new trees. Planting the right type of trees can help provide a habitat for wildlife. People can grow trees from seeds or plant saplings (young trees). Planting native trees (the kind that grow naturally in our area) conserves our trees. Seeds can be collected from local trees in autumn and winter and planted about 1 inch deep in damp compost. When the seedling reaches about 4 inches in height, it can be planted outside.

Other helpful ways to conserve trees include recycling paper and paper products, buying recycled paper products, reusing paper bags, and adopting a tree near your home. By adopting a tree, you can do your part to protect the tree and watch it grow through the seasons. Remember, every little contribution helps if each individual participates in conservation.

Prelab Questions

1. Explain the difference between a conifer forest and a deciduous forest.

2. List five or more ways trees are useful to society.

3. What is the difference between deciduous trees and evergreen trees?

4. List three ways you can help conserve the trees of the world.

5. List three reasons humans are destroying tropical rain forests.

6. List three reasons humans are destroying deciduous forests.

Materials

Cardboard (from a box or crate) at least as long as your arm

Tape measure or ruler

Masking tape

Chair or stool

White paper

Crayons (of any color)

Guide books of native trees in your area

String

Scissors

Explanation of the Activity

In this activity, you will adopt a tree. You will perform a variety of investigations on this tree to write its life history. You should take care of your tree for the remainder of the

© 1994 by The Center for Applied Research in Education

year. Be sure it has adequate water. If it is a deciduous tree, select one with some leavesstill on the limbs. At the start of this activity, you should go outside and select your tree. After you have identified your tree (no one else should have the same tree you select), perform the following procedures and fill in the requested information on the Adopted Tree Data Sheet.

Procedure

Part A—How Tall Is Your Tree?

1. Obtain scissors, string, a tape measure, and a piece of cardboard at least as long as your arm.

2. Hold your left hand straight out in front of you at eye level. With the tape measure, measure the distance from your eye to your outstretched hand.

3. On the cardboard, draw a rectangle the length of the distance you measured and about 2 or 3 inches in width. Use your scissors to cut the rectangle out of the cardboard.

4. This cardboard rectangle will be used to estimate the height of your tree.

5. Locate your adopted tree and hold the rectangle upright at arm's length in front of you. Move backward and forward until the rectangle is lined up exactly with the top and bottom of the tree (see the illustration in Figure A).

6. Now take the string and lay it from the base of the tree to where you are now standing.

7. Using the tape measure, find the length of the string from where you are standing to the base of the tree. This will be the height of the tree. Record this information on the Data Sheet, Part A.

Part B—How Old Is Your Tree?

You can easily tell the age of a tree when it is cut down by counting the xylem growth rings. Each ring represents a year of growth. But it becomes a little more difficult to determine the age of a tree before it has been cut down. Instead of cutting the tree down to determine the age of the tree, you can measure its girth. The girth of the tree is the distance around (circumference) its trunk at a height of 5 feet from the ground. On average, most trees increase their girth by about 1 inch each year. The number of inches you get for the girth will be the approximate age of the tree in years.

FIGURE A

Procedure

Part B—How Old Is Your Tree?

1. Obtain a string, tape measure, and a chair.

2. Go outside to your adopted tree and measure up 5 feet from the base of the tree.

3. At this 5-foot point, you will use the tape measure to find the distance around the tree (its girth).

4. Wrap the string one time around the girth of the tree. You may have to stand on a chair or stool to accomplish this if it is uncomfortable (see the illustration in Figure B).

FIGURE B

5. Take the amount of string it took to perform this task and use the tape measure to find the circumference of the tree in inches. This will be the age of the tree. Record this information on the Data Sheet, Part B.

Part C—What Kind of Tree Have I Adopted? Bark and Leaf Rubbings

Different trees will have different bark patterns and leaf venation patterns. By looking at the pattern of a tree, you can determine the type of tree you are studying. You can use field guides of native trees in your area to help identify the tree in question.

Procedure

Part C—Bark and Leaf Rubbings

1. Obtain a crayon, your data page, and a tree field guide book.

2. To make a bark rubbing of your tree, place the section of your data sheet marked "Part C: Diagram of the Bark Rubbing" face up on the bark of the tree. Use your crayon to rub over the paper with steady pressure. You will have made an imprint of the bark.

3. Repeat this process by placing the section of the data sheet marked "Part C: Diagram of the Leaf Rubbing" face up on top of one of the leaves from your tree. Rub the crayon over the top of the paper to form an imprint of your leaf.

4. Use your tree field guide and the rubbing you did of the leaf and the bark to figure out what type of tree you have adopted. Write the name of the adopted tree in the blank that says "Common name of your tree."

Procedure

Part D—What Other Tree Trivia Exists?

Obtain the Adopted Tree Data Sheet and write your answers in the Adopted Tree Data Sheet under Part D—Trivia.

a. Are there any scars or unusual formations on the tree? If so, describe them.

b. Are there any nuts or fruits on or under your tree? If so, describe them.

c. Is there any evidence of animal life around your tree? If so, what is it?

d. What other information can you include about your adopted tree?

LIFE STORY OF A TREE *(continued)*

ADOPTED TREE DATA SHEET

Name of parents (your name): _____

Vital statistics of adopted tree

PART A: HEIGHT OF TREE

Length of the cardboard rectangle in inches	Distance from your eyes to the base of the tree in inches	Height of the tree in inches

PART B: GIRTH OF THE TREE

Length of the string required to go around the girth of the tree in inches	Age of the tree in years

LIFE STORY OF A TREE *(continued)*

PART C: DIAGRAM OF THE BARK RUBBING

LIFE STORY OF A TREE *(continued)*

PART C: LEAF RUBBING

Common name of your tree: _____

279

Life Story of a Tree *(continued)*

PART D: TRIVIA

Question A	Question B	Question C	Question D

LIFE STORY OF A TREE *(continued)*

Postlab Questions

1. If your adopted tree was ever cut down, how could you check to see if you estimated the age of the tree correctly in this lab?

2. List some things you could do to take care of your tree over the next year.

3. Taking into consideration the area in which your tree is located, list the agent that most threatens the life of your tree.

4. What animals might be affected if this tree were cut down? (To answer this, you may have to read about the animals that inhabit trees of this type.)

5. Look up your tree in the field guide and record the following information about your tree:

Scientific name of the tree: _____

Average height of an adult tree: _____

Average diameter of an adult tree: _____

Color of bark of the tree: _____

Fruits, berries, or nuts common to the tree: _____

Venation (distribution or arrangement of veins—simple, compound, palmate, pinnate) of the leaf of the tree: _____

Uses of the tree to humans: _____

_____

_____

_____

_____

_____

_____

_____

_____

_____

_____

_____

_____

Lesson 22: Ecology

22–1 RELATIONSHIPS IN LIFE
Content on Ecology

Populations and Communities

Nothing exists on this earth in isolation. Every living thing is part of a community of organisms that affect each other and their environment. In the field of ecology, people study the relationships between organisms and their environment, which includes both the physical and biological conditions under which an organism lives. The term *relationship* refers to interactions with the physical world as well as interactions with other organisms.

A group of the same organisms composes a population, and several populations living in an area form a community. An example of a community is a pond, which might contain populations of bluegills, bass, turtles, snakes, water striders, algae, and cattails. Tumbleweeds, cacti, rattlesnakes, kangaroo mice, skinks, and hawks might be members of a desert community.

Types of Relationships

The relationships among organisms in a community are both complex and varied. Some species develop symbiotic relationships with other species (that is, two or more organisms live together). There are several forms of symbiosis.

Mutualism. If symbiots help each other, the relationship between them is called mutualism. The clown fish and sea anemone have a mutualistic living arrangement. The sea anemone is a marine invertebrate that is attached to rock or coral. Its poisonous tentacles wave through the water in search of small fish as prey. The tiny orange and white striped clown fish swims freely into the dangerous anemone tentacles to rest or hide, and it is never stung (see Figure A). The anemone provides protection for the clown fish, and the clown fish often brings food particles to the anemone.

Commensalism. If two symbiots do not help each other, the relationship between them is called commensalism. The orchid plant is a commensal of trees in the rain forest. The orchid is an epiphyte, a plant that does not grow roots into the ground but gets all its nutrients from the air. The host tree is not benefited by its epiphyte, nor is the epiphyte helped by the tree.

FIGURE A. Clown fish and anemone.

Competition. Resources like food and space may be in short supply within a community, and many organisms compete with each other for access to these resources. One form of competition is predation, in which one organism (the predator) kills and eats another organism (the prey). Lions are predators that eat any animal they can catch. Another form of competition is parasitism, in which one organism (the parasite) feeds on another organism (the host). Tapeworms are very specialized parasites that live in the digestive tract of many organisms. Parasites rarely kill their host but may weaken it. Parasitoidism is a form of competition in which the larvae of one animal develop inside another animal, consuming the host as they grow. Many wasps lay their eggs inside the bodies of caterpillars. The eggs hatch and begin eating the caterpillar from the inside out.

The Sun's Energy

All living things require energy to maintain life, move, eat, digest, reproduce, and perform a host of other activities. The energy that keeps organisms alive comes from the sun. A very small fraction of the sun's energy shines on earth, but that little bit is enough to sustain life on this planet. Green plants, or autotrophs, have the ability to absorb the sun's energy and change it to chemical energy in the process of photosynthesis. They can do this because they contain the green pigment chlorophyll, and chlorophyll can capture the sun's energy so that carbon dioxide and water vapor are changed into glucose and oxygen. The sun's energy is then tied up in the bonds of the glucose molecules. When plants need energy for respiration, they use some of this glucose.

Energy Moves Through a Community

Organisms that don't have chlorophyll, like animals and fungi, cannot capture the sun's energy and make glucose and are called heterotrophs. Heterotrophs get the sun's energy by eating glucose-rich green plants. In the process of respiration, heterotrophs break down glucose into carbon dioxide, water vapor, and energy. Heterotrophs need energy just like plants for maintenance, growth, movement, and other life activities.

This transfer of energy from one organism to another is called a food chain. When a grasshopper eats a blade of grass, it is the first or primary consumer in a food chain. If a frog eats the grasshopper, the frog is the secondary consumer. The frog does not get as much energy from the grasshopper as the grasshopper got from the grass; therefore, the frog must eat several grasshoppers to maintain life. A food chain is a small part of a much larger picture called a food web. In reality, frogs are not the only organisms that eat grasshoppers. Birds also eat grasshoppers and are therefore secondary consumers also. Birds themselves may be eaten, or they may eat small frogs. This set of interrelationships between organisms creates a food web (see Figure B).

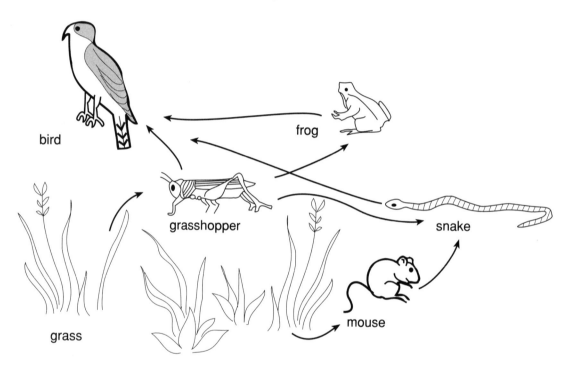

FIGURE B. Food web.

It is easy to visualize grazing food webs, those above ground. We can generally see all the organisms involved and have often witnessed their predator and prey relationships. However, a tremendous amount of energy falls to the ground in the form of dead vegetation, and this vegetation supports the detrital food chain. Detritus is dead or decaying matter. Organisms in this food web are extremely small, and we are often unaware of their existence.

Detritivores

The detrital food chain can be found in all ecosystems (communities of living things and their nonliving environment). Of the total amount of energy captured by some trees, 50% is used by the tree for respiration and maintenance, 13% is used by the tree for growth, 2% is consumed by plant eaters (herbivores), and 35% falls to the ground and enters the detrital food chain. The forest floor supports a detrital food web that includes mites, millipedes, springtails, cave crickets, and snails as herbivores. Earthworms live in the soil and eat bits of decaying organic matter. Predatory mites and spiders prey on these and other organisms. Saprophages, organisms that live on dead material, include fungi and bacteria. These organisms aid in the decomposition of leaves and other organic matter. During decomposition, some organic material is changed into animal, plant, fungal, and microbial tissue. Other material is broken down into simple compounds and returned to the soil. These compounds can then be used in different food chains (see Figure C). Decomposition is influenced by moisture, temperature, exposure, and other variables. Warm temperatures and plenty of water greatly increase microbial activity.

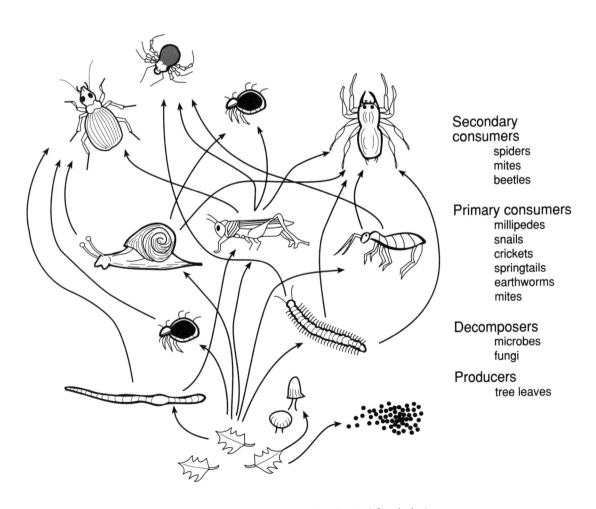

Secondary consumers
  spiders
  mites
  beetles

Primary consumers
  millipedes
  snails
  crickets
  springtails
  earthworms
  mites

Decomposers
  microbes
  fungi

Producers
  tree leaves

FIGURE C. Organisms in the detrital food chain.

Restoring Natural Cycles

Many people are learning that the decomposition of organic material is an important natural cycle in nature. When matter is removed from this cycle, there may not be enough nutrients available to sustain other food chains. Backyard and countywide composting is one way that we can help keep nutrients and organic matter in the soil. Most Americans send their garbage to landfills where it is entombed in layers of plastic and covered with soil. In sanitary landfills, no decomposition occurs because water and sunlight never reach the garbage. Some of our garbage can be composted. Composting is the biological decomposition of organic waste generated by people, such as food scraps, grass clippings, and leaves. Composting helps reduce the amount of garbage that we send to landfills.

ECOLOGICALLY SPEAKING—VOCABULARY ACTIVITY ON RELATIONSHIPS IN LIFE

Directions

Use the clues to fill in the following blanks. A message will appear in the vertical box when all clues are recorded.

1. _ _ _ _ _ _ _ _

2. _ _ _ _ _ _

3. _ _ _ _ _ _ _ _ _

4. _ _ _ _ _

5. _ _ _ _ _ _

6. _ _ _ _ _ _ _ _ _

7. _ _ _ _ _ _ _

8. _ _ _ _ _ _ _

9. _ _ _ _ _

10. _ _ _ _ _ _ _ _ _

11. _ _ _ _ _ _ _ _ _ _

12. _ _ _ _ _ _

13. _ _ _ _ _ _ _ _ _

14. _ _ _ _

15. _ _ _ _ _ _

VOCABULARY ACTIVITY ON *RELATIONSHIPS IN LIFE (continued)*

Clues

1. ___ consumers eat primary consumers.

2. ___ is the study of relationships between organisms and their environment.

3. When resources are limited, there is ___ between organisms.

4. A ___ kills and eats its prey.

5. An orchid is a(n) ___ that lives in a tree but does not help or harm the tree.

6. ___ are organisms that can make their own food.

7. ___ is dead or decaying matter.

8. Organisms that eat plants are ___.

9. A community of living and nonliving things forms a(n) ___.

10. The green plant pigment that can capture the sun's energy is ___.

11. ___ are organisms that cannot make glucose from carbon dioxide and water.

12. ___ is organic matter from kitchens and yards that decomposes.

13. ___ are ground-dwelling invertebrates that eat decaying organic matter.

14. The transfer of energy through a community is a food ___.

15. During decomposition, ___ matter is converted into animal and microbial tissue.

22–2 WHO LIVES IN OUR TRASH?
Activity on Composting and Food Chains

Objectives

Students practice deductive reasoning, learn the roles of organisms in food chains, and create a compost pile.

Teacher Notes

This lab is designed to teach students how to compost and is generally an outdoor activity. Since many teachers do not have access to an outdoor area, an indoor version of composting is presented in Part A, followed by an outdoor version in Part B. In Part A, students should put the same amounts of food and paper scraps in each soda bottle so that comparisons at the end of the activity will be valid.

To introduce students to the concept of food chains in a fun way, you can write the names of all members of a food chain or web on cards. Tape a card to each student's back. Cards with names of autotrophs should be green. Primary consumer names could be printed on yellow cards, secondary consumers on red cards, and decomposers on brown cards. Allow students to question each other to determine what name is taped on their backs. Students should ask questions that can be answered either yes or no and they should ask each person in the class only one question. When students discover the name taped to their back, they can put the card on their chest.

Have students arrange themselves in a four-level food chain, with all the autotrophs on one level, primary consumers on a second level, secondary consumers on a third level, and decomposers on a fourth level. Relationships among organisms on different levels can be indicated with yarn. If an organism (student) eats or is eaten by another organism (student), connect those two with a yarn string. Very quickly a complex set of strings and relationships is established. To extend this activity, pretend that one organism in the food web (caterpillar, for example) has been killed by a farmer's insecticide. Have that organism (student) drop all of his or her strings. What happens to the rest of the food web?

WHO LIVES IN OUR TRASH?
Activity on Composting and Food Chains

Introduction

Composting has regained popularity in the United States in recent years. Before the days of landfills and garbage haulers, everyone threw their food scraps and yard wastes into vacant fields and forests. The material decomposed there, and nutrients in the material were released to return to the soil.

Today we live in apartments and houses that are closely arranged. Since organic matter thrown into the yard is unsightly and undesirable, we package our trash and send it to the landfill. Landfills of the 1990s are not just holes in the ground. Our new sanitary landfills have layers of clay and plastic on the bottom to prevent contamination of water supplies. After garbage is added to the landfill, it is covered with soil and more plastic. Engineers design landfills to keep water and sunlight out. Unfortunately, garbage cannot decompose under these cool, dry conditions. Garbologists have found readable, 40-year-old newspapers and pink, edible-looking hot dogs in sanitary landfills.

Organic matter should be returned to the earth so that minerals and nutrients tied up in that material can be reused. We can help nature's recycling process by composting our own organic wastes. Food scraps, leaves, and grass clippings are ideal candidates for the compost pile. Organisms that are members of the detrital food chain will move into the decaying matter and speed up the decomposition process.

Part A—Indoor Composting

Materials

Three soda bottles with caps

Three sheets dark construction paper

Masking, electrical, or packaging tape

Plastic wrap

Soil from outdoors (Potting soil has been sterilized and will not work.)

Four or five worms

Packet of yeast mixed with warm water

Food scraps (Omit meat because it produces bad odors.)

Newspaper, torn into tiny strips

Three thermometers

Rubber bands

Procedure

1. Soak the three soda bottles in hot water to remove labels and base. Discard labels.

2. Punch holes in the caps and in the sides of the bottles. Cut off the bottom of each bottle.

© 1994 by The Center for Applied Research in Education

3. Label the bottles 1, 2, and 3.

4. Put the caps on the bottles, and invert them into the base (see Figure A).

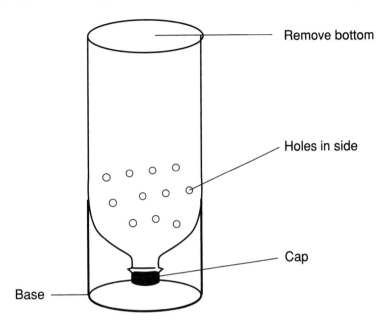

FIGURE A. Inverted soda bottle compost container.

5. Fill the bottles as follows:

    Bottle 1: Layer of dirt
    Layer of food and paper scraps
    Layer of dirt

    Bottle 2: Layer of dirt
    Layer of food and paper scraps
    Tablespoon of yeast and water mixture
    Layer of dirt

    Bottle 3: Layer of dirt
    Layer of food and paper scraps
    Four or five worms
    Layer of dirt

6. Insert thermometers into each bottle. Record the temperature in each bottle in the Temperature Data Table.

7. Cover the open end of each bottle with plastic wrap and secure with a rubber band. Wrap each bottle in dark construction paper.

8. Put the bottles in a warm place. Remove the plastic wrap and sprinkle the soil with water if it appears dry. Replace the plastic wrap.

9. Check the temperature in each bottle weekly. Record temperatures in the Temperature Data Table.

10. After 6 to 9 weeks, pour out the contents of all three bottles and compare the amount of decomposition that occurred in each.

Data and Conclusions

1. Record temperature changes in the Temperature Data Table.

TEMPERATURE DATA TABLE

	Bottle 1	Bottle 2	Bottle 3
Week 0			
Week 1			
Week 2			
Week 3			
Week 4			
Week 5			
Week 6			

2. Create a line graph that shows the temperature changes in each bottle over the experimental period. On your graph, draw Bottle 1 in red, Bottle 2 in blue, and Bottle 3 in green.

3. In which bottle did the most decomposition occur? Why?

4. Which bottle got the warmest during composting? Why?

5. Yeast is a fungus. Why was it added to Bottle 2?

6. What did the yeast in Bottle 2 eat?

7. What other organisms are in these bottles? From where did these other organisms come?

Part B—Create a Compost Pile Outdoors

Materials

Rake
Pitchfork
Leaves, grass clippings, wood chips, food scraps
Soil (not potting soil)
Thermometer
Wire fencing and four posts (optional)
1-gallon milk jug with cap, rinsed
Scissors
Petri dish or saucer
Alcohol or Bioperm™
Lamp

Procedure

1. In an area about 4 feet by 4 feet, clear the soil of weeds and grass. Build a fence around this area, if desired.

2. Cover the area with leaves and loose soil. Add a layer of food scraps, then more leaves and soil. Continue layering to a height of 3 feet. (Layers can be added all at once or over a period of weeks.)

3. Wet the compost pile until slightly moist.

4. Push the thermometer deep into the compost pile. Record the temperature in the Temperature Data Table.

5. Continue to record the temperature weekly.

6. With a pitchfork, turn the compost pile weekly to circulate air. This speeds up the process of decomposition. Sprinkle with water as needed.

7. After 6 to 9 weeks, spread out the compost pile and examine the contents.

8. Create a Soil Critter Catcher for collecting soil organisms by cutting the gallon milk jug in half. Punch holes in the cap and replace it on the top half. Invert the top half of the milk jug into the bottom half. Put a shovel full of compost soil and scraps in the inverted milk jug.

9. Put a lamp directly over the soil and a petri dish or saucer of alcohol or Bioperm™ under the cap (see Figure B).

10. Leave the soil in this position for 24 hours.

11. Remove the petri dish and place under the dissecting microscope.

12. Count and sketch the different kinds of organisms that you see.

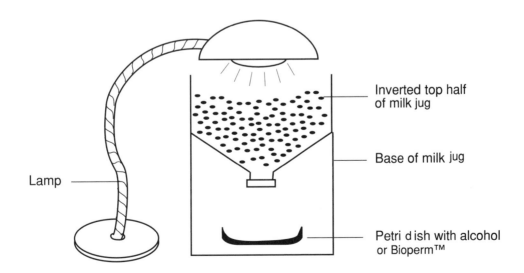

FIGURE B. Soil Critter Catcher made from an inverted milk jug.

WHO LIVES IN OUR TRASH? *(continued)*

Data and Conclusions

1. Record temperature changes in the following data table.

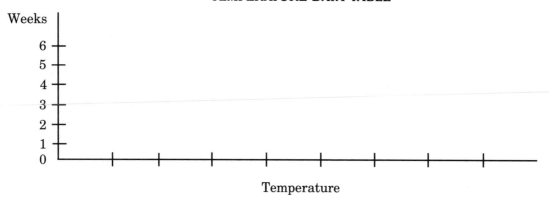

TEMPERATURE DATA TABLE

2. Graph the data from the Temperature Data Table. Put "Temperature" on the Y-axis and "Weeks" on the X-axis.

3. How did the temperature change in the compost pile over the experimental period?

4. What caused this change in temperature?

5. When you spread and examined the condition of food scraps placed in the compost pile, how had they changed?

6. What caused these changes in the composted material?

7. What organisms did you find living in the compost pile?

8. These organisms are members of the detrital food chain. From where did these organisms come?

9. What organisms do you suspect are present that you cannot see in the detrital food chain?

10. What would life on earth be like if there were no detrital food chain?

Answer Keys

Acrostics Vocabulary

```
 1   2   3   4   5   6   7   8       9  10  11  12  13  14  15

                         m
     b           a       o   m       f           p
     e   v   l   s   l   u   a       o   m   p   a   t   d
[f] [l] [o] [a] [t] [i] [n] [g]     [s] [a] [u] [c] [e] [r] [s]
 a   t   l   v   h   t   t   n       s   n   s   i   c   i   i
 u   s   c   a   e   h   a   e       i   t   h   f   t   f   n
 l       a       n   o   i   t       l   l       i   o   t   k
 t       n       o   s   n   i       e           c   n       i
 s       o       s   p   s   c                   i           n
                 p   h                           c           g
                 h   e                           s
                 e   r
                 r   e
                 e
```

KEY 1–2
Rockin' and Rollin' in the U.S.A.

Prelab Questions

1. Scientists compute the arrival time of shock waves at three or more stations around the world to locate the epicenter.

2. A seismologist studies earthquakes, while a geologist studies the makeup of the earth.

3. A P wave would accomplish this in 82 seconds (16.4 × 5), while an S wave would require 122 seconds (24.4 × 5) to accomplish this.

4. The greater the difference in arrival time, the farther the station is from the epicenter of the earthquake.

5. The place where the stress energy changes to wave energy, or the point of origin of an earthquake, is the focus. The point of the earth's surface directly above the focus is the epicenter.

6. Stored energy waiting to be released into moving energy

7. Scientists measure the energy given off by the earthquake on the Richter scale.

DATA TABLE

New York	57 seconds	712.5 km
Louisville	40 seconds	500 km
Pittsburgh	32 seconds	400 km

Postlab Questions

1. Pittsburgh; New York

2. Either North Carolina or Virginia would be acceptable answers.

3. Before. It would be closer to the epicenter than New York was.

4. Around 1120 km.

FIGURE B. Answer Key—Rockin' and Rollin' in the U.S.A.

KEY 2–1
The Scoop on Soil Vocabulary

1. Bedrock
2. Humus
3. Topsoil
4. Glacier
5. Abrasion
6. Gravity
7. Ventifacts
8. Migration
9. Windbreak
10. Sand
11. Dunes
12. Stream load
13. Vegetation
14. Conservation
15. Contour
16. Terracing
17. Mature
18. Weathering
19. Roots
20. Granite
21. Oxidation
22. Carbonization
23. Rust
24. Iron oxide

Word Trace Puzzle

Examples

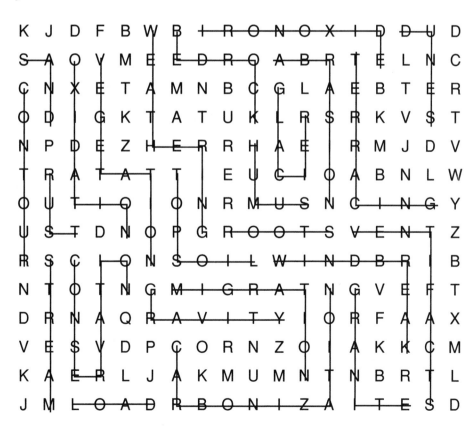

KEY 2–2
Lab on Weathering of Rocks

Prelab Questions

1. Physical weathering does not alter the composition of the rock, only the size. Chemical weathering creates new substances in its process.

2. Ice wedging is the movement of water into the cracks and pores of rocks. The water expands as it freezes and can crack and break rocks apart by this process.

3. Carbonization is the action of carbonic acid on rock materials. Carbonic acid can dissolve certain minerals such as calcium carbonate in limestone to create openings like the limestone caves.

4. Sandstone is more porous than granite.

5. Limestone contains calcium carbonate, which can be dissolved by acid; granite does not have this compound.

6. Type of rock, type and hardness of minerals in rock, and the climate

Results on the Data Table

Answers will vary, but the following should be noted:

In water, sandstone will be the only rock to gain mass. The other rocks will stay fairly constant in their measurements.

In vinegar, sandstone and granite will remain unchanged, but both marble and limestone will decrease in mass.

Postlab Questions

1. Sandstone. It is more porous and absorbs more water.

2. Limestone or marble. It is dissolved by acid.

3. Granite

4. Vinegar is stronger and quicker to work than carbonic acid.

5. Sedimentary—limestone, sandstone, marble; Metamorphic—granite

6. Yes. Climatic factors and materials in the air can cause rocks to weather more quickly.

7. Water represented rain and water flowing over rocks on earth, and vinegar represented the action of carbonic acid on rocks.

KEY 3–1
Crossword Puzzle

KEY 3–2
Hygrometer Lab

Prelab Questions

1. Relative humidity is a comparison between the actual amount of water vapor in the air, and the maximum amount of water vapor the air can hold at that temperature.

2. At 75% relative humidity, the air can only assume 25% more moisture before its maximum state is reached.

3. It would be more comfortable to jog in the higher temperature, lower humidity than the lower temperature, higher humidity. Jogging in higher humidity will make it seem much hotter due to sweat not evaporating from the skin. This prevents cooling, which normally takes place at lower humidities.

4. A saturated atmosphere is completely full of water vapor at that temperature. At this point the relative humidity is 100%.

5. The hot, sticky feeling you get in humid weather results from the accumulation of sweat on the skin. The failure of this sweat to evaporate prevents the body from cooling itself adequately.

Postlab Questions

1. Dry bulb. The wet bulb has moisture that, as it evaporates from the bulb, cools the bulb.

2. Slight. When the temperature is very close for the dry and wet bulbs, this indicates the air is already so full of moisture that it is not accepting much water vapor by evaporation.

3. When there is no difference in the two temperatures, it indicates that the air is completely saturated with water vapor.

4. Increase. This would indicate that the air temperature is hot and full of moisture.

5. Answers will vary.

6. Answers will vary.

KEY 4–1
Water Words

1. s u n

2. l o (a)⁹ d

3. e r o d (e)³

4. (c)⁴ l o u d s

5. a q u (i)⁵ f e r

6. r e c h a r g e

7. w a t e (r)² s h e d

8. (p)¹ o l l u t a n (t)¹⁰ s

9. s u b l (i)¹¹ m a t i o n

10. h y d r o l (o)¹² g i c

11. e v a (p)⁶ o r a (t)⁸ e

12. c o n d e (n)¹³ s e

13. g l a c (i)⁷ e r

14. l i q u i d

15. c y c l e

p r e c i p i t a t i o n
1 2 3 4 5 6 7 8 9 10 11 12 13

KEY 4–2
Bearly Raining

Conclusions

TABLE 1

Rain on Little Dipper High School Campus

Annual rain volume in cubic feet	Monthly rain volume in cubic feet	Weight of annual rain in pounds	Weight of annual rain in kilograms	Weight of monthly rain in pounds	Weight of monthly rain in kilograms
8,406,048	703,363	525,378,000	238,521,610	43,960,200	19,957,931

2. 1250 feet

3. Answers will vary. Additions that include concrete or blacktop increase the volume of runoff because rain cannot percolate into the soil. Farms, feedlots, lawns, golf courses, and nurseries increase the amount of pesticides and fertilizers in the runoff. Industries and businesses have varying effects on runoff, depending on the nature of the business.

4. Answers will vary.

5. Answers will vary. Generally, water degradation increases in proportion to the number of people living in an area. All living things are dependent on water.

6. Removing ground cover and vegetation increases the amount of erosion that occurs. Roots, dead leaves, and other plant matter slows the impact of rain and prevents soil from being carried away by runoff.

KEY 5–1
Wave Vocabulary

1. The _____ *frequency* _____ of a sound wave determines a sound's pitch.

2. Ocean waves are _____ *transverse* _____ waves because the water and the waves move at right angles to each other.

3. In a longitudinal wave, the space where there are few particles of medium is called a _____ *rarefraction* _____.

4. Some _____ *bats* _____ can produce ultrasonic sounds, which they use for navigational purposes.

5. A _____ *wave* _____ is a disturbance that moves energy through space or matter.

6. Sound is a _____ *longitudinal* _____ wave because the medium moves back and forth in the same direction as the wave travels.

7. The _____ *crest* _____ of a transverse wave is the highest point, or point of maximum displacement, of the wave.

8. The sound of an approaching train whistle increases in pitch because of the _____ *Doppler* _____ effect.

9. Sounds that people cannot hear are called _____ *ultrasonic* _____ sounds.

10. Air is one _____ *medium* _____ through which sound can travel.

11. The frequency of sound waves is measured in units called _____ *hertz* _____.

12. In a sound wave, the space where air particles are pushed together is called a _____ *compression* _____.

13. A _____ *sound* _____ wave is produced by a vibrating object that causes the air molecules to vibrate.

14. The intensity or loudness of a sound is measured in units called _____ *decibels* _____.

15. Wave _____ *amplitude* _____ refers to the maximum distances medium molecules are displaced.

16. The lowest displacement of a wave is called the wave's _____ *trough* _____.

17. A rocket engine produces a wave of high _____ *intensity* _____, which registers 200 on the decibel scale.

18. Dogs can hear _____ *ultrasonic* _____ sounds in the 25,000-Hz range.

19. FM radio stations broadcast at frequencies in the mega-_____ *hertz* _____ range.

20. Sounds above 85 _____ *decibels* _____ can damage our ears.

© 1994 by The Center for Applied Research in Education

KEY 5–2
Good Vibrations

1. (a) Answers will vary.
   (b) Answers will vary.

2. (a) The string with the highest pitch is the tightest string.
   (b) The string with the lowest pitch is the thickest string.

3. Answers will vary.

KEY 6–1
Atomic Shake Crossword Puzzle

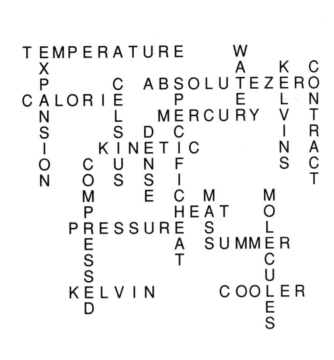

KEY 6–2
Up, Up, and Away

Prelab Questions

1. It has less mass than cold air.

2. As cold air moves underneath warm air, the warm air rises and creates a current effect.

3. Air pressure below a region of warmed air is greater than the pressure above this region. As a result, the air is buoyed upward.

4. Warmed gases expand and push outward on the container.

5. Hot water. Warm vapor would rise into the balloon and expand. The balloon would expand as a result of this.

Postlab Questions

1. Answers will vary.

2. Answers will vary.

3. Answers will vary.

4. Answers will vary.

5. Answers will vary.

KEY 7–1
Word Find

1. speed
2. odometer
3. average
4. inertia
5. force
6. inversely
7. frame of reference
8. displacement
9. vector
10. acceleration
11. instantaneous
12. gravity
13. reaction
14. deceleration
15. friction
16. scalar
17. rest
18. second
19. sun
20. mass

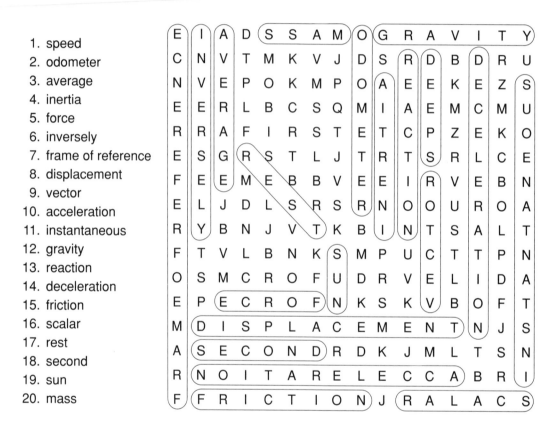

© 1994 by The Center for Applied Research in Education

KEY 7–2
Solving Your Problems in Motion

1. $S = d/t = 25/15 =$ a. 1.67 miles/min   b. $1.67 \times 60 = 100$ miles/hr

2. $S = 25/20 =$ a. 1.25 miles/min   b. $1.25 \times 60 = 75$ miles/hr

3. $V =$ displacement/time = 100 miles/hr west

4. $V = 75$ miles/hr east

5. A. a = final velocity – initial velocity/time = 60 miles/hr – 0 miles/hr /2.5 sec
    a = 60 miles/hr /0.0007 hr = 85,714 miles/hr/hr
    (*Note:* 2.5 seconds must be converted to hours by dividing by 3600 in this problem.)

    B. First change 60 miles per hour to miles per second by dividing by 3600. This will give you 0.017 miles/sec
    a = 0.017 miles/sec/2.5 sec = 0.007 miles/sec/sec

6. a = 0 – 120 miles/hr/4 sec = –120 miles/hr/0.0011 hr = –109,091 miles/hr/hr

7. 10 miles

8. 3 miles (displacement from the house to Max's)

9. S = 10 miles/2 hr = 5 miles/hr

10. V = 3 miles/2 hr = 1.5 miles/hr south

11. Final velocity = initial velocity + acceleration × time
    V = 0 + (10) (2.5) = 25 m/sec

12. d = $S \times t$ = 250 miles/hr × 1.5 hr = 375 miles

13. t = d/S = 20 miles/60 miles/hr = 0.33 hr × 60 min = 20 min

KEY 7–3
The Ball Drop

Prelab Questions

1. 1/2 (10) (8) (8) = 320 m

2. Air resistance will prevent it from falling at 10 m/sec/sec.

3. Change in velocity over time

4. The pull of gravity is different.

5. Timing will not be exact; object must be placed in a vacuum to get an exact value.

6. Answers will vary.

Postlab Questions

1. Answers will vary.

2. Answers will vary.

3. Tall

4. 1/2 (10) (4) (4) = 80 meters

KEY 8–1
Energy Unscramble

1. power
2. Newton
3. kinetic
4. pitch
5. friction
6. joule
7. acceleration
8. energy
9. horses
10. height

11. velocity
12. machines
13. lever
14. knife
15. horsepower
16. direction
17. seesaw
18. work
19. kilogram
20. final velocity

KEY 8–2
Golf Balls and Their Potential

Prelab Questions

1. a.   PE = mgh = (2 kg) (10 m/sec/sec) (20 m) = 400 J
   b.   On top of the fence
   c.   At the bottom; speed increases as objects fall.

2. Answers will vary.

Postlab Questions

1. Increased. Increased distance from the cup, so d is greater in the $W = F \times d$ formula.

2. KE = 1/2 mv^2. As the ball assumes motion, it obtains kinetic energy.

3. Inclined plane

4. Velocity would have increased, resulting in greater kinetic energy.

KEY 8–3
Problems with Energy

1. $W = F \times d$ = 20 N × 80 m = 1600 J

2. $P = W/t$ = 1600 J/6 sec = 266.7 W

3. KE $= 1/2\ mv^2 = 1/2$ (10 m/sec/sec) (2 m/sec)^2
   $= (5$ m/sec/sec) (4 m^2/sec^2)
   $= 20$ joules

4. KE $= 1/2$ (70 kg + 2 kg) (1.2 m/sec) (1.2 m/sec) $= (36)\ (1.44) = 51.8$ joules

5. You cannot compute this because acceleration due to gravity is not 10 m/sec/sec due to the effect of air resistance from the parachute.

6. $W = F \times d = 80$ kg $\times 70$ m $= 800$ N $\times 70$ m $= 56{,}000$ joules
   $P = W/t = 56{,}000$ J/3.5 sec $= 16{,}000$ watts

7. a. PE $= mgh = (6)\ (10)\ (22) = 1320$ J
    b. $\qquad\qquad = (25)\ (10)\ (10) = 2500$ J
    c. $\qquad\qquad = (50)\ (10)\ (30) = 15{,}000$ J

8. $E =$ output/input $= 100$ J/500 J $= 0.20 = 20\%$

This is low efficiency, because you only get out one fifth of the work you put into operation of this equipment.

KEY 8–5
More Power to You

Prelab Questions

1. In order to do work, we must possess energy.

2. Power. This indicates how long you performed the exercise.

3. $W = F \times d = (100$ kg $\times 10$ m/sec/sec) (2 m) $= 2000$ J

4. $P = W/t = 2000$ J/2 sec $= 1000$ W

5. PE $= mgh = 100$ kg $\times 10$ m/sec/sec $\times 2$ m $= 2000$ J

Example of some possible data for the chart. Answers will vary.

Student	Mass of student	Distance of step from floor	Up steps—1 min
Sue Ann	60 (kg) or 132 lb	12 inches (0.305 m)	40

Postlab Questions

These answers will vary depending on the data in the data table. The following answers have been based on Sue Ann's results listed in the sample data table.

1. $W = F \times d$ = (mass × acceleration due to gravity) (height of step in meters)
   W = (60 kg × 10 m/sec/sec) (.305 m) = 183 joules

Note: Students can convert their weight in pounds to mass in kilograms by multiplying pounds by 0.454. Students can convert inches of the bench height to meters by dividing the inches by 39.37.

2. $P = W/t$ = 183 J/0.75 sec = 244 watts

The 0.75 seconds was found by dividing 60 seconds (amount of exercise time) by the number of steps completed (40 for Sue Ann) and then dividing 1.5 by 2 to account for only the upward steps.

3. Yes. Heavier persons burn more calories than lighter persons.

4. The heavier person was working at a quicker rate.

KEY 9–1
AC–DC

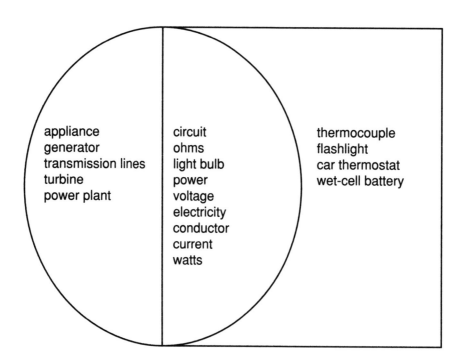

appliance	circuit	thermocouple
generator	ohms	flashlight
transmission lines	light bulb	car thermostat
turbine	power	wet-cell battery
power plant	voltage	
	electricity	
	conductor	
	current	
	watts	

KEY 9–2
Paying the Bills

1. First 650 kilowatts hours @ $.04782/kWh	$ 31.08
Next 350 kilowatts hours @ $.04104/kWh	14.36
Over 1000 kilowatt hours @ $.04040/kWh	90.21
Base charge	7.50
Fuel recovery cost for 3233 kWH	48.50
Total charges	$191.65
Tax (5%)	9.56
Total due	$201.23
2. First 650 kilowatt hours @ $.04782/kWh	$ 30.13
Base charge	7.50
Fuel recovery cost for 630 kWh	9.45
Total charges	$ 47.08
Tax (5%)	2.35
Total due	$ 49.43
3. First 650 kilowatts per hour @ $.04782	$ 31.08
Next 350 kilowatts per hour @ $.07948	27.82
Last 1995 kilowatts per hour @ $.08184	163.27
Fuel recovery	44.93
Base cost	7.50
Total charges	$274.60
Tax	13.73
Total due	$288.33

4. Electricity is most expensive in the summer. The more electricity one uses, the more expensive the electricity.

5. Answers will vary.

6. Utilities discourage families from using a lot of electricity in the summer by charging high prices.

KEY 9–3
Shocking Solutions

1. $I = V/R$
   $I = 8$ volts/20 ohms
   $I = 4$ amps

2. $I = V/R$
   $I = 6$ volts/1200 ohms
   $I = 0.0049$ amps

3. $P = V \times I$
   $P = 120$ volts $\times 10$ amps
   $P = 1200$ watts

4. $I = V/R$
   $R = V/I$
   $R = 120$ volts/7 amps
   $R = 17$ ohms

5. $I = P/V$
   $I = 2300$ watts/120 volts
   $I = 19$ amps

6. Washing machine:
   $E = P \times t$
   $E = 1.8$ kW $\times 0.5$ hours
   $E = 0.9$ kWh

Dryer:
   $E = P \times t$
   $E = 5$ kW $\times 1$ hour
   $E = 4$ kWh

Total kWh used = 0.9 + 4.0 = 4.9
   Cost = kWh $\times$ cost/hour
   Cost = 4.9 kWh $\times$ \$0.06
   Cost = \$.294

KEY 10–1
Planet Unscramble

1. terrestrial
2. Uranus
3. Mercury
4. Pluto
5. Saturn

6. nitrogen
7. Venus
8. craters
9. winds
10. comets

KEY 10–2—CHART 1
Bringing the Solar System Down to Earth

Object	Diameter (km)	# times smaller than sun	Scaled-down diameter (mm)
Sun	1,380,000	———	1000 mm
Mercury	4989	277	3.6 mm
Venus	12,392	111.36	8.98 mm
Earth	12,757	108.17	9.24 mm
Mars	6759	204.16	4.898 mm
Jupiter	142,749	9.67	103.4 mm
Saturn	120,862	11.42	87.58 mm
Uranus	51,499	26.797	37.32 mm
Neptune	44,579	30.956	32.3 mm
Pluto	2414	571.66	1.75 mm

KEY 10–2—CHART 2
Planet name distance from sun AU equivalent scaled down

Planet name	Distance from (in millions of miles)	AU equivalent	Scaled-down distance (mm)
Mercury	36	.39	390 mm
Venus	67.27	0.7	700 mm
Earth	93	1	1000 mm
Mars	141.7	1.52	1520 mm
Jupiter	483.9	5.2	5200 mm
Saturn	887.1	9.54	9540 mm

KEY 10–2—CHART 2 *(continued)*
Planet name distance from sun AU equivalent scaled down

Planet name	Distance from (in millions of miles)	AU equivalent	Scaled-down distance (mm)
Uranus	1783.98	19.18	19,180 mm
Neptune	2795.5	30.06	30,006 mm
Pluto	3675.3	39.52	39,520 mm

KEY 11–1
Star Puzzle

KEY 11–2
Star Chamber

Conclusions

1. Polaris is the North Star, which indicates the position of celestial north. Someone who is lost might be able to use the North Star as a reference point.

2. We study constellations because they are one way to learn about stars and other heavenly bodies.

3. Answers will vary.

4.
   1. b
   2. c
   3. a
   4. b
   5. b
   6. d
   7. f
   8. b
   9. c
   10. g

KEY 12–1
Lunar Message Creation

1. s e a
2. k i n e t i c
3. l u n a r s
4. t h i e f
5. s e r e n i t a t i s
6. m o o n i t e s
7. a n g l e
8. m a r i a
9. l a v a
10. p e a k
11. h e a t
12. r a y s

13. r i m
14. d u s t

15. v o l c a n o e s
16. l u n a t i c
17. C o p e r n i c u s
18. g r a v i t y
19. v a p o r i z i n g

KEY 12–2
Moon Madness

Conclusions

1. Answers will vary.

2. Peas and beans thrown from an angle have the lowest angle of impact. However, this angle does not affect the shape of the crater.

3. Answers will vary.

4. One student is appointed as the one who throws the peas and beans to reduce variability in throwing.

5. The oldest crater has rays that are partially covered by the rays from younger craters.

6. The moon's craters were probably formed by an explosion of meteor material. The crater was created when rock and soil in the area of impact were thrown out in a circular pattern.

7. Yes. Rays are made of ejecta blanket, or material that is thrown out of the crater.

KEY 13–1
Landing Spacecraft

1. Byrd
2. Sputnik
3. adapter module
4. Friendship
5. only used when near the sun
6. Food floats around galley
7. highly trained astronauts
8. gasoline
9. shower stalls
10. laundry
11. loss of memory
12. visits planets

KEY 14–1
Fat Words

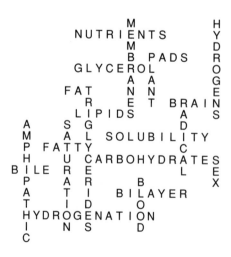

© 1994 by The Center for Applied Research in Education

KEY 14-2
Fat Foods

Prelab Questions

1. Americans eat less fat now than they did in 1972, but more than they did in 1900.

2. Student answers will vary. Americans have received a lot of education from the media about dangers of too much fat in their diets.

3. Student answers will vary. Americans have a very affluent life style and can afford any food they want.

4. Skinless chicken and turkey, leg of lamb, and fish are very lean meats. Ground beef, steaks, hot dogs, and specialty meats are high in fat.

5. From a quarter pound of hamburger, you get 112 calories of protein and 207 calories of fat.

Data and Conclusions

2. Student answers may vary. Ground beef contains more fat than ground chuck.

3. Artheriosclerosis and obesity are two health problems associated with high fat intakes.

4. Cooking meat separated the fat from the protein, allowing the fat to float to the top.

5. Skinless chicken would have less fat than ground beef or ground chuck.

KEY 15-1
Water Word Find

1. cohesion
2. soap
3. cation
4. plastic
5. hydrophilic
6. hydrophobic
7. gravity
8. adhesion
9. glass
10. surfactant
11. anion
12. skin
13. concave
14. spherical
15. air
16. weaken
17. insoluble

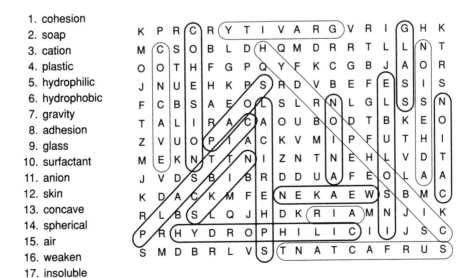

KEY 15–2
Surface Tension

Prelab Questions

1. Surface tension is the skinlike texture that forms on top of water. It forms in response to cohesion of molecules.

2. Temperature—increases the forces of attraction between water and air vapor molecules. Surfactants—reduce the cohesion of water molecules.

3. The water striders have a hairlike coating on their feet that keeps their feet from getting wet, making them able to walk on the skin of water.

4. Cohesion is the attraction of water molecules toward each other.

5. Substances such as soap and detergent that reduce surface tension are called surfactants. These substances increase the spreading and wetting property of water. This enables water to remove dirt more effectively.

Chart 1 Results

Answers will vary. The room-temperature tap water will hold by far the most gem clips. The heated tap water will hold the second most, followed by the room-temperature detergent water. The fewest clips will be held by the heated detergent water.

Part 1—Postlab Questions

1. Cup D. It had its surface tension lowered by both heat and a surfactant.

2. Cup A. It had nothing added to lower surface tension.

3. It lowers it.

4. They lower it.

5. The skin formed due to cohesion and held the water at the surface in a dome.

Part 2—Postlab Questions

1. Student designs will vary.

2. It prevents the feet from getting wet.

3. The insect would sink.

4. The insect sank.

5. The surface tension had been lowered and the skin broken on the water surface.

6. They could not walk nearly as easily on the pond surface.

KEY 16–1
A Tri-ing and Hairy Experience

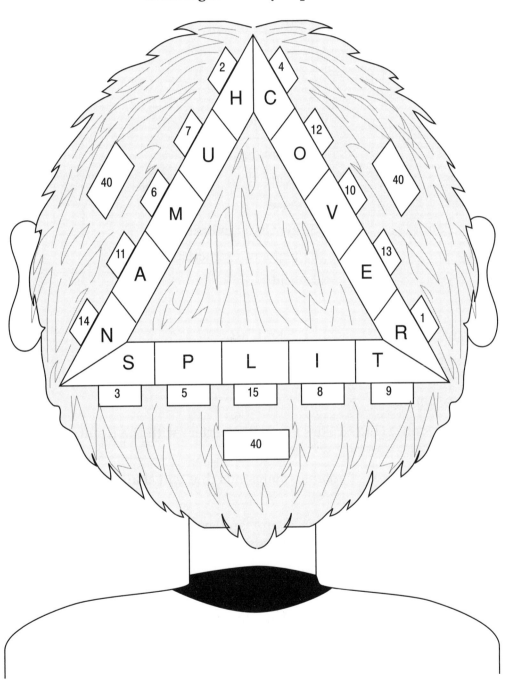

KEY 16–2
Homemade Hair Perms

1–4. Sketches will vary.

5. NaOH is a strong base that causes the cuticle of hair to swell and open. The hair is then more porous, and the NaOH molecules can enter the cortex, where they disrupt the sulfur bonds between cysteine molecules.

6. The acetic acid neutralizes NaOH.

7. Answers will vary.

KEY 17–1
Petal Pickin'

1. indicators
2. alkaline
3. neutral
4. anthocyanin
5. acid

6. strong acid
7. acids
8. bases
9. synthetic indicators
10. pigment extraction
11. acid

KEY 17–2
Cabbage Patch Indicators and the Petal Papers

Prelab Questions

1. These substances have colors that will interfere with the results of the test. Clear substances work much better.

2. Indicators are types of organic compounds that will change colors as the pH of the environment changes.

3. Natural indicators come from plants, and synthetic indicators are made in the laboratory from various chemicals.

4. As hydrogen ion concentration increases, the acidity increases. As hydroxyl ion concentration increases the alkalinity increases.

5. Strong acids will be a darker color, while the strong bases will be a lighter color.

Data Chart 1

Answers will vary, but the pH 1–3 will be red; pH 4–6 is usually violet; pH 8–10 is usually blue-green; and pH above 12 is yellow. These colors will vary but should fall somewhere in that range.

The substance the teacher selects for use can vary, but some guidelines are as follows:

Name of teacher choice	pH
Soda water	4
Limewater	11
Household ammonia	12
Shampoo	around 7
Garden fertilizer	5 or 6
Fruit juices	4–6

Postlab Questions

1. Answers will vary. The lowest pH should have been selected.

2. Answers will vary. The highest pH should have been selected.

3. Strong acids have the more red and deep colors. The strong bases will have the light, yellow colors.

4. *Caustic* means "to corrode or damage," as in "caustic to the skin."

5. Use pH test strip paper or a pH meter.

Chart 2

Answers will vary, but the results should be very similar to Chart 1. The colors may vary, but once again the deeper and darker colors are found with the strong acids, while the lighter colors are found with the strong bases.

Postlab Questions

1. They should have been almost identical in pH.

2. Answers will vary.

3. Answers will vary.

KEY 18–1
DNA Concept Map

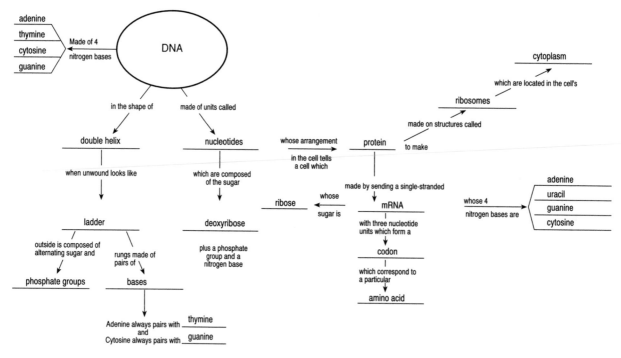

KEY 18–2
Recipe for Proteins

Conclusions

1. The sequence of bases in the DNA determines which proteins a cell will make.

2. The ribosomes hold an mRNA strand so that amino acids can be properly lined up by tRNAs.

3. tRNAs carry appropriate amino acids to the mRNA strand.

4. If amino acids are not assembled in the proper order, the resulting protein may be defective.

5. DNA sends its message for protein synthesis to the ribosomes by making a copy of itself in the form of mRNA.

KEY 19–1
The Tri-ing Cell Puzzle

1. tissues
2. erythrocytes
3. nucleus
4. ribosomes
5. nerve cells
6. mitochondria
7. lysosomes
8. centrosomes
9. endoplasmic reticulum
10. cilia
11. epithelium
12. Golgi bodies
13. bone cells
14. muscle cells
15. fat cells

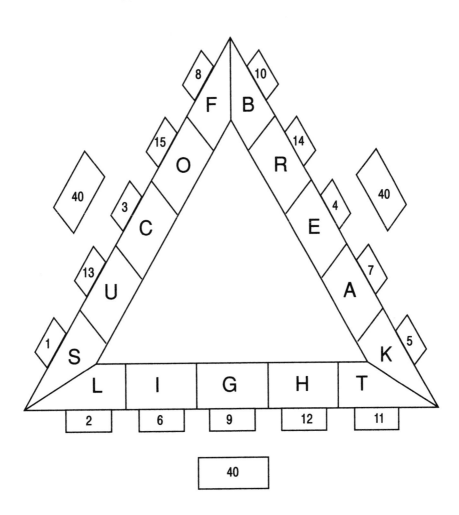

KEY 20–1
Box Puzzle Adaptations

1. genes
2. competition
3. variation
4. Darwin
5. adaptations

6. mutation
7. natural selection
8. Lamarck
9. reproductive
10. harmful

KEY 20–3
Monstrous Mutations

Prelab Questions

1. Variable characteristics in organisms produced by random alteration of DNA from the parent to the offspring is a mutation.

2. Mutations are the result of chance.

3. behavioral

4. behavioral

5. structural

6. Answers will vary.

Postlab Questions

1. Answers will vary.

2. Answers will vary.

3. Storing of food or burying food

4. Answers will vary.

5. Answers will vary.

6. Answers will vary.

KEY 21–1
Wood You Leave Him Out on a Limb?

1. wood
2. water
3. leaves
4. anchor
5. xylem
6. bacteria
7. adhesives
8. mistletoe
9. fungi
10. evaporation
11. growth cells
12. food

KEY 21–2
A Dead Ringer

1. Lighter xylem represents spring growth. Darker xylem is summer growth.

2. Xylem conducts water and minerals upward from the roots to the leaves.

3. xylem tubes

4. Lignin is material that thickens the walls of xylem tubes.

Tree stem	Age of the tree	Diameter of the tree (cm)
A	6	4.6
B	8	4.9
C	5	8.0
D	4	4.8
E	7	5.4

Postlab Questions

1. B

2. D

3. No. The size of the rings can enlarge in 1 year due to greater availability of water.

4. C

5. B

6. E

7. 1984

8. 1983

9. 1986 and 1985

KEY 21–3
Life Story of a Tree

Prelab Questions

1. Conifers are evergreen trees, while deciduous trees lose their leaves at certain times of the year.

2. Answers will vary.

3. Deciduous trees lose their leaves.

4. Answers will vary.

5. Answers will vary.

6. Answers will vary.

Postlab Questions

1. Count the number of xylem growth rings.

2. Answers will vary.

3. Answers will vary.

4. Answers will vary.

5. Answers will vary.

KEY 22–1
Ecologically Speaking

1. S E C O N D A R Y
2.   E C O L O G Y
3. C O M P E T I T I O N
4.   P R E D A T O R
5.   E P I P H Y T E
6.   A U T O T R O P H S
7. D E T R I T U S
8. H E R B I V O R E
9.   E C O S Y S T E M
10. C H L O R O P H Y L L
11.   H E T E R O T R O P H S
12. C O M P O S T
13. E A R T H W O R M S
14.   C H A I N
15.   O R G A N I C

KEY 22–2
Who Lives in Our Trash?

Part A. Indoor Composting

Data and Conclusions

3. Answers will vary.

4. Answers will vary.

5. Yeast, like many fungi, feed on dead and decaying matter. It was added to Bottle 2 to increase the rate of decomposition.

6. The yeast in Bottle 2 feeds on food scraps.

7. Answers will vary. Organisms that were living in the soil outdoors helped decompose the food scraps.

Part B. Create a Compost Pile Outdoors

Data and Conclusions

3. Answers will vary. The temperature probably increased 10 to 20 degrees Fahrenheit over the experimental period.

4. The temperature increase was caused by microbes digesting the food scraps.

5. Answers will vary.

6. Changes in composted food are caused by organisms in the detrital food web: microbes, fungi, worms, mites, etc.

7. Answers will vary.

8. These organisms moved into the compost pile from the surrounding soil.

9. One-celled organisms (protists and bacteria) and fungi are probably present.

10. Without the detritivores, dead things would not decompose and return their valuable minerals to the soil.

Bibliography

Allison, Linda, *The Wild Inside—Sierra Club's Guide to the Great Indoors,* Sierra Club Books, San Francisco, 1988.

Anthony, Catherine and Thibodeen, Gary, *Textbook of Anatomy and Physiology,* Times Mirror/Mosby College Publishing, St. Louis, Missouri, 1987.

Apfel, Necia H., *Astronomy Projects for Young Scientists,* Arco Publishing Company, Inc., New York, 1984.

Aquatic Project Wild, Environmental Education Council, Boulder, Colorado, 1987.

Borgford, Cristie L. and Lee R. Summerlin, *Chemical Activities,* American Chemical Society, Washington, D.C., 1988.

Braun, Sherry, *Biology, Laboratory Investigations,* D. C. Heath, Lexington, Massachusetts, 1989.

Brooks, Felicity, *Protecting Trees and Forests,* Usborne Publishing, Usborne Conservation Guides, London, 1991.

Christensen, John, *Global Science: Energy, Resources, Environment,* Kendall/Hunt Publishing Co., Dubuque, Iowa, 1984.

Colker, Laura J., *Energy Facts and Impacts: A Handbook for Georgia Students,* Mobius Corporation, Alexandria, Virginia.

de La Cotardiere, Philippe, *Astronomy,* Facts on File Publication, New York, 1986.

Eggen, Paul and June Main, *Developing Critical Thinking Through Science—Book Two,* Critical Thinking Press and Software, Pacific Grove, California, 1990.

Fariel, Robert, *Earth Science,* Addison-Wesley, London, 1984.

Fleming, Michael F., *Life Science Labs Kit,* Center for Applied Research in Education, Prentice Hall, Englewood Cliffs, New Jersey, 1985.

Fleming, Michael F., *Science Teachers Instant Labs Kit,* Center for Applied Research in Education, Prentice Hall, Englewood Cliffs, New Jersey, 1992.

Gallagher, Dianne and Roberts, Rope, *125 Science Activities for the Elementary Classroom,* Atlanta, Georgia Power Company, 1991.

Hamilton, Debra, *Earth Trek—An Environmental Learning Manual for Educators,* Earth Lab, The Educational Division of the Georgia Conservancy, Atlanta, Georgia, 1991.

Herbert, Don, *Mr. Wizard's 400 Experiments in Science,* Book Lab Publishers, New Jersey, 1990.

Hummer, Paul, *Probing Levels of Life, A Lab Manual,* Merrill, Columbus, Ohio, 1989.

Hurd, Dean, *Physical Science,* Prentice Hall, Englewood Cliffs, New Jersey, 1988.

Kaskel, Albert, Paul Hummer, and Lucy Daniel, *Biology, An Everyday Experience,* Merrill Publishing Company, Columbus, Ohio, 1988.

Kenda, Margaret and Phyllis Williams, *Science Wizardry for Kids,* Barron's Publishing Co., New York, 1992.

Lamb, William, *Physical Science Lab Manual,* Harcourt Brace Jovanovich, Inc., Orlando, Florida, 1989.

Leeson, C. Roland, and Thomas Leeson, *Atlas of Histology,* 2nd edition, W. B. Saunders Company, Philadelphia, Pennsylvania, 1985.

Lingelback, Jennifer, (Ed.) *Hands On Nature,* Vermont Institute of Natural Science, Woodstock, Vermont, 1986.

Mason, R. J. and M. R. Mattson, *Atlas of United States Environmental Issues,* Macmillan Publishing Co., New York, 1990.

Matthews, William, *Investigating the Earth,* Houghton Mifflin, Atlanta, Georgia, 1987.

McLaren, James E. and Lissa Rotundo, *Biology,* D. C. Heath, Lexington, Massachusetts, 1989.

Metzger, Mary and Cinthya Whittaker, *This Planet Is Mine,* Fireside Books by Simon and Schuster, New York, 1991.

Moran, J. M., M. D. Morgan, and J. H. Wiersma, *Introduction to Environmental Science,* W. H. Freeman and Company, New York, 1986.

Morrison, Robert Thornton and Robert Neilson Boyd, *Organic Chemistry,* Prentice Hall, Englewood Cliffs, New Jersey, 1992.

Namowitz, Samuel, *Earth Science,* D. C. Heath, Lexington, Massachusetts, 1989.

NASA Fact Sheets, National Aeronautics and Space Administration, Marshall Space Flight Center, Huntsville, Alabama, December 1990.

NASA Information Summaries, "The Early Years—Mercury to Apollo Soyuz," National Aeronautics and Space Administration, Marshall Space Flight Center, Huntsville, Alabama, May 1987.

NASA Information Summaries, "Living and Working on the New Frontier," National Aeronautics and Space Administration, Marshall Space Flight Center, Huntsville, Alabama, September 1991.

Needham, James and Paul Needham, *A Guide to the Study of Freshwater Biology,* Holden-Day, Inc., San Francisco, 1962.

Nolan, Louise, *Physical Science,* D. C. Heath, Lexington, Massachusetts, 1987.

Oram, Raymond, *Biology, Living Systems,* Charles E. Merrill, Toronto, 1983.

Parker, Steve, *The Marshall Cavendish Science Project Book of Water,* Marshall Cavendish Corporation, New York, New York, 1988.

Parker, Sybil, *McGraw-Hill Encyclopedia of Science and Technology,* McGraw-Hill Book Company, New York, 1982.

Powitt, A. H., *Hair Structure and Chemistry Simplified,* Milady Publishing Corporation, New York, 1978.

Project Learning Tree, Supplementary Activity Guide K–6 and 7–12, The American Forest Council, Washington, D.C., 1992.

Project Wild, Western Environmental Education Council, Boulder, Colorado, 1987.

Prusko, John, and Jody Stone, *Physical Science,* Scott Foresman and Co., Glenville, Illinois, 1990.

Ramsey, William, *General Science,* Holt, Rinehart, and Winston, New York, 1979.

Schoonmaker, Peter, *The Living Forest,* Enslow Publishers, Hillside, New Jersey, 1990.

Shea, Keith Mitchell (Ed.), *ChemCom, Chemistry in the Community,* Kendall Hunt, Dubusque, Iowa, 1993.

Smith, Sean, *Project Earth Science: Astronomy,* National Science Teachers Association (NSTA) Special Publications, Washington, D.C., 1992.

Spaulding, Nancy, *Earth Science Laboratory Investigations,* D.C. Heath, Lexington, Massachusetts, 1989.

Smith, Richard, *Chemistry,* Merrill Publishing Co., Ohio, 1987.

Smith, Robert, *Elements of Ecology,* Harper Collins Publishers, West Virginia University, 1992.

Stroub, Sharon and Jeffrey Callister, *Earth at Hand,* NSTA, Washington, D.C., 1993.

Stryer, Lubert, *Biochemistry,* W. H. Freeman and Co., New York, 1981.

Sugarman, Carol, "Americans Go Overboard with Fat-Free Foods", *The Atlanta Journal and Constitution,* p. B5, May 24, 1994.

Thompson, Henry, *Fundamentals of Earth Science,* Appleton-Century-Crofts, Inc., New York, 1960.

Van Cleave, Janis, *Physics for Every Kid,* John Wiley & Sons, New York, 1991.

Walpole, Brenda, *175 Science Experiments to Amuse and Amaze Your Friends,* Random House, New York, 1988.

Whitney, Eleanor Noss, *Concepts and Controversies in Nutrition,* West Publishing Company, New York, 1982.

Notes

Notes

Notes

Notes

Notes